Patricia Craig is from Belfast. She move
always retained strong links with her n
Northern Ireland in 1999. A leading li
she regularly contributes to the *Irish Times, London Review of Books,*
New Statesman, Independent and *Times Literary Supplement,* and
has appeared on various television and radio programmes. She
is the author of *Asking for Trouble: The Story of an Escapade with
Disproportionate Consequences* (Blackstaff, 2007) and *Brian Moore: A
Biography* (Bloomsbury, 2002), and has edited many anthologies,
including *The Oxford Book of Ireland* (Oxford University Press,
1998) and *The Ulster Anthology* (Blackstaff, 2006).

PRAISE FOR *ASKING FOR TROUBLE*

'... speaks its elegant mind'
KARL MILLER, *Times Literary Supplement,* Books of the Year

'I commend this accomplished Belfast author's
marvellously readable memoir'
CAL McCRYSTAL, *Independent on Sunday,* Books of the Year

'She has a wonderful eye and ear for the geography and sociology of
the old Belfast of her childhood ... her amiably discursive style and
encyclopaedic knowledge of Irish culture enable her to offer
the sharpest insights into the perennial "Irish question"'
STANLEY PRICE, *The Oldie*

'This is a powerfully evocative memoir of many things: life in
middle-class Belfast in the 1950s, the experiences of teenagers in a
convent school, and above all the seminal, magical *rite de passage* called
"going to the Gaeltacht" ... I found the book refreshingly angry and
totally absorbing – I couldn't put it down.'
ÉILÍS NÍ DHUIBHNE

'It's funny and sweet (in the right sort of way), so sharp in its
capturing of time and place that I believed myself to be
on the road in Rannafast with the girls.'
MARGARET FORSTER

A TWISTED ROOT

PATRICIA CRAIG

BLACKSTAFF PRESS

First published in 2012 by Blackstaff Press
4c Heron Wharf
Sydenham Business Park
Belfast BT3 9LE
with the assistance of
The Arts Council of Northern Ireland

Typeset by CJWT Solutions, St Helens, Merseyside

Printed in Great Britain by the MPG Books Group

A CIP catalogue for this book is available from the British Library

ISBN 978 0 85640 904 2

www.blackstaffpress.com

www.blackstaffpress.com/ebooks

For Harry Tipping
and in memory of my grandmothers
Sarah Brady (née Tipping), 1881–1969
Emily Craig (née Lett), 1889–1973

For history's a twisted root ...

PAUL MULDOON

CONTENTS

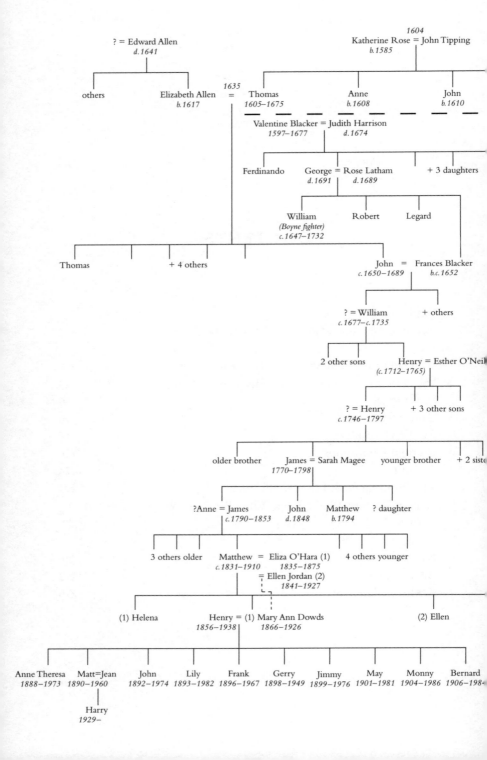

Alicia
b. 1614

William
b. 1617

1640
= Margaret O'Hoole

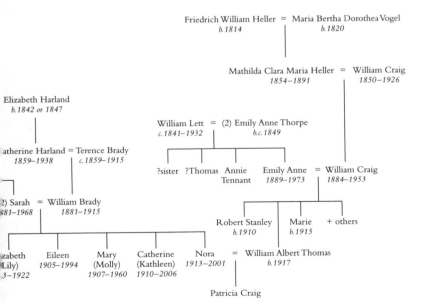

Friedrich William Heller = Maria Bertha Dorothea Vogel
b. 1814   *b. 1820*

Mathilda Clara Maria Heller = William Craig
1854–1891   *1850–1926*

Elizabeth Harland
b. 1842 or 1847

William Lett = (2) Emily Anne Thorpe
c. 1841–1932   *b.c. 1849*

:atherine Harland = Terence Brady
1859–1938   *c. 1859–1915*

?sister ?Thomas Annie   Emily Anne = William Craig
                  Tennant   *1889–1973*   *1884–1953*

2) Sarah = William Brady
:81–1968   *1881–1915*

Robert Stanley   Marie   + others
b. 1910   *b. 1915*

:zabeth   Eileen   Mary   Catherine   Nora   = William Albert Thomas
Lily)   *1905–1994* (Molly)   (Kathleen)   *1913–2001*   *b. 1917*
3–1922   *1907–1960* *1910–2006*

Patricia Craig

INTRODUCTION
THE DANGEROUS EDGE OF THINGS

If there's one single unalloyed good that has come out of the overdone debates about historical 'revisionism', it's the idea of the historian as subversive. We should be seeking out the interactions, paradoxes and sub-cultures ... if only to rearrange the pieces in more surprising patterns.

R.F. Foster, *Varieties of Irishness*

Thoughts of history present themselves constantly. What version of history do we accept, though, if any?

Derek Mahon, 'Dark of the Moon'

Some years ago, I wrote a memoir called *Asking for Trouble. A Twisted Root* is not a sequel, but there's a sense in which it grew out of certain preoccupations of the former book. The memoir is centred on an alarming event of my early life: being expelled from a convent school in Belfast at the age of sixteen for a miniscule misdemeanour. The crucial episode of misbehaviour, with its disproportionate outcome, occurred in the Donegal Gaedhaltacht, in Rannafast, where I'd gone with some friends and fellow pupils of St Dominic's High School, in August 1959, to polish my Irish. It involved some carry-on with local boys. When word of this small carry-on reached the ears of St Dominic's nuns, they threw up their hands in horror and promptly cast out of the school the three ringleaders in the affair (as it seemed to them). I believed at the time, and still believe, their reaction was crazed and their treatment of the three of us ruthless and unjust. Others will disagree – indeed, some readers of *Asking for Trouble* did disagree, with varying degrees of vehemence. They rushed into print or went on the air to stick up for nuns, claiming that convent pupils all over Ireland and, indeed, Britain, had been summarily expelled from other schools for lesser offences. What did we expect, they snorted. Kissing boys behind turf stacks, and being caught at it, had put us beyond the pale.

Those were the sniffy brigade. Other readers, those who had suffered horrors under a convent regime, thought I hadn't gone nearly far enough in my castigation of that educational system. 'More could be told' – uttered darkly – was the verdict of the convent-afflicted. At this point, it looked as if the title, *Asking for Trouble*, might relate to the reception of the book no less than the activities evoked in it.

That title – hmmn. I was not exactly happy with it. I feared it might be a contender for a Kate Adie award for unoriginality. But I stuck with it, due to its slightly ironic bearing on the theme of the memoir, and also because I had it in mind that it referred not only to the particular events I was writing about, but to an entire society on the verge of falling apart. Given the conditions prevailing in the North in the late 1950s – economic, social, religious and political conditions – it was clear that something had got to give. And, for a brief moment in the following decade, it looked as though the inevitable upheaval might actually engender a more equitable, just and progressive reshaping of Northern Irish society – but as we know, it didn't happen. What happened instead exceeded the direst anticipations of the most pessimistic observers of Northern Ireland's sectarian ethos. James Simmons puts it succinctly in his poem entitled 'The Ballad of Gerry Kelly': 'Sixty-nine the nightmare started./Loyalist anger rose.'

Loyalist anger rose, and at the same time, republican anger rose to meet it. Things fell apart. The death toll rose too. Destruction by bomb and fire overtook not only the centre of Belfast, but the centres of many pleasant historic towns, small towns, country towns, seaside towns. 'Now with compulsive resonance they toll,' John Hewitt wrote in his bitter 'Postscript' to the celebratory 'Ulster Names' of the late 1940s:

Banbridge, Ballykelly, Darkley, Crossmaglen,
summoning pity, anger and despair,
by grief of kin, by hate of murderous men
till the whole tarnished map is stained and torn,
not to be read as pastoral again.

Living in London, and well out of it, as I thought, I watched from afar
with horror and despair as my native province blew itself to pieces. I
was uncertain as to where my loyalties lay – or if loyalties were even
relevant in the infernal imbroglio. I had long discarded the crusading
republicanism of my teenage years. Civil rights, the People's Democracy,
had seemed to offer a rational alternative to out-and-out 'Irish-Ireland'
affiliation; but those well-intentioned bodies had failed to withstand
the warring objectives of people aligned to them. It all came down to
sects and factions as conduits to chaos. And in the resulting meltdown
it was sometimes hard to distinguish between ideologists and cynical
exploiters of civic unrest. It was hard not to feel sympathy for the killed,
bereaved, afflicted, of whatever persuasion or degree of complicity. It
wasn't hard to deplore the vicious sectarian instinct that flourished like
bindweed among the ignorant, depraved and psychopathic. I'm thinking
of gangs like the Shankill Butchers and its leader named Murphy. Sects
and factions – but with Northern Irish individuals and their ancestry, it
is often hard to tell where one sect ends and another begins.

While I was writing *Asking for Trouble*, I became aware that the
central story, the expulsion story, was surrounded by others endemic to
the place I grew up in, and some of these had to do with family history
and the way it had of throwing up oddities and ironies. Thanks to the
researches of two intrepid cousins, Harry Tipping on my mother's side
and George Hinds on my father's, I came into possession of a good deal
of information previously unknown to me – or at best, only partially
known and haphazardly assimilated. At some point it occurred to me that
some of this information might be amplified to form a separate volume
– not, I should say, a family history as such, but a book whose *raison
d'être* is to indicate how interlocked we all are in the north of Ireland,
whether we consider ourselves to be exclusively Protestant, Catholic,
Presbyterian, Mormon, Shaker, Quaker or high-caste Brahmin. What I
had in mind was a kind of Ulster cat's-cradle constructed from history
and identity and literature, image and allusion and invention – all woven

together with whatever verve I could muster. I was partly inspired by a marvellous book, *Rebellions* by Tom Dunne (2004), which has the kind of density and balance I was aiming for, with its blend of history and family history, autobiography and social comment. *My* undertaking (I repeat) is not a family history. It is illustrative rather than genealogical, even though it focuses to an extent on the lives of some of my own ancestors, those who begin to emerge with a degree of clarity from the nearly impenetrable mists of the past. I'm interested in the past and its implications for the present, in historical ironies, in revelations dismantling preconceptions about attachment to this or that tribe, or other *idées fixes*. On a personal level, I'm excited by discoveries concerning aspects of my own background, and keen to insert these into the general picture. If I've got it right, each of the following chapters should tell a good – a pertinent – story about the way things were at a particular time in the past. Extracting the personal from the historical (and vice versa) is one of my objectives, even if I'm bound to fall short in certain areas (those of characterisation and verisimilitude, for example). And I'm delighted to find my direct and indirect forebears turning out to be a wonderfully heterogeneous lot – down and up the social scale (mostly down), in and out of church and chapel, Lurgan Papes and Wexford Prods, hanged and hangmen, street-brawlers and scholars, full-blown Orangemen and republican activists. I have to say that the 'fíor-Gaedhalach', true-Irish, strain in my ancestry is the most exiguous, but it does exist (I think), courtesy of an umpteen-times great-grandmother named Esther O'Neill. Well, I'm laying claim to it along with other things that can't altogether be verified.

Graham Greene was fond of quoting a couple of well-known lines from Browning, which he said could stand as an epigraph to all his novels: 'Our interest's on the dangerous edge of things, / The honest thief, the tender murderer, / The superstitious atheist.' In the context of Northern Ireland, we might adapt these lines to accommodate the Protestant Fenian, the principled rioter, the unchristian cleric, the merciless Sister of Mercy (and I'm happy to say I've uncovered none of the last among my ancestral connections). 'The dangerous edge', for me, suggests above all an edge of complexity, a subversiveness, that makes a nonsense of the monolithic certainties on which the entire structure of our centuries-old conflict is based.

An Orange procession in the early years of the twentieth century

Earlier, I quoted the Simmons line about loyalist anger. Loyalist anger is the standard response to any perceived threat to Ulster's status quo. From Thomas McKnight writing in 1896 about 'armed assemblies of Orangemen' and 'Mr Parnell' taking note of what he called 'tumultuous and riotous gatherings of Orangemen wishing to murder the Irish Catholics' to the burning of Bombay Street and Conway Street in Belfast, in August 1969, by a mob in the throes of loyalist anger, the past has always risen up, like a ghoul from a burial mound, to overwhelm any current egalitarian impulse. Whenever it showed the least sign of subsiding, atavistic outrage was easily reignited by some energetic demagogue like the Reverend Henry Cooke – described by one commentator as 'the framer of sectarianism in the politics of Ulster'[1] – whose entire being was geared to opposing what he called 'fierce democracy on the one hand and more terrible popery on the other'.

Dr Cooke in his antique clerical garb is a kind of cartoon embodiment of nineteenth-century Ulster illiberalism; but in fact, as well as contributing to the diehard Protestant ethic of the day, Cooke was also articulating sectarian doctrines to which many people subscribed, overtly or covertly. 'You know,' they might have whispered, 'there's something in what he says.' This behind-hands quotation from John Hewitt's poem 'The Coasters' takes us forward a century or so and refers to a different set of circumstances – but the author puts his finger on a continuing, low-grade, passive bigotry, a bigotry of boardrooms and suburbs, which played its part in contaminating the whole of Northern Irish society, to a point of dissolution. 'You coasted along,' the accusing poem goes:

> You even had a friend or two of the other sort,
> coasting too: your ways ran parallel.
> Your children and theirs seldom met, though,
> being at different schools.
> You visited each other, decent folk with a sense
> of humour. Introduced, even, to
> one of their clergy. And then you smiled
> in the looking-glass, admiring, a
> little moved by, your broadmindedness.
> Your father would never have known
> one of them. Come to think of it,
> when you were young, your own home was never
> visited by one of the other sort.

The 'you' addressed by Hewitt is of course a Protestant Ulsterman, but I'm not suggesting that an equal amount of bigotry, aggression, name-calling or nepotism didn't exist among 'the other sort' – the Catholics of Ulster. The novelist Brian Moore (1921–99), who grew up in Clifton Street, Belfast, recalled his doctor father's refusal to allow any member of his household to adorn the table with 'a Protestant loaf of bread' – that is, one made by the Ormeau Bakery rather than Barney Hughes's. Think of the episode in St John Ervine's novel of 1927, *The Wayward Man*, when young Robert Dunwoody strays into Catholic territory in the back streets of Belfast, and is set upon by 'a gang of rough youths' who exact a tribal betrayal from him: ' "Curse King William, you Protestant *get*, you!" They crowded round him, ... pulling his hair and beating his skull with their knuckles. ... He could see the vicious face of the leader of the gang turning more vicious still.'

Or take the moment in a considerably inferior work of fiction published in 1911, *The Belfast Boy* by Agnes Boles, when a couple of Protestant girls succumb to terror on catching sight of a body of men coming towards them over Peter's Hill. ' "Look!" cried Maggie Reilly,[2] "It's the Catholics coming to wreck the Shankill." ' Confronted with all this coming from both sides, you might find yourself harbouring a degree of sympathy with the author of an even worse novel, James Douglas, when he took a look at Edwardian Belfast and its goings-on and renamed the deplorable city 'Bigotsborough'.[3] 'The clash of broken glass was a familiar sound in the streets of Bigotsborough.'

Sectarian noise was not confined to Belfast. Let us take a look at Portadown. The late George Watson, academic and literary critic, published a pointed essay in the *Yale Review* in 1986 about his experiences growing up as 'a Portadown Pape'. Each day, coming home from primary school (he says), he and his friends had to fight Protestant boys who taunted them with the epithet, 'Fenian scum'. Now – if you gave it any thought at all in this respect – you would take 'George Watson' to be a Protestant name. If you then found out that Watson's father was an RUC constable, the family's Protestantism would seem to be assured. But it wasn't so. Both his parents, in fact, were Catholics from the South, from Kilkenny and Connemara respectively, and his father (born in 1898) had got himself transferred North from the old Royal Irish Constabulary after 1922. Members of the RIC were at risk of assassination in the South, and Catholics were at risk of assault in Portadown. It seemed there was no escape from sectarian violence anywhere – well, anywhere apart from the family home, especially when the radio was on and a sonorous *English* voice, reading the shipping forecast or delivering a cricketing commentary, disseminated a tremendous sense of well-being and security.

'Cultural confusions' is George Watson's pertinent subtitle. As far as he was concerned, England was the great good place, a view compounded by his boyhood immersion in English public school stories such as *Teddy Lester's Chums* and weekly story papers like the *Champion* and the *Rover*. 'In that world,' he writes – that is, the world of honour, fair play and English uprightness – 'you would not see, with that sickening lurch of the heart, three shadowy figures detach themselves from a wall and saunter towards you, while you realised that your mental navigation had let you down ... and you had blundered into an Orange street. In Teddy Lester's world, you would not get a half brick on the head because you were a "Papish".'

The self-perpetuating momentum of sectarian misdoing was the thing that engendered the greatest despair in the hearts of liberals and social reformers of all persuasions, in the past and later. No citizens of Belfast, Benedict Kiely wrote in 1945 in his book *Counties of Contention*, 'could congratulate themselves on the uncouth, vicious thing that comes to life at intervals to burn and kill and destroy'. He wasn't singling out one faction as being more reprehensible than the other, at least at street-fighting level – but of course, as a general rule, liberal opinion in Ireland has always come down on the side of Catholicism. I don't mean the religious system, indeed, but the elements of society coming under that heading, since social oppression (roughly speaking) was a prerogative of the other side. 'Avaunt his verses be they ne'er so fine, / Who for the Catholics – REFUSED TO SIGN,' William Drennan wrote in 1811 about a clergyman-poet who'd declined to add his signature to a petition calling for Catholic Emancipation (see p. 93–4 below).

However, no one should be in any doubt that forms of Catholic bigotry exist which are just as virulent and excluding as their Protestant counterparts. If the latter seem to have more aggression about them, it's probably through being more insistently thrust in our faces. At any rate, this was true in the past. It's hard to forget incidents like the one described by James Connolly's daughter, Nora Connolly O'Brien, as she watches a terrified young shipyard worker pelting along Royal Avenue in Belfast with a gang of fifty men, all dressed in dungarees, in hot pursuit. 'Islandmen chasin' a Papish,' she is told off-handedly when she asks a passer-by what is going on.[4] Such things were still going on when Sam Thompson brought them to the attention of an audience outside Belfast with his play, *Over the Bridge* (see p. 242 below), first produced in 1960. And long before the days of political correctness you had a shoemaker in Belfast who advertised his wares with the unambiguous slogan, 'Wear Kelly's Boots to Trample the Papists'.

Well! By the time you reach this stage of bare-faced provocation, you've gone beyond bigotry and into some indigenous realm of robust street-assertion – and actually interdenominational entertainment. As a piece of unrepentant Ulster lore, the 'Kelly's Boots' injunction is fit to be cherished by all, along with 'The Oul' Orange Flute' and the story about the Orangeman on the Liverpool boat listening politely to a stranger who was singing the praises of the pope, describing the pontiff as a great statesman and a worthy gentleman personally into the bargain. 'What you say may be true,' says the cautious Orangeman eventually. 'It may be true, but I have to tell you, he has a very bad name in Portadown.' ... All right, I know I'm getting into a mode of Ulster quaintness here, but bear with me for a moment: I don't intend to overindulge in it. My aim is simply to indicate a tiny portion of the Northern Irish inheritance common to all of us, whether we kick with the right foot or the wrong foot — or whatever manufacturer's boots we wear to do it. It would, indeed, be a very po-faced Catholic and nationalist who would fail to be amused by the 'Trample the Papists' legend.

And there's another, more serious point to be made in connection with that egregious advertisement (and here, at last, I'm getting to the central theme of *A Twisted Root*). Consider for a moment the name Kelly — or Ó Ceallaigh, as it would have been in its original form. It's hard to think of anything more suggestive of Irish-Ireland, Gaelic and nationalist and Papist to the core. Somewhere in the background of your ultra-Orange bootmaker a change of allegiance must have occurred. And this, I'm convinced, would prove to be true of most of us in the north of Ireland. It's only necessary to go back a generation or two, in many cases, to find some abhorrent antecedent popping up to alarm any would-be factional purist — or delighting those of an ecumenical disposition. ... A few paragraphs back I mentioned Brian Moore's father and his aversion to Protestant bread. Dr Moore was a very prominent figure in Belfast Catholic circles in the 1920s and 30s, and utterly wrapped up in churchly activity — but, as it happens, his own father was a Catholic convert, and Dr Moore had a pair of nineteenth-century Protestant grandparents from Ballyclare to keep under his chapel-going hat.

That's just a tiny example of the pervasiveness of ancestral exogamy. Another occurs in the opening poem of Seamus Heaney's pungent sequence 'Clearances', from *The Haw Lantern* of 1987. It concerns his Protestant great-grandmother whose name was Robinson.

A cobble thrown a hundred years ago
Keeps coming at me, the first stone
Aimed at a great-grandmother's turncoat brow.
The pony jerks and the riot's on.
She's crouched low in the trap,
Running the gauntlet that first Sunday
Down the brae to Mass at a panicked gallop.
He whips on through the town to cries of 'Lundy!'

... And 'lapsed Protestant' Glenn Patterson, in his engaging book about his Lisburn grandparents, *Once Upon a Hill* (2008), doesn't have to go to any great lengths to uncover the Catholic lineage of one of them (see p. 189–90 below). And again: take the Falls Road, Catholic, Irish-speaking Carson family, and you find Liam Carson in his memoir *Call Mother a Lonely Field* (2010), and Ciaran Carson in various places, making no bones about claiming a great-grandfather – another turncoat – who started his adult life as an Orangeman in Ballymena. 'And all of us thought him a stout Orange blade.' Another memoir, the generically titled *Protestant Boy* (2004) by Geoffrey Beattie, evokes a true-blue, working-class upbringing in Ligoniel – but what the young Protestant Beattie doesn't grasp for years is the fact that his favourite uncle, his Uncle Terry, is 'one of them': a Papist. (It's true that Uncle Terence's name, O'Neill, which he shares with a prominent Ulster politician, suggests an uncertainty about his denominational origin.)

I could go on. And I will return from time to time to this melting-pot aspect of our heritage which exists as a strong undercurrent in Northern Irish life, even if many of us aren't aware of it (or would fiercely repudiate any such integrationist commonplace). As I have indicated, I intend to underscore the point by highlighting a couple of strands of my own ancestry, which for the purposes of this book may be taken as representative. I am endlessly intrigued – without, I hope, falling too easily into an 'ironies-of-history' mode of perception[5] – by the way things often work themselves out in an unexpected form; and when it comes to Northern Ireland and our sectarian divisions, it could be argued that the whole state of contention is based on a fallacy, the fallacy that every one of us is irreversibly and unequivocally attached to one tradition or the other. (I mean attached by genetics as well as political orientation.) As Irish-German Hugo Hamilton suggested in the title of his 2005 memoir, we are all 'speckled', streaked or piebald to a greater or lesser extent.[6]

So: 'Am I an Irishwoman?' This is the question Brigid Brophy put to herself in one of the wry and spirited essays which she published under the title *Don't Never Forget* (1966). Is she? Am I? Once, I'd have firmly believed I had a better right to that designation than a person born and brought up in London, but now I'm not so sure. In my case – and Brigid Brophy's, and everyone else's – Irishness, Englishness or whatever is only a part of it. If I go back far enough I find I can call myself Scandinavian (Blacar/Blacker), German (Heller, Stolzenbach) or Latvian (Lett). But if I do, I'll be in danger of disappearing up my own family tree, of taking off from its highest branches into some Never-Never Land at the top, where nationality and concomitant characteristics are watered down to nothingness. I'm really not interested in *global* interconnections; I just want to stick to one tiny spot (Northern Ireland), and try in a small way to undermine its internecine incompatibilities by emphasising all the composite undercurrents running through it.

As for those ubiquitous 'ironies of history' – sometimes something so overwhelming occurs along these lines that it can hardly be assimilated. Sometimes, too, it may get just a bit distorted to improve its impact. For example – the historian R.F. Foster has pointed out that William of Orange's victory at the Boyne 'was *not*, as so often claimed, greeted ... with a Te Deum in Rome'.[7] What a pity – however, it remains true that, due to the intricacies of seventeenth-century politics, the pope of the day made common cause with Protestant William rather than Catholic James. *Te Deum* or not, William's victory at the Boyne caused rejoicing in the Vatican. Not that it makes a whit of difference in the streets of Ballymena or Portadown. You don't see an image of Pope Alexander VIII, William's ally, borne aloft on any Orange banner.

Sixteen-ninety: let's go back a century or so from that significant date, to the 1590s and the Elizabethan Wars in Ireland. Don't worry, I'm not planning to present a potted history, either backwards or forwards: I just want to point out another staggering historical irony that's come to my attention. Everyone agrees that the outstanding enemy of Elizabethan rule in Ireland was Hugh O'Neill, Baron of Dungannon, Earl of Tyrone, last of the great Gaelic overlords of Ulster. O'Neill was a formidable strategist, well versed in 'shifts and devices', half 'civilised' by his boyhood exposure to the ways of the English court, half Irish 'savage' in the eyes of his military adversaries. For Queen Elizabeth I O'Neill was 'the fly in the ointment, the crack in the mirror, the thorn in the flesh' (I'm quoting from Elizabeth Bowen's 1943 review of Sean O'Faolain's book *The Great O'Neill*). Elizabeth's Deputy, Lord Mountjoy, saw the Irishman as 'the most ungrateful Viper to us that raised him'; and the queen herself labelled him a 'villainous Rebel'. All that – and Queen Elizabeth too (had she but known) might have echoed the cry of Macbeth when Banquo's descendants appeared before him in all their illustriousness: 'What, will the line stretch out to the crack of doom!' Elizabeth, of course, was childless and the Tudor line died out with her. O'Neill, on the other hand, was prolific in progeny and his descendants are innumerable. One of them sits on the English throne at the present time.[8] Queen Elizabeth II is not descended from Elizabeth I. She can, instead, count Hugh O'Neill, that jagged thorn in England's flesh, among her direct ancestors in the maternal line. Some kind of large dynastic wheel has come full circle here – though whether to the joy or dismay of Irish republicans I can't be sure.

Of course none of us, including the queen of England, can help our ancestors, the whole mixed bunch of them – though some in the north of Ireland, when it comes to a question of identity, may choose to believe they are indissolubly one thing or the other. They are not. One of my aims, when I started work on *A Twisted Root*, was to elevate the dark horse above the sacred cow, to argue for fusion rather than segregation, complexity instead of fixity. Here's John Hewitt, Belfastman, Irishman, native and settler, again: 'Kelt, Briton, Roman, Saxon, Dane and Scot, / time and this island tied a crazy knot.'

CHAPTER 1
WE HAD TO BUILD IN STONE FOR EVER AFTER

Famine and pestilence, grief, greed and slaughter ...

Anthony Cronin, *Letter to an Englishman*

Not long ago I was reading, with great pleasure, Germaine Greer's book about Shakespeare's wife.[1] This attempt to rehabilitate Anne Hathaway has much to recommend it, not least the aplomb of its central admission, that every one of its conclusions in favour of its subject is 'probably neither truer nor less true than the accepted prejudice'. The accepted prejudice is that Shakespeare, as far as he could, washed his hands of his disappointing spouse. But the meagre known facts of this enigmatic marriage will bear a different interpretation, as Germaine Greer shows. Not that facts alone come into the picture. Greer has gone about the work of scrutinising every available piece of documentary evidence relating to a particular time and place – the Warwickshire market town of Stratford-on-Avon in the second half of the sixteenth century – and assessing the extent to which her findings are applicable to Mrs Shakespeare. Inspired conjecture is the method – and in the hands of an author as adept as Germaine Greer, it makes for a fascinating account. Every bit of her book is interesting and informative – but it wasn't until I'd reached page 269 that I was jolted

1

out of the usual engaged but disinterested reader's mode. There appeared on that page a name which held significance for me personally. Katherine Rose.

Katherine Rose is listed among thirty-nine girls who were born in Stratford in 1585 and baptised at Holy Trinity Church in the town. Another is Shakespeare's daughter Judith. Of the remaining thirty-seven, Greer tells us, thirteen died young, in accordance with the usual pattern of childhood mortality. Another died unmarried in her early twenties. Most of the other Elizabethan Stratford girls in Greer's list disappear from the records, probably as a consequence of moving out of the district. They might have gone into service or married elsewhere, Greer thinks. Their subsequent history is lost to posterity, unlike that of Katherine Rose (at least in outline). She – my unimaginably-distant, multiply-great-grandmother – was married at eighteen or nineteen to a local tradesman, a cutler named John Tipping, who either came from Stratford itself, or from one of its outlying villages, Alcester, Alderminster or Leek Wootton, possibly. The marriage took place at the same Holy Trinity Church on 10 June 1604.

Was Judith Shakespeare, Katherine's contemporary and perhaps her friend, among the members of the congregation attending that summer wedding in the second year of the reign of King James I? It would please me to think so, but that's one fact among millions that can't be ascertained. Was Katherine's hair worn spread on her shoulders for the last time, before, as a married woman, she had to put it up and cover it with a kerchief? Did bridesmaids waken her that June morning by singing outside her window – her latticed window – 'The Bride's Goodmorrow'? ... And by envisaging an episode of early Jacobean revelry (with pastoral elements – in Stratford!), am I resorting to a piece of nursery-rhyme indulgence? Very likely; and I'm now about to make things worse by tying up the unreal picture I have in my head with a different set of pre-nuptial traditions and indigenous *joie de vivre*. In her wonderful book about the people, songs and traditions of Oriel[2] (*A Hidden Ulster*, 2002), Pádraigín Ní Uallacháin discusses at length a couple of spellbinding songs – among many others – '*Amhrain na Craoibhe*' ('The Garland Song') and '*Thugamar Fein an Samhradh Linn*' ('We Brought the Summer With Us'), both associated with ritual Gaelic forms of merrymaking, rejoicing in the arrival of summer, and rife with courtship and fertility implications. '*Amhrain na Craoibhe*', with its resonant chorus – 'Haigh do a bheir i 'bhaile's haigh di' ('Hey to him who takes her home, hey to her') – is extraordinarily delicate and at the same time, racy. One heady summertime festival, at Forkhill, County Armagh, at which that particular song would have been sung, is dated precisely to 9 June; and it was probably taking place at the same time as the Rose/Tipping wedding, in another country. ... But similar jollifications held an important place in rural communities all over Europe; is there any more than a generic connection between the two different forms of celebration I've singled out here? Well, the connection is arbitrary, indeed; but perhaps not quite as arbitrary as all that. The descendants of Katherine Rose and John Tipping did reach County Armagh, but not for some time.

My mother died in September 2001. The night of the 21/22. It was an unreal time. At her funeral a few days later, at the Catholic church of Kilclief, County Down, where I absolutely did not want to be, I overreacted to the generic jabber of the young officiating priest who knew nothing at all about her, her kindness to cats, her relish for local, comic turns of phrase, the poems she could quote. 'True to her faith'; 'respected in the community': these were the clichés he spouted. Well, she was a Catholic in as much as she was anything, but for the last thirty-odd years of her life she had ceased to be a practising Catholic, in response to the pressures and influences of the modern world. Religion did not play a great part in her life. Only in the run-up to her miserable death in the Medical Assessment Unit of Downpatrick Hospital did the trappings of her Catholic girlhood begin to creep back, as something to hold on to in a disintegrating world. When a nun entered the ward and sat down by her bedside, my mother claimed to have been 'brought up' by nuns, turning herself in retrospect into an orphan and banishing her own resolute mother, and her older sisters, from a selective image of the past which she at that moment held in her head. What she should have said was 'educated by nuns', her education running in tandem with a perfectly adequate and not excessively religious home life. But her brain had softened. She was eighty-eight. She thought she was on holiday – 'This is a nice hotel, isn't it?' Then she thought she'd been stuck in some unsuitable location with a lot of drivelling pensioners. 'There's nobody my age here. They're all old people.' This was shortly before she sank into unconsciousness and ceased to think anything at all. Friends and relations came and went, stroked her hand and exchanged hopeless glances across her hospital-issue coverlet. Through it all, my father, four years her junior and in full possession of his faculties, exhibited remarkable patience and tact (he is not a patient man), going to endless lengths to tempt her with titbits and bolster her spirits. For a long time he believed that, if he got her home, he'd be able to bring her back to herself. But it was plain to everyone else the way she was going.

Her decline had come on slowly, and then accelerated towards the end. A couple of broken hips contributed to the process. It was out the window with her unique, engaging personality, her charm, resourcefulness, humour, efficiency and kindness, all the things that marked my mother off from the general run of mothers and schoolteachers, in my experience. All the things the platitudinous priest knew nothing about. His mealy-mouthed tributes could have fitted anyone, and no doubt did. When I rose up, at the funeral, to say my piece (reluctantly allowed to do so because, with my father, I was the chief mourner: the Church, it seems, doesn't really care for any form of secular speaking within its sacred precincts) – when I rose up, I began by declaring, 'One thing it's true to say about my mother –' (I stressed 'one thing') – 'is that all her life she was a Shakespeare enthusiast.' I then quoted from memory the opening verse of the funeral song for Cloten from *Cymbeline*, which begins, 'Fear no more the heat o' the sun'. In my overwrought state I could only manage one verse, but I hoped it was enough to make the point that what I said was true and pertinent and *particular*.

My mother's bible was A.C. Bradley's *Shakespearean Tragedy*, a book she'd studied closely during her golden years as a student at Queen's University, Belfast, in the 1930s. She lived at the time in a house in Sandhurst Gardens, in the middle of a dingy terrace sloping down towards the Lagan with its damp fogs immortalised by Maurice Craig (see p. 211): damp fogs were then a feature of Belfast, wrapping its workaday streets in murk and mystery, engendering a good-humoured exasperation in pedestrians bumping into one another, or stumbling for the twentieth time over the stumpy base of a green-ribbed metal lamppost with outstretched arms like an elongated scarecrow. Belfast could seem, then, like 'old, murky Edinburgh' with its Burke-and-Hare atmosphere relished by Sean O'Faolain in his *Irish Journey*. Its seasons were distinctive. At Queen's, for instance, summer was tied up with the carnival carry-on of successive rag days, 1933, '34, '35; a bench in the cloisters between lectures, flirtation, gossip with friends;[3] and the lectures themselves, delivered with aplomb or eccentricity by professors with plentiful initials, R.M. Henry, H.O. White and H.O. – again – Meredith.

My mother, Nora Brady, took her studies seriously. She understood that hard work was necessary to gain her degree, and applied herself unstintingly to everything required of her – but naturally some parts of the course held more appeal than others. And at the top of her personal pantheon was Shakespeare – in particular, the tragedies; and of the tragedies the two that spoke most compellingly to her were *Hamlet* and *Macbeth*. And Bradley's sensible, character-based approach to the plays struck a chord with her, from the moment his book was brought to her attention. The full glory of every line of Shakespeare's was ingested by my mother, linguistic, dramatic and all. She didn't need to have a gloss imposed on every textual ambiguity; mystery, impenetrability, held its own appeal. She simply took it all in. Whole passages from Shakespeare came to her aid in times of anxiety or upheaval. ... And because of all this, it's a cause of chagrin to me that she died without knowledge of her own slight personal connection with the world of Shakespeare, a connection unfolding through her ancestors in the direct line who were Shakespeare's fellow-townsmen, members of the same Holy Trinity Church, and quite possibly attended the playwright's funeral there in 1616.

When I was twelve and a pupil in Form 2A at St Dominic's High School on the Falls Road in Belfast, a performance of *Macbeth* was put on at the Grand Opera House next door to the Hippodrome in Great Victoria Street. The year is 1955. One morning after assembly in the study hall comes an announcement of a treat in store for the school. Well, not the whole of the school. Pupils en masse, from Form 3 upwards, will be privileged to enjoy an evening performance of *Macbeth* (those who can afford to pay for a seat in the stalls, that is). English teachers, one per class, will shepherd the lucky theatregoers into their plush-velvet rows and block any access of overexcitement before it can get a hold. That is the unspoken agreement: the emphasis that morning is placed on the educational and recreational sides of the outing. Marks and larks. I don't know if many at the school are theatrically inclined, but a rare sense of impending festivity grips the upper forms and creates a buzz. And what of the rest of us? The excluded children of Forms 1 and 2 are left feeling resentful and flat. The edict concerning our unsuitability as playgoers especially gets up the noses of myself and my friend Fiona

5

Devlin, since we are actually reading *Macbeth* in English class and gaining a lot of enjoyment from it — old enough to study the play, it seems, but not to view it. So it's in an aggrieved frame of mind that I go home at lunchtime, catching a number 12 bus as usual outside the Royal Victoria Hospital and alighting at St James's Park, tearing down the Park, pigtails flying, turning right at St James's Avenue and in through our back gate, to solicit sympathy from my reliably partisan mother. 'Why can't we go as well? ... It isn't fair.'

It isn't, she agrees, and proceeds to do something about it. It is then too late to obtain a seat in any part of the Opera House except the gods. So up and up we go, on the night in question, my friend, my mother and myself, up flights and flights of stone steps to emerge at last, with a jolt of vertigo, into an unexpectedly steep area that has us hanging on to one another while we find some solid seats to sit down on. Relief! And there below us, when we nerve ourselves to peer over the edge, are the assembled upper forms of St Dominic's — there is Miss McVerry, identifiable by her turquoise hat.

I am a little disorientated; the Opera House is a pocket of opulence in the lustreless city, not what I am used to, an overwhelming extravagance of decor. But from the moment the curtain rises on the wild and incantatory witches gathered round their cauldron, I am transported. It's not aesthetic or theatrical excitement that grips me, exactly, but rather poetic — the lines, the words of Shakespeare and the way they are spoken. I am lifted out of myself and out of the downbeat ambience of Belfast. And all the way home, on the bus and on foot, a particular sinister and overpowering passage is ringing in my ears:

> Light thickens, and the crow
> Makes wing to the rooky wood.
> Good things of day begin to droop and drowse,
> Whiles night's black agents to their preys do rouse.

Night's black agents. In his poem 'The Colony', John Hewitt refers to 'a terrible year when, huddled in our towns, / My people trembled as the beacons ran / From hill to hill across the countryside, / Calling the dispossessed to lift their standards.' One town in the north of Ireland sheltering a huddle of menaced settlers was Lisburn, or Lisnagarvey as it was then: the year was 1641 and the dispossessed were on the rampage.

Among the inhabitants of Lisburn at that time we find the Stratford Tippings – two, or possibly three, generations of them – some, no doubt, taking part in the fighting which broke out at the end of November, others seeking safety wherever they could find it. To discover what brought the Tippings to this ill-omened place it's necessary to go back twenty years or so, to Sir Fulke Conway and his assembly of hardy adventurers, fifty-one families from Stratford and thereabouts, who, giving in to persuasion, had turned their backs on everything steady and familiar, every *English* blessing, and set off for unknown, remote and dangerous territory. Probably the group, in a general mood of apprehension mixed up with optimism, would have sailed from Bristol and landed at Bangor, then struck inland through the mud and murk of bedevilled Ulster – territory utterly new to them and not immediately holding out a prospect of welcome. 'One can imagine the wayside camp in the rain and mud, watched over by a weary sentinel; for that woodland on the hillside might well hold a swordsman or two; and if there were no swordsmen in it there were surely wolves ...'. You can't say historian Cyril Falls's imagination is running away with him when he envisages this scene in his 1936 account of *The Birth of Ulster*.

Sir Fulke Conway of Ragley Hall in Warwickshire was an industrious planter of the lands in South Antrim granted to him in 1609 by King James I, including the manor of Killultagh and the castle and village of Lisnagarvey. The castle had belonged to a deposed grandee of the O'Neill dynasty, but where the villagers were when Sir Fulke put in an appearance, or what state the 'village' was in, we haven't a clue. We do know that forest as impenetrable as anything out of Grimm was the first thing to be noted about the area. Well, the name tells us as much, Killultagh – *Coille Ultagh* – meaning simply the woods of Ulster. These pre-Elizabethan woods were dense. It was said that, if you'd had a mind to, you might almost have walked from MacArt's Fort[12] to Lisnagarvey across the tops of trees, oak and elm and spreading chestnut. And down below, among the gnarled trunks and the loamy undergrowth, lurked all kinds of menaces, natural and supernatural. Wolves and wild Irishmen and shadowy bogeymen. So the colonists' first task was to clear the land for ploughing and building, to fell as many trees as possible and divest the forest of most of its sinister associations. These 'modern' imperatives would have taken shape in Planter minds as a way of dealing with age-old dangers and superstitions.

Move forward to 1622 and we have to wonder if Sir Fulke Conway's new wave of settlers had the least idea of what they were coming to. What lay behind them was a place, a region of England filled with lush hedgerows and deep country lanes, catkins swaying in the breeze, plum orchards and cider vats, neat villages complete with manor house, grey Norman church and outlying farms, as placid as a child's picture book, at least on the surface, and destined to find a place in the minds of beset Irish incomers, perhaps, as a glowing Elizabethan idyll incomprehensibly relinquished. And in front of them ...? Well, recent history supplied an image of an utterly bereft and barbarous country, ruin and desolation on every side, multitudes of starved Irish strewn dead about the countryside, their mouths all green from eating shamrocks, nettles and dock leaves; violence and misery inflicted and reciprocated. '[W]e do continually hunt all their woods, spoil their corn, burn their houses, and kill as many churls as it grieveth me to think it is necessary to do so.' So wrote Lord Mountjoy before he left the country in 1604 – the year of the Tippings' wedding – bequeathing to his successors a legacy of remorselessness towards all Irish 'rebels', and an odd way of implementing the 'civilising' mission decreed by England for the benefit of outlandish Ulster.

The Tippings and their fellow-Plantees, in the throes of an absolute break with the past, probably would have understood little about the circumstances causing land in a foreign country, a remote outpost, to become available to them, just for the asking. It's unlikely they'd have heard of the Earls and their exodus, or the great defeat that preceded the 'Flight' from Lough Swilly's shores, and subsequent appropriation, by the Crown, of all the forfeit lands. Actually, the most concise and witty summing up of the situation – and its outcome – that I'm aware of, occurs in a recent poem, 'The Yaddo Letter' by Derek Mahon:

> ... I'd wander round the hills above Kinsale
> Where English forces clobbered Hugh O'Neill
> In Tudor times, wrecking the Gaelic order
> (result, plantations and the present Border) ...

Result, all those indeed. And here, unwittingly contributing to the long-drawn-out process, were some innocent Planters – I'm assuming they were innocent of any genocidal or even warlike tendencies – arriving in a desolate part of the north of Ireland with their portable belongings, prepared to the fullest extent for arduous labour, eyes firmly fixed on the long-term advantage. Having no alternative, once they'd got there, they dug in their heels and settled. The ground on which they established their exiguous settlement would evolve in time into the considerable town of Lisburn; but first it was necessary to engage in building work, land cultivation and evasion of onslaughts from the outraged Irish – all the things they'd come prepared to tackle, and a few extra besides.

Possibly the Tippings, then in their late thirties, were accustomed to manual work. They may have been employed previously as tenant farmers or servants on the Conway family's estate at Arrow, near Stratford-on-Avon, if they didn't live in the town of Stratford itself. We know they were married in it, at Holy Trinity Church, but not the location of their first home, or what persuaded them to become immigrants into the unknown.

It seems likely that invitations to proceed to Ireland would have been issued first of all to those possessing invaluable construction skills, bricklaying, plastering, carpentry and so forth, and perhaps a skill in the making and selling of knives was considered an asset too. We needn't assume, with old-style nationalist historians, that some discreditable motive underlay the Planters' willingness to uproot themselves – that Ireland, unknown and unimaginable, offered an escape route out of some sticky situation prevailing at home. It hardly seems fair to label the whole lot of them the 'scum' of two countries (England and Scotland), as some contemporary commentators did. Their aim was probably no different to that of emigrants before or since – to gain a better life. The lure of unexplored territory was strong at the time, and there was Ireland, Ulster, on their doorstep, so to speak, without the bother of going the whole way to America. These new, hopeful colonists would hardly have been aware, at least to start with, of moral ambiguities surrounding their presence in Ulster – though no doubt native hostility soon became apparent to them. We know, however, that accommodations were worked out – that it wasn't entirely a case of the native Irish being rounded up and deposited on hills and in bogs, wherever the land was scrubby and unproductive, while crowing colonists lorded it over them. The colonists hadn't exactly marched in and grabbed the good Irish lands from under the noses of their rightful owners, though there was enough truth in the perception of wholesale dispossession to fuel antagonisms for centuries to come. Scrupulous historians, from about the mid twentieth century on, have been at pains to restore complexity to what had come to be seen as a simple matter of right and wrong, with these interchangeable entities depending totally on the standpoint you viewed them from. Planter civility versus native barbarism: this was one of the accepted oppositions. Native integrity versus foreign oppression was another.

Foreign oppression. A collection of poems by Francis Carlin, published in 1918, includes a resonant contribution to the 'wronged Irish' ideology. It is called 'The Ballad of Douglas Bridge':

> On Douglas Bridge I met a man
> Who lived adjacent to Strabane,
> Before the English hung him high
> For riding with O'Hanlon.
>
> 'Before that time,' said he to me
> My fathers owned the land you see,
> But they are now among the moors,
> A-riding with O'Hanlon.'

... The ghostly speaker in the Carlin poem embodies a persisting and romantic sense of grievance about stolen lands and enforced degradation. Carlin's historical imagination embraces an idea of Ulster – we've now moved forward to the late seventeenth century – as a wilderness still populated exclusively by wronged natives and ruthless colonists, with Redmond O'Hanlon, a sturdy defender of the dispossessed, singled out as the epitome of lawlessness in a good cause. He was a man in the grip of a mission: to inflict the utmost aggravation on strangers imposed on Irish acres. Robin Hood. The Irish Rapparee. Well, 'Rapparee' is not the word, exactly. The term only became current in the 1690s, some years after O'Hanlon was shot dead. You can trace the anachronism back to the nineteenth-century novelist William Carleton who based a work of fiction on O'Hanlon and gave it the subtitle 'The Irish Rapparee', when he should have known better. He should also have known not to extend O'Hanlon's principled brigandage into the late 1690s, if he wished to stick to the historical facts. But did he? With *Redmond Count O'Hanlon: The Irish Rapparee* we're in a Sherwood Forest scenario, adapted to fit Armagh. The normally serious and impassioned Carleton has somehow slipped into a different mode, the bad-but-colourful-old-days bagatelle. This is someone who denounced the diehards of his own day in his novel of 1845, *Rody the Rover; or, The Ribbonman*. But he takes a very different attitude to the bandits of the past, whom he makes as honourable and invincible as the original *Fianna Éireann*.

Redmond O'Hanlon – with Carleton's help or without it – has bequeathed his name to a particular Planter hazard: a fear, amounting to obsession, of secretive wild men in rough garb relying on local knowledge to effect their deadly objectives. Anachronistically or not, he's the quintessential rapparee. Throughout the frantic seventeenth century an image took shape in Planter minds of marauding Irish lurking in the undergrowth intending harm to their supplanters. And after 1641 it gained a hellish and concrete crystallisation. 'There was great slaughter then, man woman, child, / With fire and pillage of our timbered houses; / We had to build in stone for ever after', John Hewitt wrote in 'The Colony', a pointed monologue in which the narrator sticks up for Planter entitlements, while admitting the justice of aboriginal affront: 'for we began the plunder'. Hewitt's apparent Roman legionary is of course meant to be taken as an Ulster incomer of the seventeenth century: a far-seeing man, and one endowed with a liberal consciousness.

Incidentally, the name O'Hanlon carries more than one connotation. Members of that clan, only a generation back from the dashing Redmond of Carleton and Carlin, were deeply implicated in the unholy activities of 1641, having a hand in the notorious shoving of Protestants off Portadown Bridge and generally contributing to the cruelty and mayhem of the age. Mary Hickson (see p. 15 below), writing at the end of the Victorian era, dissociates herself strongly from the outlaw glamour conferred by posterity on this plunderer and son of plunderers and murderers. In Ireland, there are always contradictory ways of looking at things, and always many outlets for savage indignation.

Before the anticipated eruption occurs – to return to the newly arrived Tippings where we left them, maybe digging the foundations for a house in a future high street, or helping to plot out the fortified tower house of their patron Sir Fulke Conway, with its gardens and orchards sloping down to the River Lagan – before the year of wholesale slaughter, the settler drive to wrest order from the wilderness is making headway. Hewitt again:

We planted little towns to garrison
the heaving country, heaping walls of earth
and keeping all our cattle close at hand ...

The site chosen for the Conway mansion had previously been known
as *Lios na gCearrbach*, Fort of the Gamblers, though who or what the
eponymous gamblers were is a mystery. Were they servants or retainers
attached to the stronghold nearby, so addicted to games of chance that
they never stopped playing until they'd gambled the clothes off one
another's backs? Or outlaws taking a break from their depredations on
the earliest wave of settlers? Different accounts have different surmises
to offer. But whatever the truth of the matter, the name took hold – and
perhaps it wasn't too wide of the mark in settler terms as well. The whole
new way of life for the ordinary colonists was a gamble, as to whether
they would prosper, or go under.

We don't know, either, how 'Lisnagarvey' turned into Lisburn –
Lisbourne, Lisburne in early documents – 'burn' having no obvious Irish
derivation. It is surely too literal-minded to relate it to the burning of
the town in 1641. But 'burn' it became, and stayed. And while I'm on
the subject of obscurities and inconsistencies, I should mention that the
Conway castle at Lisnagarvey was either the old O'Neill castle renovated,
or a fortified manor built from scratch; that it was either Sir Fulke, who
died in 1624, or his brother Sir Edward, who undertook the necessary
refurbishment, or demolition and reconstruction (you can take your
pick). It's certain, though, that by 1630 – when Sir Edward died in his
turn – an anglified structure had taken the place of the original Gaelic
castle. Its gardens, outbuildings, brewhouse, oathouse, powderhouse and
office were enclosed within a wall, while the stables, stable yard, kitchen
garden and slaughterhouse stood outside. With the flower gardens and
orchards mentioned above, and the salmon-filled river, it was certainly
an idyllic habitation.

The indigenous Irish may have watched with amazement as radical
alterations to the landscape and native architecture took place around
them; and we know that many of them were not too set in the ways of
Gaelic feudalism to accept employment with the newcomers. The old
world was giving way to the new; and no amount of Gaelic recalcitrance,
or allegiance to the past, was going to halt the process. For those of a
pragmatic cast of mind, the way forward was clear enough, and entailed

adapting to current circumstances. At the same time, they'd have waited to see if the overthrow of the Gaelic world might not be followed by a reversal: who knew what plans for a coup or a military campaign were being fomented from above! They, the ordinary Irish, certainly had cause to resent the labels – 'barbarous', 'savage', 'churls', 'bandits' – foisted on them by colonists unfamiliar with the intricacies and sophistications of the Gaelic way of life. Settler presumptions of superiority, and contempt for an old and alien civilisation, didn't make for an easing of suspicions and hostilities.

The basic obstacle to meaningful communication between settler and native was of course the language difficulty, with the edict coming down from the new administrative class that inclusion under the heading 'civil Irish' depended on a person's command of the English language. If you couldn't speak English you were seen as nearly Neanderthal. Well, Edmund Spenser in the previous century had taken the view that the only way to deal with the entire unruly population of Ireland was to exterminate it or anglicise it, that extermination wasn't too dire a fate for those who wouldn't be anglicised. But it often happened instead that settlers became gaelicised, though it could take a few generations for the process to get truly under way.

When John and Katherine Tipping uprooted themselves from well-regulated Warwickshire and headed for the woods of Ulster, they brought with them a family of five children aged between four and seventeen. The oldest, Thomas, was born in 1605; then came Anne (1608), John (1610), Alicia (1614) and William (1617). All English-born, all attuned (we may suppose) to the enlightened civilities of the age. One would like to think these younger Tippings regarded the Irish enterprise as a great adventure. Did they exhibit a *Children of the New Forest* type of resourcefulness once they'd reached their own new forest, Killultagh? Was the strangeness of Ireland, the dark aboriginal woods sheltering mysterious ill-wishers, will o' the wisps, the beehive-shaped huts housing seeming savages, the gloomy days of winter, the fraught silences punctuated by snatches of a foreign tongue – were these things an enticement or a cause of nightmare? Did they hanker after a Warwickshire peace and quiet? Or did they soon begin to feel at home? They had their little community around them to keep the worst of the colonists' perils at bay – or so it seemed – and there in front of their eyes a whole new town was taking shape, with castle, church and street of houses.

The earliest map of Lisburn, preserved in the Dublin Rent Office and dated to 1640, lists the names of the original builders of the town. Alongside 'John Tippen' we find a George Rose who can't have been other than the Tipping children's uncle, Katherine's brother; and probably there were cousins too, in the little settler enclave. Most of the names on the builders' list are clearly English in origin (Dobbs, Bones, Butterfield), a few are Welsh (John ap Richard, Owen ap Hugh), and there's even one Irish name, Peter O'Mullred (O'Mullan, Ui Maol Riada?), to bring in a suggestion of a rudimentary democracy operating at the time (democracy, or sycophancy: again, you can take your pick). The same map shows the Tippens (Tippings) established at No. 12 the High Street (the present Castle Street), with Bridge Street on the other side of the castle descending pleasantly to the River Lagan. In 1640, this was the whole extent of the town.

Perhaps the younger children attended school in the centre of the Market Place, getting up early in the morning and, after a breakfast of porridge and buttermilk, crossing the road with their satchels and hornbooks. In winter, they might have carried lanterns to see them safely home. In the long days of summer, there were abundant fields behind the houses to play in, or to gather herbs for cooking and healing. Would the older ones have learned to read and write before they left Stratford? We have no way of telling – or of envisaging what kinds of commerce and social activity the adults engaged in. Was their aim to make a replica of an English town? More than a century later, in 1759, an English traveller called Willes compared Lisburn to Stratford-on-Avon – but by this time the town had been destroyed twice, and twice rebuilt, and descendants of the first inhabitants were long dispersed. Nevertheless, perhaps something survived, in Lisburn's layout and atmosphere, of the settler impulse to create a home-from-home; and, in the peculiar conditions of seventeenth-century Ulster, a pocket of sanity and calm amid the general disorder.

Bridge Street today (2009) is a sorry sight. Its straggle of rickety houses and shops has a dank, abandoned look about it. Redevelopment, not conservation, is horribly in the air. Well, Lisburn, now a city, is no less prone than anywhere else in the North to modern forms of crassness and philistinism. (I'm talking architecture here.) But up until a couple of years ago, there was at least one good reason for visiting Bridge Street. Right at the top, on the corner opposite the present linen museum (the old market house) stood a second-hand bookshop run by a Church of Ireland minister named William Harshaw. The Old Bookshop, Lisburn, had everything to gladden the heart of a collector. You could hardly get in for the piles of books crammed in every corner and cranny. Books spilled over from the sagging shelves and colonised large sections of floor space. Falling on them with a whoop, if your eye was caught by some desirable title wedged in the middle, might cause the whole tottery structure to topple over – but it didn't matter. The helpful, knowledgeable, laid-back proprietor was only too happy if you'd lighted on something you were looking for.

The Old Bookshop was not exactly run as a commercial concern and so it became unsustainable, in the brutal days of rising rents and rates. Its alluring abundance of bibliomaniac's *desiderata* has been transported elsewhere. Like the old Smithfield Market in Belfast, foremost resort of the bric-a-brac addict, it had about it a ramshackle headiness: you were always certain to emerge from these eccentric premises with your arms overladen. Both rarities and standard works in any subject were copiously on offer. I don't know what led me to the Old Bookshop (other than an instinct for acquisition), but shortly after I'd moved back to Northern Ireland, after long years in London, I could count myself among William Harshaw's most persistent customers. My book interests are eclectic: first editions of the twentieth century, poetry, detective fiction and what-have-you. I'm principally a children's-books accumulator, and hard-to-find titles by Mabel Esther Allan, Elinor Lyon, Winifred Darch, Evadne Price and others were apt to turn up here. Children's books – yes. But I'm also always on the look-out for material to do with Ireland, past and present, and in this respect too the Old Bookshop turned up trumps. *Ulster and Ireland*, by J.W. Good, published by Maunsel in 1919; the Talbot Press edition of Ferguson's poems; *The Truth about Ulster*, by F. Frankfort Moore; the Northern Banking Company's Centenary Volume of 1924 ... all these, and more, many more, arrived on my shelves by way of Bridge Street, Lisburn. And among them was Mary Hickson's *Ireland in the Seventeenth Century* – published in 1884 – which describes in some detail 'the Irish Massacres of 1641–42'. What I didn't know, when I first read Mary Hickson's account of this atrocious episode, was that an ancestor of my own, a Tipping in-law, was conspicuous among the massacred. His name was Edward Alleyn, or Allen, and he lost his life in horrific circumstances, and as a consequence of the Irish, with their exterminatory instincts aroused, paying no heed to chivalrous rules or merciful strategies available in wartime.

Between 1622 and the autumn of 1641 the Tippings seem to have lived peaceably enough in their two-street town with the broiling countryside beyond it, the ageing parents and the growing children, who, in due course, followed the impulse to found families of their own. (The two girls, alas, as is generally the way with female siblings and the female line, disappear from the story.) By the 1630s, Stratford-on-Avon would likely have faded in the minds of all the High Street and Bridge Street immigrants, especially those of the younger generation. Ulster was the here-and-now, and a kind of social order and civic consciousness was being established in Lisburn itself and in all the little Planter towns, in small ways and according to an English pattern. The Protestant religion loomed large as an aspect of the 'civilised' life, as much for what it stood for, among a rudimentary bourgeoisie – the past, moderation, respectability – as for its value as a theological comfort.

But Irishness wasn't an insurmountable obstacle to the forming of attachments. The first Tipping to marry outside the tribe was the youngest son of John and Katherine, William, whose bride's name, Margaret O'Hoole (O'Toole, Ui Thuathail?) suggests a different type of upbringing and family background. (This is an assumption – and so is a good deal of what follows.) William, we remember, had only had four years of being a little English boy in the reign of King James, before the woods of Ulster closed in on him, bounding his horizons and perhaps endowing him with a degree of sympathy for the local underdog, the ill-treated Irish. … However it came about, the marriage of William and Margaret in the summer of 1640 is recorded in the sole surviving fragment of the earliest register of Lisnagarvey Parish Church, St Thomas's – so the bride can't have been of an unshakeably Catholic faith. No children are attributed to the couple, but that's not to say they didn't have any: we simply don't know. William went on to become an officer in the Royalist army and after the Restoration of 1662 he was granted lands in County Leitrim and County Armagh, as we shall see. But in the year of the uprising the twenty-four-year-old William was probably still in Lisburn, along with his brothers John and Thomas. All three were married by this time; John was the father of an infant daughter, and Thomas had four young children (a fifth, a girl, had died shortly after birth). ... Apart from a few brief mentions later on, the middle Stratford son, John, at this point passes out of my Tipping narrative, I am thankful to say: there are far too many Johns and Williams and Thomases making it difficult to disentangle one from t'other. One might have wished for a tad more originality in the matter of the naming of offspring; where are the Hercules and Horatios and Henriettas who might have made things easier for a future chronicler (not to mention reader)?

But now the autumn of 1641 is creeping up on us, and we have the whole lot of the Ulster Tippings – not yet multiplied immeasurably – assembled in or near the original settlement (I think). Settler fears of a native outbreak had never been entirely allayed, although – as I've suggested – life in Lisburn and other embryo towns had assumed as far as possible a flourishing character. Prophetic voices like that of Sir Thomas Phillips, governor of Coleraine, had warned against complacency: 'It is fered that they will Rise upon a Sudden and Cutt the Throts of the poore dispersed British.'

The signs were there, and eventually the time was right. It's recorded in *The Montgomery Manuscripts* that, on the afternoon of 23 October, a man, 'half-stript', dismounted from his horse and came running to the Montgomerys of the Ards bearing a missive from Bishop Leslie in Lisburn to the effect that all hell had broken loose. 'Insurrections, Murthers, and burnings' were being carried out by 'ye Irish' on all sides. The first messenger was swiftly followed by further out-of-breath runners bringing the alarming news of 'Crewell Massacres of divers persons'. Panic set in, and soon the countryside was alive with the terror-stricken settler population fleeing in droves towards reputed places of safety, towns such as Lifford, Strabane and Derry. Their houses, lands, hay, corn, farming implements, furniture, clothes ... everything they had owned was in flames behind them. 'There hath been seen great fires so near as were discerned from this place,' Lord Edward Chichester in Belfast wrote in agitation to the king on 24 October.

Two days previously, a section of the Ulster Irish under the leadership of Sir Phelim O'Neill had launched a surprise assault on major fortified positions in the North, and by now nearly the whole of Ulster, from

Newry to Donegal, was in Irish hands. The game was afoot. And some of the Irish were running amok. Most people nowadays would agree that the rising was not planned as a wholesale massacre of English and Scottish settlers – that it wasn't the 'fiendish Romish massacre' of popular Protestant mythology. But it also seems clear that the military commanders quickly lost control of headstrong recruits whose pent-up angers and resentments had finally gained an outlet – a savage outlet. The settlers, it seemed, were fair game. They could be slaughtered, robbed, stripped of their clothes and possessions, and driven naked into the wilderness with impunity. They were paying a terrible price for the depredations wrought earlier in the century on the orders of Lord Mountjoy and Sir Arthur Chichester. 'We have killed, burnt and spoiled all along the lough within four miles of Dungannon,' the latter had written in 1601. 'We spare none of what quality or sex soever, and it hath bred much terror in the people.' In Irish eyes, the long-awaited vengeance was justified in matching 'excess with excess'. I'm quoting here from the Colville Papers of 1717, in a different context but with equal relevance: 'for as we know savage customs always beget a corresponding darkness of the soul'.

As days and weeks went by, the horror stories proliferated. Lurgan was burnt to the ground, Portadown was the scene of a hellish event, when about a hundred of the settler community were flung into the River Bann and drowned, and more helpless victims were burned to death by a sept of the Maguires at Lisgoole Castle in County Fermanagh. What, we might wonder, went through the attackers' heads as they put whole communities violently to death? Did they think of themselves as avengers, heroes? The final sight to meet the eyes of many of those cut down would have been their mad malignant faces glorying in a homicidal frenzy. The imprint of these occurrences must be etched into the landscape, branded for ever on the places where the worst of human impulses erupted.

The reality was terrible enough, but it wasn't long before rumour and fabrication spewed up ever more gruesome enormities. Colonel Manus O'Cahan, a commander in the Irish army, for example, was envisaged gorging himself at the breakfast table on the heads of murdered Protestants (like a worse version of the giant in *Jack and the Beanstalk*). The bridge at Portadown soon acquired an evil reputation as cries and howlings, believed to signal a ghostly re-enactment of the drownings, made it a place to avoid after dark. (A more prosaic explanation for the

A contemporary image of the massacre of settlers at Portadown

eerie nocturnal noises put them down to wolves, or to packs of dogs made homeless by the murder of their masters.)

Meanwhile, back in Lisburn. ... The townspeople, including, no doubt, the able-bodied Tippings, were rallying against the menacing Irish forces. Some among the Planters were rather disposed to stand their ground than to fly for their lives, and among them was a Captain Robert Lawson who beat a drum through the emptying streets of Belfast calling for volunteers. Having 'gathered in all about 160 horse and foot', Captain Lawson then proceeded to Lisburn, where he and his men beat off an attack on the town by Sir Conn Magennis. It was the night of 25 October. Reinforcements arrived, led by Lord Montgomery and Lord Hamilton, and by Sir George Rawdon, the current Lord Conway's agent in Ireland. In all, up until the evening of 28 November, when the ground was covered in ice and the dregs of snow, three assaults on the town took place, and all were repelled. Even stampeding a herd of cattle at the town gates didn't achieve the attackers' objective. In the aftermath of the third attack, led by Phelim O'Neill himself, Bridge Street and High Street were chock-a-block with corpses of both factions, lying where they'd been struck down. The lovely meadows behind the houses had become a killing ground too, a place of pure horror.

Soon houses, meadows and corpses were all gone, all burned to ashes, reduced to smouldering ruins. The retreating Irish set fire to the town on the night of 28 November; and the following day, for good measure, they burnt George Rawdon's house, Brookhill (built before 1611 by our old acquaintance Sir Fulke Conway, whose library went up in smoke with the rest). ... Had the women and children of Lisburn been moved to some place of safety? Were they – and I'm thinking particularly here of the female Tippings – among those residents who, with the Bishop of Down who sent the warning to the Ards, 'fled towards Belfast' with whatever they could carry? (I'm quoting from Lord Ernest Hamilton's *The Irish Rebellion of 1641*.) There are no records of non-combatant casualties in Lisburn at this time – and we know the Tippings survived, though at least one of their kinsmen by marriage didn't. This was Edward Allen, mentioned above (p. 16).

A wild and forsaken part of Ireland in the early seventeenth century was the Leitrim/Longford area, and it was decided, in 1621, to try to bring it under English control by importing strong colonists. Among them was a Humphrey Alleyn, or Allen, who was granted 810 acres in Toomonahan townland in the barony of Carrigallen on the shores of Garadice Lough, by edict of King James I. This Humphrey had a son, Edward, whose daughter Elizabeth, eighteen years old, came to Lisburn in 1635 to marry the thirty-year-old Thomas Tipping. This makes Elizabeth Allen from Garadice Lough the first Mrs Tipping to marry in Ireland; and she embarked on her wifely occupations with a will (for all we know to the contrary). Actually, of course, our ignorance concerning the private lives of Thomas and Elizabeth is illimitable. We can't tell how the marriage came about, with the two of them living, as they did, at a considerable distance from one another. How did they get acquainted in the first place, and what drew them together? Was it an arranged marriage? Did Thomas have business that took him to Longford? Was he a cutler, like his father? We have nothing to go on, to further speculation – just the stark fact contained in the St Thomas Church register. They married, and had children (the youngest, John, the most crucial to my purposes, hasn't yet put in an appearance, but he will shortly). And wherever Elizabeth and these children had taken refuge during the days of wrath, she must have been frantic with worry about her father and the rest of her family back in Longford – and with good reason.

'The Irish massacres of 1641 became part of European history, and held a place of infamy by the side of the Sicilian Vespers and the Massacre of St. Bartholomew.' This sententious sentence occurs in J.A. Froude's introduction to Mary Hickson's book, *Ireland in the Seventeenth Century* (see p. 15 above), which consists of extracts from the thirty-two volumes of depositions taken down from Protestant survivors of the bloody events. Through the centuries, doubt has been cast on the authenticity of these documents, or at least on accuracy of recollection, or concern for unvarnished veracity, on the part of some of the informants. Many people, at the time and later, had political or sectarian axes to grind, and accordingly tried to minimise or magnify the scale of the atrocities. But somewhere between the view that no massacres at all took place, and the contradictory view that entire Protestant populations were wiped out at a stroke, you might find an approximation to the truth.

The depositions, exaggerated or not, make harrowing reading; but I'm only concerned here with the murder of my umpteen-times-great-grandfather Edward Allen. The first relevant deposition has him down as Edward Allen, Gent., of Longford – so perhaps Elizabeth and his other children enjoyed a more or less urbane upbringing in a seventeenth-century house in a town, not in isolation on the sodden shores of a desolate lake, with reeds swaying in the water and curlews crying overhead. Perhaps, as time went on, the family came to believe that their lives were relatively secure and fixed in an ordained course, before disaster struck and sent them scurrying for shelter to the newly built castle of Lord Aungier in the centre of Longford, vigorously pursued by the dispossessed O'Farrell clan.

The uprising has reached the Irish midlands, and the warlike O'Farrells are out in force to repossess the lands compulsorily impounded. In their fearsome battle-garb and surrounded by Gaelic uproar, they converge on the castle where distraught Planter families are holding out – holding on for dear life until, in the first week of December, hunger and other miseries drive Longford's besieged Protestants to enter into negotiations with their hell-raising adversaries. The Irish, armed with swords, pikes, pistols, skeans and what-not, make a sight to strike terror into the hearts of their beholders. They are far from having 'Gent.' appended to their names. They are not great upholders of clemency.

A four-man delegation, including Edward Allen, is suffered to emerge from the castle and conducted under armed guard to a nearby house where terms are thrashed out and agreed in writing, signed by all parties. The lives of the English settlers will be spared, and all of them assured of 'safe convoy to Ballimowe, in the County of Westmeath ... [where] Sir James Dillon was to come ... with some English forces from Dublin.' For the starved and frightened refugees in the castle, it must have seemed as if the worst of the ordeal was over. But the worthless guarantee of safety, written down or not, is only a ruse to flush the settlers into the open. Like beaters driving game birds upwards to be shot for sport, the Irish have arranged a victory for the most unscrupulous of tactics. As the tragic procession of men, women and children staggers out from the place of refuge, they are set upon, stripped of their clothing and slaughtered on the spot – though a few get away in the ensuing melee, and live to recount the ghastly story.

My extremely distant forebear Edward Allen does not give in without a fight. Outraged and terrified, bleeding from the head where an Irish skean has struck him, he leaps into the River Camlin hoping to swim to safety. But Brian O'Cane of Longford hauls him out of the river – or maybe this person has shoved him into it in the first place; accounts become hopelessly confused at this point. O'Cane may have tried to drown an English enemy; or it's even possible he was trying to help. Still Edward Allen isn't dead. Half-drowned, bloody and exhausted, he gets himself to the house of a man named Bartholomew Nangle – the house in which the mendacious negotiations had taken place – and gains a momentary respite. It is very short. A murderous bunch of Irish avengers, scenting blood, is coming up behind. Threatened with arson and goodness knows what other acts of violence, Nangle and his brother-in-law Thomas McGeoghegan part company with the fugitive. Rather than dying with him, they send him to his death. They know what they are doing, but what else can they do? 'He forced us to take him in – here he is.' The next act in the frightful drama sees Edward Allen chained in a dungeon, two days and two nights of appalling incarceration, before his maddened enemies drag him out and hang him from a gallows in front of Longford Castle. The fate of Edward Allen's wife and younger children, who are mentioned in the depositions, is not known.

When I was young and in thrall to a nationalist imperative I'd never have wanted to hear anything bad about the Irish. This was Belfast in the 1950s, and the thing most dear to my heart was the noble conspiracy in a back room up a rickety staircase. Inspired, pipe-smoking conspirators in Donegal tweed jackets devoted to Ireland's cause. I was exhilarated by the idea of a principled lawlessness. It was as much a matter of leaning as breeding. I mean, I knew that half my ancestry was Protestant. But the other half, I believed, was Catholic Irish and Gaelic through and through, and that was the side I chose to affirm. It suited me to claim connections with Irish patriots – however far-fetched – just as it suited me to block out the Orange affiliations of my father's family, whose merits as human beings I fully acknowledged. These were my dear aunts and uncles, not oppressors or bigots or appliers of rude epithets to the pope. No member of the Craig family had the least wish to withhold from myself and my peers the package of social advantages which was increasingly coming to be known as our civil rights. Indeed, any news of our deprivation in this area would have startled and mystified my paternal relations. Aside from periodic ructions in the back streets, they'd have argued, didn't life, for all of us in the north of Ireland whatever our religious persuasion, proceed in much the same non-controversial way? At one level this was indisputable – but for those of us, historically- or crusader-minded, who craved a cause to get our teeth into, the North provided plenty of scope for indignation and right action. We were ripe for recruitment to the dissenting ideologies of the time and place.

Whenever I think of Ireland, when I am sixteen, a picture comes into my head of a country wronged, violated and mutilated (six counties lopped off), but rising above every abuse to keep its mystique intact. Its personifications are poignant and alluring. Kathleen Ni Houlihan. The Poor Old Woman. Roisin Dubh. Replete with romance and secrecy, they confer an edge of glamour on our everyday existences. The history we respond to has the fullest nationalist slant imposed on it. It's a story of unbroken rectitude on the part of the true Irish, against every kind of colonists' and oppressors' enormity and iniquity. For seven hundred years the Irish nation had suffered heroically and marshalled its resources, over and over, in a doomed but gallant revolutionary endeavour. In every generation, as it was said, Irish blood – copious and uncontaminated Irish blood – was spilt for the country's sake. Patriotic verses enshrined the ensanguined. O'Neill and O'Donnell were the names, Sarsfield, Emmet, Wolfe Tone, Mitchel, Pearse. In our iconography, the emphasis will always fall on Boulevogue not Scullabogue, on the Yellow Ford and never the Orange Boyne. We envisage a state of affairs stretching back and back to ancient times, in which freedom and Erin, or some such concept, is perpetually opposed to the Saxon and guilt.

Enlightened disaffection, edifying unrest, are modes of being we uphold and immerse ourselves in. We can't be talked to about complexity or impartiality. It's simply a case of us and them. Of course, you can choose to align yourself with the incorruptible Irish cause even without the unblemished ethnic credentials some might call for – think Mitchel, Emmett, Plunket, Tone – but those best entitled to republican kudos have names like Maguire, McMahon, O'Reilly, O'Kane. ... And where does that leave me, Irish and Gaelic, as I consider myself, to my fingertips? 'Craig' does not exactly endorse that bit of wishful thinking. In my part of the Falls district of Belfast, 'Craig' has unfortunate associations. It proclaims the very thing I am anxious to repudiate: an affinity as Orange as a Belisha beacon.

'Brady' creates a better effect: my mother is Nora Brady, and in my head is some vague genealogical commonplace, neither verified nor discredited at the time, about an Irish Brady connection to County Cavan. My grandfather Brady had married a Tipping, and the Tippings, I know – in so far as I know anything at all about them – are staunchly republican. If I think about it, though, that name too is a worry: it doesn't exactly have the Gaelic ring I'd have relished. (My cousin Harry Tipping, the family historian and a silent collaborator in this enterprise, mentions in one of his papers a desperate attempt on some family member's part to gaelicise the name by turning it into something like O Tiomhpanaigh. The version he prefers, Harry says, is O Tarbhchach – literally, bullshit.)

Around the turn of the twentieth century – I learn from my mother on an occasion in the distant past – some of our Tipping relations go in for a bit of genealogical excavation, but hastily abandon the family history project once they get back to the 1650s and uncover the shocking fact that the founding father of the family is Oliver Cromwell. It's nonsense of course, my mother says, her assumption being that an ancestral 'Cromwellian soldier' had somehow, by a process of Chinese whispers, got transformed into the old executioner and villain of Irish history himself. She's right, as it turns out – but for her, as for me, *any* Cromwellian connection is a thing to keep very dark. It would be vastly preferable to claim descent from the wonderfully named Cormac Mac Ross O'Farrell, clan chieftain and besieger of the English settlers at Longford Castle – not that any of us, at the time, know a thing about that particular episode in English/Irish relations, with expected roles of victims and aggressors reversed. My mother, like me, would choose to be as Irish as possible; although, as a teacher of history, she holds a less deluded view of historical rights and wrongs (and, indeed, many aspects of English history have a strong fascination for her, as strong as anything in her own country's past). But our lineage, as it happens, as far as pure Irishness is concerned, is worse, much worse, than she and I could ever have imagined.

I am an expert on 1641 – or so it seems to me, in my sixteenth year. I know the risen Irish have the right of it. If your lands are filched by invaders with brutal armies at their disposal, your aspirations reduced and your culture derided, you'd have to be pretty pusillanimous not to take some retaliatory action if the chance arose. Foreigners planted on stolen lands had it coming to them, in my vehement opinion. Besides, I know – everyone knows – reports of atrocities on the part of the Irish were magnified from the start for a partisan purpose. It is of course a different matter if the atrocity in question is down to the other side. An event I'm familiar with through a poem by Ethna Carbery[5] makes my hair stand on end. It concerns the slaughter of almost the entire population of Islandmagee, blameless people wiped out by soldiers of the garrison at Carrickfergus in an orgy of bloodletting. That is a true atrocity of 1641, I think (or of early 1642: the date of the Islandmagee massacre is disputed, as, indeed, is the source of the attack). I am horror-stricken by the brutality involved. The poem evoking it, 'Brian Boy Magee', is written from the point of view of the sole survivor of the Clan Magee. Coming to his senses in the aftermath of the slaughter, 'Great Christ! [he exclaims] Was the night a dream?'

> In all that Island of Gloom,
> I only had life that day.

Death covered the green hillside,
And tossed in the bay.

The terrible Phelim O'Neill of the Protestant tradition, commemorated in an Orange jingle:

Remember the steel of Sir Phelim O'Neill
Who slaughtered our fathers in Catholic zeal –

that bugbear of Protestants and unionists gets a different incarnation here. Ethna Carbery's poem goes on:

I shall go to Phelim O'Neill
With my sorrowful tale, and crave
A blue-bright blade of Spain,
In the ranks of his soldiers brave.
And God grant me the strength to wield
That shining avenger well –
When the Gael shall sweep his foe
Through the yawning gates of Hell.

The antiquated diction – 'shining avenger', 'crave', 'wield' – procures an uplifting effect; at least, it uplifted me as high as the peak of Errigal, while I wallowed in its romantic implacability. (I'm quoting the thing from memory; it has stayed with me.) I'd have been ready with my besom, myself, by those orotund infernal gates, given half a chance. In my book, the redressing of wrongs carries an especially thrilling charge. I might even have regarded the burning of Lisburn, on the orders of Phelim O'Neill, as an excusable act of war (not knowing I had any ancestral input into the business). I might have admitted, under pressure, that neither side in the interminable vicious conflicts had an absolute monopoly on honourable or on atrocious behaviour; but I'd always, in my besotted youth, have stood four-square behind the Irish troops, the Irish names.

The Cromwellian soldier preposterously conflated with Cromwell himself to loom menacingly and embarrassingly amongst the topmost branches of our family tree – this soldier can be identified as Thomas

Tipping, husband of Elizabeth Allen, son-in-law of the murdered Longford negotiator and father of John Tipping whose line of descent includes myself and the Lurgan Tippings (about whom more anon). 'Cromwellian soldier', though, doesn't seem quite right: it implies that Thomas came over to Ireland with Cromwell's army, and as we know he did nothing of the sort. He was already established in the country and committed, no doubt, to making a go of things. Did a shift in his attitude occur after Lisburn was burnt? It is possible that Thomas and his brothers lost their occupations as well as their possessions in that calamitous year. Perhaps they hadn't the heart to start all over again in the same spot; at any rate, there's no evidence to link the Tippings with the town from this point on. They, and their families, vanish from sight for a time amid the dishevelment and uproar of the age – and when the brothers next come into focus it's as soldiers caught up in the Cromwellian wars in Ireland, though on opposite sides.

I don't propose to go into the twists and turns of seventeenth-century British politics and their tangled repercussions in Ireland (I hear you breathe a sigh of relief). But it's necessary to touch on a few of the things that happened after 1641. First of all, at the time and for the future, a virtually irremovable wedge was driven between the Catholics of Ireland and the rest of the population. It left Catholic Scottish settlers in Antrim in an odd position. Some, at the start of the uprising, had joined forces with native insurgents against Protestant Planters – but, as Scottish as well as English incomers began to be listed among the massacred, significant numbers of Antrim Scots switched sides to their fellow-countrymen and deserted their co-religionists. Other Scots followed suit after April 1642, when General Munro arrived from Scotland with his army of Covenanters poised to gain redress for the murders of Presbyterians in the only available way: reciprocal massacres. A situation was taking shape whereby Planters and indigenous Irish were eternally opposed to one another; and native Irish terrain was coming to be seen as an enclave of mad brigands (an attitude persisting in some quarters right down to the present). Once the uprising was more or less quelled, the musterers of rebel forces, once again, had their lands confiscated and sold off to English investors known as Adventurers.

By this stage (the 1640s) the ongoing troubles of King Charles I with his parliament had altered the colouring of the Irish picture. As the people of England split into two factions, Royalists and Parliamentarians, so the

English in Ireland correspondingly sided with one or the other. Add the Irish Catholic rebels who came out in support of the king, the Protestants and Presbyterians who defected *to* the king, and Ulster Catholics who became Cromwellian converts, and you get the right conditions for chaos piled on top of pandemonium. Within every discernible social grouping in the country you find variation (in outlook) and vacillation (when it comes to commitment). A sense of unstoppable movement characterises the age, movement to the country and within the country, movement of troops in all directions preparing for military action, evasive movement on the part of rebels and woodkerne, restless movement of wandering poetic beggars lamenting the overthrow of the overlords, hectic movement of settlers fleeing for their lives or towards their deaths, movement of the dispossessed, westwards movement of Cromwell-created refugees, movement of irresolute recruits from army camp to camp. And against this background of disruption, you had ordinary decent Irish people, and ordinary decent settlers, doing their best to achieve a bit of stability and get on with whatever might pass for a normal life.

It's impossible for us, at a distance of more than four and a half centuries, to fully comprehend the massacres of 1641 and after. We can, of course, experience intellectual outrage on behalf of anyone caught up in annihilating events; but emotional outrage eludes us, when these events occurred so far in the past. There's only so much horror you can properly respond to before it loses its impact. After a time, the dreadful details contained in the 1641 depositions hardly seem to relate to flesh-and-blood suffering, but belong more to the realm of statistics (well, either to that or to some blood-bolter'd genre of historical sensationalism).[6] So many hacked to pieces, such-and-such a number incarcerated and burnt alive, a further lot stuck with pikes as they try, half-drowned, to scramble from the River Bann. These scenes from hell are as remote from us as Hieronymus Bosch. We can – and must, as I've said – deplore the cruelties of this incredibly historic time; but the fullest emotional involvement evades us, the recognition that these things really happened to real people.

It was all so unimaginably different, as Louis MacNeice said about the ancient Greeks, and all so long ago … and this means I can't (for instance) realistically attribute any kind of personality or domestic circumstances to my great-grandfather-at-an-immeasurable-remove, the atrociously executed Edward Allen, or to his Carolean in-laws the Tippings, since he and they are essentially unknowable, if not entirely unimaginable (*pace* MacNeice). Something of their stories can be imagined, by building on the information we have, the bare bones, the meagre outline – and for that, the available data, enormous thanks are due to the record-keepers of old, and (personally speaking) to the ancestral detective work of my scholarly second cousin Harry Tipping.

A hanged ancestor: now there's a ghost that could haunt you, if you let it. It could come supernaturally dragging the ball and chain that secured it in a dungeon, bleeding from its head-wound – a spectral presence and nightly embodiment, or disembodiment, of accusation, re-enacting its deathly predicament by the sole surviving outer wall of Lord Aungier's castle, as avid for vengeance as Brian Boy Magee in Ethna Carbery's poem. Or, more subtly, it could insinuate itself into the brains of susceptible descendants, colouring their attitude to enormities of the past. But I don't think so. I think Edward Allen, Gent., of Longford, would wish to dissociate himself from a lurid afterlife. I think he'd like the emphasis to fall on his orderly and upright existence, not his awful death. (Sheer guesswork here, again: it's just the 'Gent., of Longford' bit that's prompting this supposition.) But the effect of his murder on those closer to him in time, his children and grandchildren – to stick with those two generations – would naturally have been vivid and extreme. (His posthumous grandson John, my particular concern, will have his say – or what can pass for it – in Chapter Two.)

For numerous succeeding generations, my own included, the knowledge that Edward Allen was hanged, not for being a law-breaker, but simply for being who and what he was (a Planter and a Protestant) – this deprives our ancestor of any of the delinquent glamour his death might have carried in other circumstances. He never lived a life of sturt and strife – or so I believe. Basically, he died for attaching credence to the binding nature of a pledge of clemency, never suspecting it to be as worthless as a wandering beggar's rags. An upsurge of hysteria and blood-thirst had O'Farrell's followers in its grip. And no supposed invader of Irish lands need expect humane treatment from them, or fair dealing. From a perspective in the present, the fate of Edward Allen can only be contemplated sombrely, the tale told with intentness and dispassion.

CHAPTER 2
VALENTINE BROWN AND
VALENTINE BLACKER

...Winding-sheet and swaddling-band
Were one. Needle-flute and thimble-drum
Stitched the way to kingdom-come, to Derry,
Aughrim, Enniskillen and the Boyne:
Rat–a–ta–ta, rat–a–ta–ta, rat–a–ta–ta,
Humdrummery of history.

W.R. Rodgers, from Epilogue to *The Character of Ireland*

The great Munster poet Aodhagán Ó Rathaille (O'Rahilly) (1670–1726) has a bitter poem whose ironic adaptation of an English name – 'Bhailintín Brún' – sounds a note of increasing weariness and contempt. I first read this poem as a simple indictment of an unwelcome infiltrator into seventeenth-century Gaelic Munster; and Frank O'Connor's adept translation of three verses, under the title 'A Grey Eye Weeping', confirmed me in this view.

That my old bitter heart was pierced in this black doom,
That foreign devils have made our land a tomb,
That the sun that was Munster's glory has gone down,
Has made me a beggar before you, Valentine Brown.

O'Rahilly, says O'Connor, 'would have considered "Valentine" a ridiculous name for anyone calling himself a gentleman, and as for "Brown", he would as soon have addressed a "Jones" or a "Robinson".' Well – not quite. O'Rahilly's preferred patron would certainly have been one of the country's traditional Gaelic elite, the MacCarthy Mór – of a clan now dispossessed and dispersed. But the poet's relations with the Browns, new Lords of Kenmare, were perhaps not altogether as clear-cut as the poem called 'Valentine Brown' suggests. By one of those historical ironies I'm constantly invoking, the Catholic Browns were both supplanters and supporters of the MacCarthy sept, and adversely affected in their turn by King James's defeat at the Boyne. Sir Nicholas Brown, Sir Valentine's father, is lamented in one of O'Rahilly's poems as 'the prince who sheltered me' – but with the son it's a different matter. The son, educated in England, arrives in Kerry displaying his total ignorance of the Gaelic world and its system of patronage of the arts. O'Rahilly, an *ollamh*, a scholar and a poet, an aristocrat of the intellect if nothing else, gets short shrift when he comes within the orbit of 'Sir Val'. Sir Val, the fool, takes the great, learned poet for a beggar, in his tattered coat held together with a sugan belt. Hence O'Rahilly's litany of reciprocal insults, the 'foreign devils', the 'foreign raven' preying on the native birds, the blighted streams devoid of fish. The poet's sense of a shattered Irish world throws up abundant images of desolation: a clouded sun, a waste of scrub and heather, a drift of feathers, a palace forsaken, an *ollamh* relegated to the margins of society. The ultimate triumph, however, belongs to O'Rahilly. Valentine Brown has gone down in history – at least, in literary history – as a deplorable parvenu, an importer of new and uncongenial manners and customs into regal Kerry. O'Rahilly has set him up for perpetual ridicule, 'Sir Val' of the oafish vainglory.

Now another seventeenth-century Valentine is coming into focus, a Valentine Blacker. (I can't resist the coincidence of the forenames, even if there's little else to link the two.) Captain Valentine Blacker was a Royalist officer from the village of Poppleton, near York, who came to Ireland some time in the early seventeenth century and never went home again. He was also, to bring in a personal element once more, another of my far-back forebears. At this point I should, perhaps, make it clear that I'm not about to embark on a genealogical jamboree. My purpose is different – and besides, anyone on the trail of ancestors knows that the further back you go, the more selective you have to be (if selectivity weren't already imposed by the quantity of information available). Once you've got to some reasonably remote era of the past, the possibilities for uncovering distant progenitors are extended ad infinitum, with thousands and thousands of anonymous begetters branching off into an infinity of consanguinity. It's enough to derange one's equilibrium. In the interests of sanity, if nothing else, you have to stick to a particular familial line – with allowance for twists and meanderings and even dead-end diversions. Of course, anyone susceptible to the lure of continuity will get a tremendous kick out of placing themselves in an actual, personal historical sequence – and I'm no exception. It's great to be able to single out a few distinctive forebears among the myriads who, of necessity, must remain unidentifiable and irreclaimable. All vanished – some of them utterly, attenuated to nothingness, some bequeathing a fact or two, nothing more, to future generations, many existing as nothing more than a name on a document, or a gravestone. ... Judith Harrison, for example, daughter of Sir Michael Harrison of Ballydargan, County Down, who became the wife of Valentine Blacker and the mother of two sons and three daughters, who lived through the wars and massacres of the mid seventeenth century. ... What was her family doing in County Down? Were they part of the Old English colony in east Ulster, or new English adventurers? Did she grow up in the townland of Ballydargan? What was life like for a Jacobean Ulster girl? Did she witness terrible occurrences? Where did her loyalties lie? ... I'm lumbering myself with a lot of unanswerable questions here. One thing is certain, though, and disconcerting to a would-be Irishwoman. If I make a list of my known female ancestors of the seventeenth century – Katherine Rose, Judith Harrison, Elizabeth Allen, Rosa Young, Rose Latham, Frances Blacker (I'll get to the last two in a minute) – what strikes me about this list is the unequivocal *Englishness* of the names. Ah well.

Valentine Blacker. A little book, *For God and the King*, written by J.S. Kane and published by the Ulster Society in 1995, traces the history of the Blackers of Carrickblacker. A lot of my information about the family comes from this source, and I'm grateful for it. ... It starts with a Viking raider named Blacar, or Blacaire, a cousin of King Sitric III, sailing up the River Bann towards the future site of Portadown on a night unlike the one evoked in a heartfelt quatrain of the eighth or ninth century, translated by F.N. Robinson:

> Fierce is the wind tonight,
> It ploughs up the white hair of the sea.
> I have no fear that Viking hosts
> Will come over the water to me.

A calm night for the warrior Blacar, then, horrors for the preyed-on Irish, with a furious battle to follow; the defeat of a sept of the O'Neills, and a temporary Viking settlement in a townland called Drumlisnagrilly, which Kane translates as 'the fort of the dagger': 'broadsword' (*greillean*) would be closer. So Blackers – Blacars – were on the spot in the tenth century before making tracks for the north of England; and then, seven hundred years later, a Royalist descendant returns to Ireland 'to claim his ancient lands', as Kane has it. These ancient lands, true enough, include Drumlisnagrilly along with six other townlands. One of these, Ballynaghy (*Baile an Achaidh*, the Townland of the Plains), soon becomes the site of a manor house known as Blacker's Bawn.

'Blacker's Bawn' takes us up to the 1660s: Cromwell dead, one king executed and another restored to the English throne, and Valentine Blacker's career as a Royalist officer long in the past. He was pretty elderly by this stage – well over sixty – though energetic enough to undertake the building of his new manor house, as well as setting in motion the restoration of the Church of Ireland parish church at nearby Seagoe. The earliest church on this site – according to Kane – had been built by English settlers during the reign of Queen Elizabeth. When the alien edifice appeared in the landscape it didn't go down too well with the native Irish, who promptly made short work of it. By 1609 the church was in ruins. Settler tenacity raised it up again, and again an Irish assault destroyed it. Its second demolition occurred during the uprising of 1641, when many of Seagoe's beleaguered parishioners found themselves rounded up like a herd of cattle and driven to the bridge at Edenderry to meet their deaths in the Bann, whose level rose with the numbers of corpses crammed into it – shot, stabbed, piked, bludgeoned, whipped to death or simply drowned. (A grisly reminder of this atrocity shook the people of Portadown nearly three hundred years later, in the 1930s, when workers laying out a new bowling green near the site of the massacre turned up hundreds of bones from the Edenderry victims.)

It was due to Valentine Blacker that Seagoe Church got rebuilt yet again, and he and his wife were granted the first pew in the church when it opened for worship in 1662. In the following decade, it became their burial place. So Valentine Blacker can be judged a benefactor of his adopted Northern Irish community, and a notable presence in the locality – even if, like that other Valentine, Valentine Brown, he probably had little acquaintance with native Gaelic traditions in the area, seasonal rituals with song and dance and girls garlanded with flowers, fertility rites, mourning customs and so forth: all hidden from Protestant incomers but flourishing around them none the less. *Tugamar Fhein an Samhradh Linn*.

It is time to return to the mid seventeenth-century wars, and the brothers Tipping. The youngest, William, is listed among 'the '49 men' – that is, those who backed the king's cause in Ireland before 1649 (when the execution of Charles I took place). William's brother John was also a Royalist recruit. What caused the eldest, Thomas, to take up the cudgels for Cromwell isn't known, but probably it had more to do with expediency than ideology. Given the uncertain and insane conditions prevailing at the time, it might have seemed prudent to have at least one family member on the winning side, whatever that should turn out to be.

The outstanding Royalist in Ireland was the Protestant Earl of Ormond, James Butler, of the prominent Old English Catholic Butler family (Ormond was a Protestant convert). Lord Ormond commanded forces for the king – and with the Catholic Confederates and Puritan Parliamentarians thrown into the mix, not to mention deserters and tergiversators – the scope for mayhem and slaughter was intensified. Were the Tipping brothers in the thick of it? How much actual fighting did they do? Did they ever come face-to-face in a skirmish? Where did they settle their wives and children once they'd gone for soldiers? What happened after Cromwell came, with his assumption of a God-given licence to wipe out the perpetrators of 1641, and his terrible subduing tactics? It would be horrendous to think that Thomas Tipping had any part in the massacres at Drogheda and Wexford. One hopes (and this is likely) he was quartered elsewhere in the country; and at least we know that, Parliamentarian or not, he didn't come over with Cromwell's invasion force, which was chiefly responsible for the indiscriminate slaughter. No, I think I can absolve my ancestor of military brutality on the scale it erupted in these Irish towns. Drogheda and Wexford: the names remain conspicuous in the catalogue of horrors inflicted on the Irish. It was the number of civilian victims laid at Cromwell's door that consolidated his reputation for creed-condoned mercilessness and ethnic abhorrence, at least as far as Ireland is concerned. ... Cromwell is, of course, in one sense an anomalous figure. In England, as Elizabeth Bowen puts it in her book, *Bowen's Court*, 'he had fought for the English conception of "freedom"; in Ireland he fought against the Irish conception of it'. No Irish republican, indeed, would want to claim Cromwell as an ideological ancestor, but it's a different matter if you're an anti-monarchist in England.

The Irish conception of freedom included the freedom to be as Catholic as Mary Tudor. Even as late as the mid twentieth century, integrity in Catholic circles was measured by the way the faith had been adhered to, through thick and thin (or dungeon, fire and sword, as in the hymn we sang at school). Turncoats in one's lineage were a cause of shame. One of my great-grandmothers, Ellen Jordan, used to boast of an unfaltering Catholicism in her family, stretching back unbroken to the days of the Normans. No recusants among the Jordans! Considering what's emerged in other sections of my adulterated ancestry, though, I am not sure how far her claim to an entirely Catholic descent will stand up. (I am not sure, either, that it *won't* stand up; it's just that, given her forthright and argumentative nature, I can't help envisaging a sturdy Protestant or Presbyterian element creeping in somewhere.) Following the Jordan line, I can only get back as far as Ellen's parents, Edward Jordan of Tannaghmore West and Susan McCorry of Moyraverty, born *c.*1812 and 1815 respectively. My great-great-grandparents – and I love the pungency of those placenames, Tannaghmore West and Moyraverty, both of them well off the beaten track, in the hidden seductive depths of leafy north Armagh.

(Susan McCorry could not be more obscure but I'd like to think she might have left something commensurate with the twang of her name – a needlework sampler of the 1820s, say, painstakingly embroidered with a red plain-fronted house, three windows and a door, and perched on the chimney of its slanting roof, an exotic bird, twice the size of the door. On the right-hand side, a tree filled with smaller birds, and another, like a parrot, charmingly out of scale; and beneath the tree, a pair of storybook figures, male and female, in Georgian get-up, dwarfed by an enormous flowerpot. The whole quaint picture worked within a decorative border round the linen rectangle, with the letters of the alphabet across the top and right at the bottom, a small perky dog, and perhaps more flowers in flowerpots. And the signature of the youthful stitcher: Susan McCorry Aged 12 Years. 17 August 1827. ... I'm making this up. Still, I suppose young Susan might have attended a local interdenominational school run by some charity or other, and sat among a roomful of good little girls from Moyraverty, stitching away at a pious verse or maxim to show her needlework skills. She might have depicted a pair of angels hovering above a church, like those on a sampler in my possession, the work of a Susanna Cottrill in the relevant year, 1827. ... On the other hand, it's unlikely that a child of impeccable Catholic lineage, as her daughter Ellen Jordan asserted, would have been let near a classroom filled with potentially proselytising Protestants. No, I think I have to let her return to the chores of the day: fetching water, carrying turf, digging potatoes, gathering wild strawberries or mushrooms in the fields with a string of younger children behind her.)

Cromwell. When I was sixteen the first volume of Walter Macken's historical *Irish Trilogy* was published. I don't remember how it came to my attention, but it wasn't long before a copy of *Seek the Fair Land* came into my hands. I'd arranged to borrow it from the handsome Carnegie Library on a dusty stretch of the old Falls Road, one of my haunts. From the opening section of Macken's story, in which the life of a roaring Connaught chieftain is saved by a mild man living in Drogheda, I was enthralled. By chapter three, and the ominous date of September 1649, when the mild man stumbles on his wife lying dead in a blood-rippled street in the wake of the Ironsides' onslaught on the town, I knew I was reading a version of history – fictionalised or not – that chimed with my deepest beliefs about the suffering Irish and exterminating English. It was an old and emotional way of thinking. You couldn't but be on the side of the desperately wronged and courageous population. ... And it did no harm to Walter Macken's sales figures that his novel is an adventure story, a survival story. That mild man from the North, Dominick McMahon, leads his remaining family, a young daughter and son, out of despoiled and perilous Drogheda towards the sanctuary of the Gaelic west. It requires immense resourcefulness to evade the Cromwellian depredators along the way.

To make matters even more difficult, Dominick is burdened with a fugitive priest, Father Sebastian, who more than once endangers the little party by stopping to perform some rite of the Catholic church, administering the last sacrament or digging a grave for the dead. Gradually, however, Dominick's exasperation with Sebastian turns to admiration for the priest's continuous affirmation of a Catholic spirit, a national virtue. Dominick's children, his sparky daughter Mary Ann and mute son Peter, take the priest to their hearts unequivocally. It is clear that it's Sebastian's virtues, his goodness, selflessness and obeisance to a higher power, that will save the nation, if it's to be saved at all. Some alternatives to his priestly humility are proffered and found wanting – a fighting determination in the face of oppression, the carousing instincts and sexual license of great Connaught Gaels like the O'Flahertys. No, in Macken's book, it's the spiritual dimension that defines the true Irish. This novel, with its two sequels, adds up to an unabashed romance of the Catholic nation.

Macken is a great storyteller, and, on one level, his books remain gripping even for a reader as sceptical as myself. You accept, while you're reading it, the premise of his plot. Cromwell looms in the background furnished with every excess Irish history decreed; and not far behind him in the monstrosity stakes is Sir Charles Coote, persecutor of Catholics extraordinaire. ... What happens? After many reprieves in the course of the narrative, saintly Sebastian finally falls into the clutches of Coote and is burnt at the stake. A witness to this event, Peter McMahon, regains thereby the voice he lost as a child following a blow to the head during the massacre at Drogheda. It is, of course, a Catholic, indeed a priestly, voice that's restored to Peter. Sebastian's successor, he promptly sets off for Louvain and a clerical education to help keep the fires of the true faith burning at home (and never mind what else burns in the process). You can, if you will, equate Peter with the Irish nation, wounded, belittled, indomitable, and destined for recovery with its essence of an indigenous spirituality intact. Well!

In 1652, an Act of Parliament had decreed the removal of Catholic landowners (and some Protestant Royalists), with their families, to the wild and unproductive territory west of the Shannon. Those officially dispossessed, and also unofficial refugees like the McMahon family in Walter Macken's novel, undertook the sorry trek into poor lands, where some would rebuild their lives with a measure of confidence, and some would not. It's one of the many sorrowful set-pieces of Irish history. A contemporary poet, Fear Dorcha Ó Mealláin, has a word of advice for the harried and defeated Catholic deportees. He counsels them to take it stoically.

> If they call you 'Papishes'
> accept it gladly for a title.
> Patience, for the High King's sake.
> Deo Gratias, good the name!

When I was sixteen and my head was teeming with images of desecrated Ireland, I was happy to take credit (along with my great-grandmother) for vague ancestral stoicism and fidelity to the Catholic faith. I'm not sure, though, how far I'd have gone along with Ó Mealláin's recommended passivity, if I'd been aware of his poem at the time; what he conjures up is a line of cowed and beaten people creeping westwards on their last legs, every jot of defiance knocked out of them. It's not an inspiriting picture. These are the people among whom the popular novelist found his characters – but the way Walter Macken builds them up they're far from being a lumpen mass of misery. It's a highly sentimental ideology he's upholding, indeed, but his skill is such that you swallow it and deplore it all at once. In capitulation to the mood of the narrative, you applaud the restoration of Peter's vocal faculty and its religious implications even while your secular hackles are bristling.

Another Gaelic poem, well known to me in my youth is '*Cumhadh na Mathara fa'n Leanbh*', 'The Mother's Lament for her Child'. This was written probably in the eighteenth century, long after the events evoked, and it's been attributed to the south Armagh poet Peadar Ó Doirnín (born *c*.1684). Recent commentators have praised this poem for breaking decisively with the strict and cumbersome bardic traditions of the past, striking instead a bold new 'modern' note with its economy and immediacy. In simple plangent terms it confronts the agony of a mother witnessing the slaughter of her infant, piked to death with the blessing of Cromwell. The outpouring of grief proceeds as if issuing from the mother:

> They tied me to a tree
> To watch what was done to you,
>> Child of the branches.

You were on the end of the pike
And I heard your cry
And it tore my heart
      Child of my breast.

It's an image to set against the women with up-flung arms being pitchforked into the River Bann from the bridge at Edenderry, or the burnt remains of Planters at Lisgoole. But, prone as I was to selective outrage, I thought the second or anything like it was a figment of someone's inflamed Orange imagination, while the Peadar Ó Doirnín poem (if he was indeed the author) was consistent with the historical facts as I knew them. As everyone knew them; *everyone* abominated the actions of Cromwell. There was no denying it.

There were things I'd have liked to deny, if they'd come to challenge the nationalist certainties of my teenage years, and my own entitlement to a largely Irish identity. If someone had suggested to me then that an ancestor of my own had allied himself with Cromwell's Ironsides, I'd have growled and snorted and repudiated the nonsense. (It wouldn't actually have made much difference if Thomas Tipping had been a Royalist like his brothers; these were all English Planters, not the *fíor-Gaels* I'd have relished among my maternal forebears.) If it had then been shown beyond doubt that it wasn't nonsense, that Thomas Tipping had really existed in his seventeenth-century army uniform, with steel helmet and leather breeches, riding about on a horse quelling Royalist and native Irish alike – well, then, my next state would have been a very sheepish one, very taken aback and wishful to keep the awful information dark. I mean, this wasn't the Craig side of the family, whose ancestral non-Irishness I had long accepted. I could have turned up marauding Scots or raving Calvinist preachers among bygone Craigs without turning a hair (well, more or less). But my grandmother Brady's family I'd considered sacrosanct, as far as good Catholic genes were concerned. Never, never would I have suspected the republican Tippings of ancestral Protestantism.

The ethnically dodgy Tippings (as I'd have viewed them in my purist days) came out of the Cromwellian wars rather better than they'd gone into them. All were granted lands in Ireland in lieu of army pay. By the time the final land allocations are ratified by the restored King Charles II in 1666, Thomas has acquired portions of townlands in County Down and County Westmeath; John is also a landowner in County Down and County Cavan; while William – though his name doesn't occur in the list of recipients of royal grants – has somehow come into possession of Ballynarea in south Armagh. Harry Tipping suggests that Thomas may then have sold his County Down windfall to speculators, and leased Ballynarea from his brother William; at any rate, he and his family seem to have settled there, while William is found at nearby Creggan.

Creggan: this is a district strongly associated with the poet Art Mac Cubhthaigh, or MacCooey (*c*.1715–*c*.1773), whose life overlapped with Peadar Ó Doirnín's, both of them prominent in the nest of singing birds whose songs and verses enhanced the pungent Gaelic ethos of south Armagh. Ó Doirnín, though, was a schoolteacher and respected as such, and Art MacCooey, much lower in the social scale, led a luckless life as a jobbing gardener and agricultural labourer, while bolstering himself up with visions of reversals of fortune, both for himself and for his chosen patrons, the O'Neills of Glassdrummond. Even while trundling cartloads of dung about the countryside, MacCooey can't be stopped from composing verses in praise of the O'Neills or against his enemies, mean-spirited priests and Protestant grandees alike. ... But it was '*Ur-Chill a' Chreagain*', 'The Graveyard of Creggan Church', his eloquent exercise in the *aisling* or vision mode, that made MacCooey's name. This poem strikes every romantic chord you could ask for: the poet at his lowest ebb falling asleep in the old secluded churchyard, the fairy woman enticing him away from a life of miseries and humiliations, the classical garnish, the deep historical sense, the lament for the ruined Gaels and their emblems of an ordered world. All evoked with a lyrical grandeur and aplomb. And when '*Ur-Chill a' Chreagain*' is sung unaccompanied by a great traditional singer like Mary Harvessy or Pádraigín Ní Uallacháin, it illumines for an instant the strangeness and incomparable richness of the culture from which it emerged.

A culture, though, in no position to succour its exponents. Enrí Ó Muirgheasa, who put together a collection of Art MacCooey's works in 1916, notes the ratio of Protestant to Catholic families in the parish of Creggan during the eighteenth century. Protestant 259, Papist 718 – but, of course, with the former very much in the ascendant. MacCooey was briefly employed as a gardener by one of them, the Reverend Hugh Hill of Mounthill, rector of Creggan between 1728 and 1773. 'Mounthill', as well as being the name of a house, was also the new name of the townland previously known as Ballinaghy (it seems there was more than one Ballinaghy in County Armagh: this is not the same as the one originally acquired by Valentine Blacker in the mid seventeenth century). And in it, according to Ó Muirgheasa, lived another Protestant family, 'of such consequence' – and here my genealogical instincts perk up – of such consequence that one of them is appointed a churchwarden of Creggan parish in 1741. The name of this exalted officiary is Thomas Tipping, junior. Could he have been a great-grandson of the William who settled in Creggan around 1670 (even though we don't know whether William had any direct descendants at all)? Or of the elder Thomas who was born in Stratford-on-Avon? There's nothing to go on but the name – but it's enough to attach him, if precariously, to this branch of my family tree. Perhaps I can hook him to it by the seat of his churchwarden's trousers, like a bad boy strung up by his classmates in an old-fashioned school story. At any rate, it pleases me to visualise this Thomas Tipping, Esq., passing the time of day with the lowly farm labourer Art MacCooey – one a bit resentful of the other's airs and graces, perhaps, the other unaware of the rough fellow's learning and poetic expertise. Their paths must have crossed, in such a small community, and especially with Creggan church a place of refuge for the poet. But the ways of the Gaels remained as alien to Planters as the ways of faery hosts in their raths and souterrains. It was as if an intangible barrier divided two exclusive zones, each primed to repel any interchange.

It was never as clear-cut as that, of course, and time would make it considerably less so. Proximity, common ground, the attractions of exogamy, all worked to blur the edges of the sharp divide. But what resulted was never going to be a smoothly blended community. Well – let me modify that assertion. What resulted was never going to be *perceived*, either from the inside or the outside, as a smoothly blended community. For I would argue that the latter is precisely what we have achieved, even if we don't know it; that all of us in the north of Ireland, Protestant, Catholic or what-have-you, are a compound of the same good and bad elements from brave hearts to stiff necks.

Bloodlines got diluted, or enriched if you prefer it, almost from the moment the Planters set foot in Ireland, individuals throwing in their lot with the side they hadn't been born to. Papists en masse renouncing the Mass, and plain Presbyterians opting for Catholic ritual. If these people were looked at askance, either as traitors to the tribe or as dubious recruits – well, within a generation or two their descendants would be thoroughly assimilated into the host faction, with never a notion of any genetic or doctrinal inconsistency to agitate them. And so it has gone on right down to the present, with the wretched factions – 'accursed systems', William Carleton labelled them – flourishing side by side, and their noisiest adherents often unaware of their less than absolute entitlement to denominational integrity. It's the names, of course, that furnish an obvious pointer: a notorious butcher of Catholics from the Shankill Road in Belfast called Murphy; a president of Sinn Féin with the English name of Adams. A Protestant poet – I'm using these terms in a descriptive, not a religious sense – called Mahon, and a Catholic poet called Carson. Another poet, Paul Muldoon, has a pointed small reminder of local complexities and ambiguities:

> ... Today he remarked how a shower of rain
>
> Had stopped so cleanly across Golightly's lane
> It might have been a wall of glass
> That had toppled over. He stood there, for ages,
> To wonder which side, if any, he should be on.

If any. Muldoon is referring specifically to the border between North and South, but you can extend his words to apply to the immemorial border between Catholic and Protestant, Gael and Planter, Orange and Green.

The twentieth-century Lurgan Tippings knew which side they were on, but to arrive at it they'd had to accommodate a long-ago episode of recusancy. I'll get to this eventually; but, for the moment, we're still in the Protestant seventeenth century, the 1670s to be precise. Here we have Thomas Tipping, ex-soldier, nearing the end of his life in the rainy uplands of south Armagh, with his family around him. Thomas had come a long way from his beginnings in Stratford-on-Avon, with its half-timbered Englishness and Holy Trinity Church presiding over the lives of its good Protestant populace. He was born, we remember, in 1605 and enjoyed a life-span of seventy years. When he dies in 1675 his eldest son, also called Thomas, takes over the running of the Ballynarea estate. (To digress very briefly: this second Thomas engenders a further succession of Thomases who keep on stepping up and up the social ladder, until they find themselves established as minor members of the County Louth aristocracy, with family seats at Castletown, Beaulieu and Bellurgan Park. But as for the descendants of my particular ancestor among Thomas I's progeny. ...We shall see. Harry Tipping puts it succinctly in his account of the family: 'You take the high road and I'll take the low road.')

The first Thomas had six children. The youngest of these, John, was born around 1650 and called after his paternal English grandfather who may or may not have been still alive. His other grandfather wasn't, as we have seen (see p. 22). Harry Tipping again: 'As a child at his mother's knee, John Tipping, ... founder of our north Armagh branch, must often have heard the horrific and tragic tale of how his maternal grandfather, Edward Allen, was callously murdered by the native Irish in the 1641 uprising.' And doubtless young John was endowed with an antipathy towards the perpetrators of this crime. Remembering the events of that recent year was enough to send shudders down every Protestant spine. And the worst of it was, they were still around, the inimical Irish, wolfish predators in the hills and woods, ready to do murder again at the flare of a beacon.

John would likely have grown up in a detached house built of stone or brick, surrounded by a stone bawn twelve-feet high, into which the cattle were herded at night for safe keeping. The men of the house would have been armed against intruders. The evolving 'siege mentality', cited by later historians to explain atavistic Protestant loathing and aggression, was keeping every Planter nerve on full alert. At the same time, these second- or third-generation settlers were in the process of acquiring their own complicated variety of Irishness, whether they acknowledged it or not. Ireland was all they had ever known, but Ireland was like a wicked stepmother country refusing to take them to her bosom. And worse: she was only waiting for an opportunity to make away with the lot of them. ... Picture a winter evening in the mid seventeen-hundreds, a Planter house in the townland of Ballynarea; a bitter wind from the north creating an uproar outside; flickering candlelight, and a huddle of children crouched by a smoking fire, avidly taking in horror stories concerning murdered Protestants, a hanged grandfather and the ghosts of the drowned at Edenderry Bridge. Stories carrying a powerful charge of fear and outrage. A legacy of aversion persisting down the centuries. ... Move forward nearly four hundred years, and you get 'Lynn Doyle' recalling his country upbringing in *An Ulster Childhood* (1921), an upbringing infiltrated by sectarian truisms (comically evoked). 'Home Rulers', he says, 'to my childish mind were a dark, subtle and dangerous race.' They were ready to rise at a moment's notice, he continues, diabolically poised 'to murder my uncle, possess themselves of his farm, and drive out my aunt and myself to perish on the mountains.' Never mind that there weren't any mountains within easy reach of the farm, 'in my aunt's stories it was on the mountains we always died, and I felt that we were bound to get there somehow'.

Ah, but the thrill of atavistically awful anticipations was not confined to one side only. As a counterbalance to Lynn Doyle, consider an episode from the Catholic childhood of the novelist Brian Moore, in the 1930s. The Moore family home in Belfast, oddly enough, was directly opposite the headquarters of the Orange Order in Clifton Street. Each year, on the Twelfth of July, the Moore children gather at a top-floor window to watch the Orange marchers assembling for the long triumphal trek to the Field at Finaghy. They, the young Moores, are the only Catholics in Belfast to have a grandstand view! The noise, the colour, the flute bands, the dignitaries' bowler hats, the Loyal Orange Lodges each with its treasured banner proclaiming some aspect of Protestantism or enshrining King William at the Boyne, the rousing warlike reverberations from the great Lambeg drums ... all these produce a rare excitement in the little Catholic nationalists, noses pressed to the windowpane, looking down on a vibrant gala occasion which is also a threat to their own well-being. They can't take their eyes off the massing wild men, thousands strong, strutting and swirling under their window. Knowing all the while 'that you and yours [are] the very enemy they seek to destroy'.

Between the 1640s and the run-up to the Boyne forty years ahead, Planter families in towns and townlands all over the North would wake each morning gladdened by the fact that no disaster had happened overnight, no sudden uprising, onslaught or outbreak of neighbourhood savagery. A decreasing sense of loss, a measure of confidence about the security of their lives and livelihoods, would slowly have taken them over. They were here to stay – and gradually, it seemed, there were fewer fears to possess them. Even if it should prove to be something of a chimera – which it did – this growing confidence allowed them to get on more or less undisturbed with the basic business of living, birth, copulation and death, and all the embellishments in between. … I'm now about to return to those redoubtable Poppleton Blackers, and two converging strands of my distant ancestry. Glenn Patterson, in his book about his grandparents, *Once Upon a Hill* (2008), refers amusingly to the long, long line of 'begets' to which everyone's family history boils down. Taking a cue from him, I am going to go in for a bit of 'begetting' myself. You will remember Valentine Blacker, the Royalist officer who settled in County Armagh after the Commonwealth wars and rebuilt Seagoe Church. Valentine begat George, who begat Frances, who begat William, who begat John … and so ad infinitum – or at least, so on in a straight progression right down to the present.

Valentine Blacker, as we've seen, married Judith Harrison of a local Irish Planter family, and 'begat' two sons and three daughters. The oldest son, the surprisingly named Ferdinando, led a valiant short life before dying at a young age in some battle or other, leaving his more conventionally named brother George as the sole heir. George Blacker – according to J.S. Kane – 'served his sovereign, King Charles II, as a major in the army and was later promoted to the rank of lieutenant-colonel in an infantry regiment'. Well, good for George. You can picture this upright soldierly figure in his seventeenth-century army uniform looking down his military Blacker nose at the uncouth Irish population of Ballynaghy and thereabouts. … Already well placed in the world, George goes on to make an advantageous marriage. His bride is a Miss Rose Latham, the daughter of William Latham and his wife Rosa Young. (J.S. Kane has George marrying Rosa Young, not her daughter, but I think he is wrong about this.) The newly-weds establish themselves with due ceremony at Blacker's Bawn, paying six shillings tax on the three fireplaces recorded at their home in 1662, and, in due course, after further begetting, raise a family of four – three sons and a daughter. George Blacker is eventually appointed High Sheriff of County Armagh to crown his undeviating career in solid citizenship. He is fortunate enough to reach this position just before the advent of King James II, and consequent shattering of what had passed for peace in the country.

I cannot tell for sure how George was affected by the Williamite wars before his death in 1691. I do have some information about his sons William and Robert, and I'll return to them, and one or two of William's descendants, later. But my attention for the moment is focused on George's daughter Frances, the youngest of his children, born *c.*1652.

… Who was Frances's mother? J.S. Kane, as I've said, claims that George married Rosa Young, not Rose Latham, and dates the marriage to the year 1658 – but this makes no sense at all, especially since Kane then refers to George's son William's marriage in 1666, when by this reckoning William would have been a boy of seven. Logically, we can attribute a birth date of 1622 to George, and 1647 to William … but hang on, there now arises a puzzle in connection with grandfather Valentine. If Valentine Blacker only set foot in the province in 1641 or 42, how had he married an Ulster lady many years earlier and fathered five children on her? If, on the other hand, he'd been in Ulster all along, why and when did he arrive here? … These genealogical puzzles and chronological inconsistencies are giving me a headache and I am not going to delve any further into them. I don't care if long-ago George married Rose Latham, or her mother, or her grandmother. The thing is, to keep a grip as far as possible on pungent and pertinent bits of information, and let the rest go hang. One such fact (it is a fact) concerns George Blacker's daughter Frances. In 1677 or thereabouts, Frances becomes the wife of young John Tipping and initiates a line of descent that will – eventually – be at odds in every respect with the lordly Protestant Blackers. This much I do know, and it's enough to be going on with.

For the time being, however – in the years leading up to the Boyne – the Tippings are every bit as Protestant and as strongly allied to the cause of Orange William as John's august in-laws. (Perhaps more so; the Blackers, we remember, were great Stuart supporters, at least before the advent of Catholic James.)... John and Frances, once married, set up home in a townland called Gallrock, in the parish of Tartaraghan in north Armagh. Did Frances's family object to her marriage to a Tipping? They don't seem to have bestowed much of the Blacker wealth on her, leaving her to lead a quiet farming life, which she and her husband do, undisturbed as far as we can tell, for the next twelve years or so, while they go about 'begetting' offspring. (The exact number of new young Gallrock Tippings is uncertain.) But during the years between 1685 and 1689 life starts to assume a hazardous character once again. The cause is the accession of an English Catholic king, and consequent conferring of hope for an overthrow of their disabilities on the Catholic population of Ireland. Catholic aspiration is suddenly in the ascendant, while dormant Protestant fears are about to be reawakened.

By the late 1680s, Protestants all over the North are preparing for defence, or, in the last resort, flight to some place of refuge. It's the nightmare of 1641 all over again. Had you been in a Protestant house in the last month of 1688, you'd have stood all night with a weapon in your hand, poised to repel a rebel onslaught. If neighbours had come knocking at your door, a blunderbuss thrust through a window would have greeted them, with householder nerves in tatters everywhere. ... But beyond the beleaguered houses of Gallrock and Ballynaghy, beyond the agitated towns of Derry, Armagh and Carrickfergus, great events are taking place in the constitutional and in the military sphere. By now, Prince William of Orange has appeared on the scene, with all his regalia, ready to be incorporated into Northern Irish Protestant iconography. Having landed at Torbay in the south of England in the previous month, William holds out a prospect of reinforced Protestantism, with all accompanying benefits, to the three kingdoms – and, for the most part, wins them over.

King James leaves for France in a hurry and sails from there to Ireland, landing at Kinsale in March 1689 with an army of French soldiers. Already, at the other end of the country, the gates of Derry have been slammed shut against James's Catholic troops, though the town has not yet come down decisively on the side of William. That wholehearted commitment will shortly follow. A Williamite army under the command of Frederick Duke of Schomberg arrives at Bangor in August 1689; and in the following year King William himself steps ashore at Carrickfergus and promptly sits down to take a rest on a chair which some thoughtful person has carried to the quayside. The Prince of Orange is marshalling his resources for a southwards dash, taking in Belfast along the way, towards the immemorial engagement at the Boyne.

But before this, in response to an escalating state of panic, many of the Protestants of Seagoe and thereabouts have left their homes and are hurrying northwards towards Derry, perhaps, and the safety of its enclosing walls. It's a wrong decision for many of them. The countryside is thick with roving detachments of King James's army, mostly Catholic, who take it as their mission to prey on Protestants. Terrible things can happen to those who fall into their clutches. And unlike Walter Macken's hero Dominick McMahon, in *Seek the Fair Land*, these northern refugees are not always skilled in evasive tactics. They've hurled themselves into a win-or-lose situation in which many will go under. Somehow, along the road, in the lethal year of 1689, John Tipping meets his death, and his mother-in-law and brother-in-law follow suit. (The Blacker family historian J.S. Kane includes Frances Tipping among the dead of Seagoe in the same year, but there is evidence to suggest that Frances was still alive as late as 1710 – and we know that at least one, and possibly two, of her sons survived.)

From whatever specific cause, though, John Tipping died, brought low, like his grandfather Edward Allen, by the violence and mayhem of the era. He is buried in Seagoe Church. In the meantime, his surviving brother-in-law William Blacker is undergoing adventures and misadventures of his own. Leading a party of women and children northwards towards Derry (as Kane tells the story), William comes face-to-face with some Irish army recruits. But rather than slaughtering him on the spot as a pernicious Protestant, these soldiers instead engage William's services as an emissary for King James II, positively encouraging him to press on to Derry – on condition that he carries with him the surrender terms laid down by James for the capitulation of the unruly city. ...You might wonder why these Jacobite soldiers trusted William Blacker to stick to the terms he'd agreed, once he was out of their hands. Had they required him to leave hostages behind? I think it more likely that his family's long adherence to the Stuart cause had something to do with it. We don't, of course, know what William had in mind, at the time or later – but he did reach Derry and delivered the compromising missive as instructed: whereupon he found himself imprisoned as a traitor, and one line of the Blacker dynasty nearly took an irregular turn.

But William's conspicuous survival instincts don't desert him. The next minute he's up on Derry's walls fighting off the besiegers alongside the Reverend George Walker and other luminaries of the heroic event. Did he have a change of heart? When it came to a clash between William's inherited Stuart loyalties and his Protestantism, I suppose it was never in doubt where his ultimate allegiance would lie. The next glimpse we have of William Blacker shows him fighting at the Boyne under an Orange banner, and thus, in the words of J.S. Kane, 'establishing the family's long and glorious connection with the cause of Orangeism'. He acquits himself so well in the battle that King William's 'horse furniture' from the Boyne engagement, including gloves, stirrups and an embroidered saddlecloth, is later presented to William Blacker in recognition of his military services and descends down through the family

PC's father 'Andy' Craig with his younger brother and sister outside their Dunmurry home, c.1928

until it finally ends up with the Grand Orange Lodge of Ireland 'for safe keeping'.

The Grand Orange Lodge of Ireland! There's a name to strike a chill into the heart of any young Falls Road republican embracing subversion in the middle part of the twentieth century. Or if not a chill exactly, a strong distaste for its alien and antiquated connotations, its diehard mentality and Sabbatarian stuffiness (when its adherents aren't draped in Union Jacks and prancing drunkenly around the Field at Finaghy reviling the pope). It's a quaint and ridiculous institution when it isn't vicious – and however you look at it, it is mired in the past; whereas we enlightened Catholics and socialists feel a breath from a more expansive future blowing on our forward-looking faces.

I haven't always been so dismissive of the Orange Order. Before I knew any better – that is, in my pre-school days – I'd been taken by my young Protestant father (now a Catholic convert) down to the city centre to watch the Orange parades pass the statue of the Reverend Henry Cooke, the Black Man on his plinth with his repudiating back for ever turned to the liberal ways of 'Inst'. Perched on my father's shoulders, I'd have waved a flag as merrily as any Shankill Billy-Boy, had one been placed in my three-year-old fist. As far as I was able, I responded to the pageantry of the occasion; and something of its dynamism must have stayed with me. Louis MacNeice's 'heart that leaps to a fife band' never leapt any more vigorously than mine did (and does).

My father's brother, and his uncle Freddie, would likely have been among the marchers glorying in their Protestant heritage and long-ago victory at the Boyne. Uncle Freddie's Orange Lodge, of which he was Chaplain with the title, 'Sir Knight F.A. Craig' (I have no idea what these terms mean), was St Nicholas LOL 782, and I am sure it was fully represented in these early post-war parades. The family's Orange affiliation was carried lightly, as far as I know, as lightly as the flutters in a summer breeze of the Union Jack flown from the roof of my grandparents' gate lodge at the end of Dunmurry Lane. It was in this gate lodge that my father grew up with his brothers and sisters in an uncontentiously loyalist atmosphere, enjoying the rough-and-tumble of crowded domestic life complete with horses, hens, whippets, cats, the doings of Captain Charley (for whom my grandfather worked as head groom) at nearby Seymour Hill, a rudimentary education at the Charley Memorial Primary school (founded in 1892), where he'd have been enrolled around 1923, with his older sister Marie (already a pupil at the school) to keep an eye on him. ... You'd have heard no talk of Taigs in my grandparents' household; no one made a thing of despising Catholics, with whom – I am sure – they were happy to share local amenities. All of them, Prod or Papist, had roots (some roots at any rate) in the same small corner of Ireland. And Ireland was important. My grandparents' Union Jack hoisted yearly around the Twelfth of July didn't signify a hankering after an English identity. It just proclaimed a simple pleasure and pride in belonging to the dominant – well, marginally dominant – culture of the place, unburdened by Papist superstition and Romish regulations. ... I'm trying to say, I think, that my Protestant relations never subscribed to any advanced form of anti-Catholic bigotry. But for all that it was definitely a Protestant, a Church of Ireland, household, that gate lodge at Dunmurry.

The fact that he, my father, had many Catholic friends even before he met his Catholic wife might suggest a refusal on his part to fit into a tribal mould. Or perhaps it was just that his sportive nature chimed in some essential way with Catholic conviviality. He took to mid-Falls life, with its pubs, betting shops, newsagents, greyhound racing, 'butterfly' nuns thronging the pavements, neighbours from all points along the social spectrum – took to it like a – I was going to say, an orphan to home life;

but 'orphan' is not right for someone like my father with his strong family ties. Like a happy-go-lucky traveller to a house of hospitality, perhaps, if a simile has to be proffered here. In his middle years he became an habitué of St Malachy's Old Boys' Club, due to his enduring friendship with some St Malachy's old boys. He fitted in (helped, no doubt, by his capacity for Guinness and his fine singing voice). Nevertheless, his temperament had been shaped by Protestantism, just as my mother's was shaped by the Catholic church. As for me ... nuns got hold of me in 1947, with an eventual outcome which I've recounted elsewhere. (*Asking for Trouble*, Blackstaff, 2007.) And long before I understood their significance, Orange processions through the centre of Belfast had become for me a thing of the past. Their place was taken by May processions devoted to Our Lady, Corpus Christi processions and Holy Communion dresses. In time, I would add Easter Sunday processions to Milltown Cemetery to commemorate the dead of 1916 – giving my father something to be broad-minded about, just as my mother had been broad-minded about the early Orange parades. She was broad-minded, indeed, about that and a good deal else besides – but what neither she nor anyone else suspected at the time was her own oblique ancestral connection with the Orange Order, which outdid in piquancy that of the Craigs.

The decisive victory in the Williamite wars (or defeat, if you prefer it) was not at the Boyne but at Aughrim in County Galway.

> At the Boyne bridge we took our first beating,
> From the bridge at Slane we were soon retreating,
> And then we were beaten at Aughrim too –
> Ah, fragrant Ireland, that was goodbye to you.

Frank O'Connor's translation of the poignant '*Slan le Padraic Sairseal*' ('Farewell to Patrick Sarsfield') captures to the full the demotic, plaintive note of the Gaelic original, with its Jacobite spokesman for a sorrowful and discomposed populace. With this poem, as O'Connor suggests, we hear for perhaps the first time an unadorned contemporary Irish voice lamenting the pass the country has come to – the endless defeats, the broken Treaty of Limerick, and 'Ireland's best', including Patrick Sarsfield, dispersed among foreign armies all over the continent. ('The Mother's

'Lament', mentioned above, was written, of course, long after the event it conjures up.) And the fact that it's an anonymous voice makes it all the more telling, like the Unknown Soldier's grave.

Fragrant Ireland, Catholic Ireland, is about to enter its darkest phase. With the Protestant ascendancy secured in the wake of the Jacobite disasters, measures are quickly enacted to keep the Catholic population in its place (its very constricted place). By means of the notorious Penal Laws, Catholic aspirations are obstructed in every area – property-owning, scholarship, freedom of worship, any kind of social advancement. A standard image from the era has a priest with a price on his head saying Mass on a lonely hillside with a rock for an altar, before a congregation of downtrodden peasants on their knees in the mud holding sacks across their shoulders against the terrible weather. This is what the tribe of Milesius has come down to! From 1691, and throughout the greater part of the following century, native Irish suffering and suppression make a powerful theme for historians and poets alike.

It was a different matter, of course, if you were on the winning side. William Blacker, fresh from his exertions at the Boyne, returns to Armagh to oversee the running of the family estate on the death of his father George in 1691, and begins the construction of what will become known as Carrickblacker House – described in 1909 by Robert M. Young as 'an ancient battlemented mansion bearing the date 1692 on a stone in the wall'.[1] (This architectural treasure eventually comes into the philistine ownership of Portadown Golf Club and is demolished in 1956 to make way, God save us, for a *club house*. Nearly three centuries of history eradicated at a stroke. I hope those Portadown golfers on the spot were haunted and put off their game by ghosts of the massacred settlers of 1641 spilling over from Edenderry – not to mention spectral Blackers outraged by the destruction of their family home.)

And what of William's sister Frances, Mrs John Tipping? Had she perished along with others in the ructions of 1689, as J.S. Kane invites us to suppose, Frances would surely have been buried in Seagoe churchyard alongside her husband. Instead, the Seagoe parish baptismal register for 1691 has a Mrs Frances Tippin (sic) standing godmother to an infant named Margaret Mathers. ... Move forward into the following century, and a map of 1710 shows a person of the same name, Frances Tippin, holding substantial farmlands in the townland of Collcosh just across the border with County Tyrone, seven miles north of Gallrock. Her sons, named William and George (dear God, is there no end to bloody Williams and Georges ... there are more to come) – William and George Tipping would have been in their early thirties/late twenties at this time; both were married, and probably they farmed the lands leased by their mother. Or perhaps by now they had moved to farms of their own; we simply can't tell.

These are the probable circumstances of Frances Tipping's life. Girlhood at Blacker's Bawn, with a full complement of parents, grandparents, brothers, servants and all; marriage to John Tipping (which may have represented a degree of social downgrading – he was, after all, a youngest son and had tradesmen among his immediate forebears); settling in Gallrock; motherhood; widowhood in County Tyrone; agrarian dealings and engagement in local life. Nothing out of the ordinary – well, nothing, that is, aside from the vast disruption of the pre-Boyne period, and the loss, in a single year, of husband, mother and brother.

But envisage for a moment a different scenario. Suppose that Frances does, in fact, meet her death at the hands of Jacobite soldiers in the brutal year of 1689. Say she leaves a daughter, Jane, as well as a couple of sons, and that all three children somehow scrape through, in the chaos and horror surrounding the murders of their parents. The boys then disappear from the records until they turn up as farmers in the 1700s; but two years after the fatal departure for Derry – in 1691 – the twelve-year-old orphaned Jane Tipping applies for assistance to the Seagoe Parish Church Vestry, whose members meet once a quarter to distribute alms to the poor of the parish. (Her name is there, in the church records.) And prominent among the Protestant pillars of the community charged with dispensing charity is, of course, William Blacker, Orange adventurer and poor Jane's uncle.

A plot is forming here, a standard plot beloved of authors of historical novels. It features an impoverished, even destitute, but spirited female orphan; of good pedigree though perhaps not knowing it, a victim of adversity – and the rich relation whose esteem she gains through a combination of winning ways and sturdiness of character. Certainly William Blacker, who fits one role in this story, could have afforded to find a niche for Jane Tipping in his bustling household among her boy cousins, children of his several marriages. Perhaps he did. Perhaps Jane had a room of her own in the new great house of Carrickblacker, and servants to sweeten her bed linen with sprigs of lavender. Perhaps she grew up and made a splendid marriage from her uncle's house. ... True, this story more often works itself out in a setting like rural Somerset or some picturesque region of the north of England. But what's to keep it from spawning a version in rough-hewn, factionally-beset Seagoe in seventeenth-century County Armagh? Nothing, but my own want of skill in amplifying the tale, in imposing an outline both pleasing and plausible on top of its bare bones. If I were a writer of fiction I would do it – for it is only a fiction, derived from nothing more elaborate than the final name on a list of deserving poor: Jane Tipping of Seagoe parish. That's all. I've made the rest up. To return to the facts: I think Frances Tipping did survive the wars in Ireland to resume, as far as possible, an ordinary farming life. And the likelihood is that Jane – poor Jane – was some Tipping by-blow, indigent and unwanted, nothing to do with Frances at all. She'd more likely have been twenty than twelve, and not destined to live much longer. Illness, malnourishment or unattended childbirth would have finished her off. No rich uncle would have taken her under his wing.

Frances's eldest son William Tipping (*c*.1677–*c*.1735) was himself the father of three sons, of whom the youngest, Henry (*c*.1712–1765), is the probable renegade who twitched the family line of descent into a Papist channel. This Henry is, we remember, the great-grandson of George Blacker – but by this stage, this branch of the family is diverging at high speed from Blacker aggrandisement and prosperity. (And also from the upward moving Tippings of County Louth.)

Henry at twenty-something is a Protestant farmer in the townland of Roughan in the parish of Drumcree. The whole district is part of the Brownlow estate, and Henry's farm is rented from a William Brownlow of Lurgan. Brownlow is the ground landlord, while a Bryan O'Neill is Henry's immediate landlord. By 1750, though, this particular Tipping, Henry, has become a leaseholder rather than a lowly tenant-at-will, having inherited Bryan O'Neill's rights in the Roughan property. Why? The answer would seem to be that Henry had married O'Neill's daughter Esther – making an odd case of a Protestant advancing in the world (and this in the Penal days) by means of his Catholic connections. It wasn't a very remarkable advancement, but it would do. And the price exacted? '... Turned Papish himself and forsook the auld cause ...':[2] or if he doesn't go that far, Henry at least allows the children of the union to be brought up in his wife's faith. (Nearly two hundred years later, my parents will enact a version of the same arrangement.) And after Henry's death in 1765, his Catholic widow and four Catholic sons move across the River Bann to a farm in the townland of Ballynamoney, just over a mile from Lurgan town centre. (The farm is held on a 'Popish lease' – thirty-one years in duration.) The descendants of these boys will become farmer/weavers.

The Tipping/O'Neill connection isn't absolutely watertight, though it fits the facts as far as they can be ascertained. It also fits with my purpose, and I intend to stick to it. ... 'Had I but known' of her existence in my days of hyper-Hibernianism, I'd have latched on to Esther O'Neill as a probable and desirable ancestress – a true Gael at last, among all the Planters and Blackers and Englishmen and women and Orange ditto.

The whole of County Armagh was coming down with O'Neills, some more peaceable than others;[3] and while those of Clancan and Clanbrassil (north Armagh) were distinct from the O'Neills of the Fews (south Armagh), all of them had a common ancestor in an Eoghan O'Neill who flourished in the fifteenth century. So, the Esther O'Neill whom I'm claiming as a direct forebear, would have been connected by blood to the Phelim O'Neill who instigated the uprising of 1641 and 'slaughtered our fathers in Catholic zeal'. So the patchwork of one's ancestry – anyone's ancestry – will often be found to accommodate many unlikely bedfellows.

CHAPTER 3
SCULLABOGUE

There's muskets in the thatch, and pikestaffs in the hay,
And shot in butter barrels buried in the bog,
Extrapolated powder in the tin for tay;
And everything is wrapped in blue-as-gunsmoke fog.

Ciaran Carson, 'Lord Gregory'

Among the ironies and cultural anomalies surrounding my Belfast
Catholic girlhood was my grandmother's accent. She, my father's mother,
had as strong a Southern accent as the tinkers in their gaudy caravans
parked on the old Bog Meadows near our home. She had only to open
her mouth to create a wrong impression. A rich Irish voice was not
a popular attribute in the Protestant North. It marked you down as a
rebelly Papist and contemptible alien. Whereas my grandmother, in fact,
was as Protestant as those Orange Blackers, shadowy maternal forebears
on an attenuated branch of my hybrid family tree.

She was born Emily Lett in September 1889, youngest child of a
County Wexford farmer named William Lett and his second wife Emily
Anne Thorpe. ... I'm struck again by the Englishness of these names, to
which I can add another, Eliza Stewart, my great-grandmother's mother.
Wexford, indeed, as a seaport, contained 'one of the highest densities
of Old English family names in Ireland' (I'm quoting from an essay by

W.J. Smyth in his and Kevin Whelan's *Common Ground* of 1988); and after Cromwell had finished with it, bringing its 'mediaeval era to a bloody end', the de-populated town attracted an influx of new English inhabitants. I don't know which wave of settlers my Wexford ancestors belonged to,[1] but clearly their origins were not Gaelic. I cannot attach them to ancient romantic Ireland in any of its guises. New Ross was their territory, Clonleigh in particular, and the triangle formed by it, Enniscorthy and Wexford. But the connotations of these place names worked for me in ways antagonistic to my ancestors. They, alas, were more likely to be yeomen than pikemen.[2] And rebel glamour was fodder for my adolescent view of the way things were.

'Enniscorthy's in flames', goes a line from a song that would often be running through my head (it never got outside my head since I couldn't sing):

> Enniscorthy's in flames, and old Wexford is won,
> And the Barrow tomorrow we cross;
> On a hill o'er the town we have planted a gun
> That will batter the gateways of Ross.
> And the Forth men and Bargy men march o'er the heath,
> With brave Harvey to lead on the van,
> But foremost of all in that grim gap of death
> Will be Kelly, the boy from Killane.

People who dominated my historical consciousness were those like Kelly the boy from Killane, Henry Joy McCracken hanged in Corn Market, young Roddy McCorley going to die on the bridge of Toome today, agile Father Murphy from Old Kilcormack: all the starry dead whose resistance to injustice was woven into the vast tapestry of successive Irish causes. For me, the idea of Wexford in 1798 carried all the kudos due to insurgency and idealism. It still does, in part. No one in their right mind could quarrel with the United Irishmen's principle, as articulated by Wolfe Tone: to substitute for Catholic, Protestant and Dissenter the common name of Irishman. And I've never quite divested the insurgents' emblem – the pike – of its stirring associations. Clasped in a sturdy hand, or concealed in the thatch of a radical farmhouse, the pike of 1798 is a symbol of bravery and a clandestine exhilaration. It, and other makeshift weapons, denote a magnificent foolhardiness. There's a potent early poem by Seamus Heaney, 'Requiem for the Croppies', in which the fatal confrontation on Vinegar Hill sees inadequately armed rebels 'shaking scythes at cannon' as the whole intrepid enterprise and buoyed-up resolution comes to nothing. A defeat, then, but the opposite of an inglorious defeat.

That is indisputably part of the Wexford picture, but it is not the whole picture. In 1993, in his review of R.F. Foster's *Paddy and Mr Punch* in the *London Review of Books*, Colm Tóibín has the following passage:

> The names of the towns and villages around us were in all the songs about 1798 – the places where battles had been fought, or atrocities committed. But there was one place that I did not know had a connection with 1798 until I was in my twenties. It was Scullabogue. Even now, as I write the name, it has a strange resonance. In 1798 it was where 'our side' took a large number of Protestant men, women and children, put them in a barn and burned them to death.

In that barn were people named Lett. Now, just as Armagh was awash in O'Neills, so County Wexford was home to a lot of Letts. But I'm taking it that they were all connected in some way – and therefore connected to *me*. And the place called Scullabogue – *Scoil a' Bothog*, the school at the ruined house? A wild guess[3] – Scullabogue is not many miles from the townland of Clonleigh, where my grandmother's ancestral farmhouse stands. Protestant children in the district might well have been scooped up by rogue insurgents and added to the other 'loyalist' captives in the terrible barn. A Benjamin Lett, a boy of about thirteen, was among the captives and so was his sister. (Their father was a William Lett who belonged to the Orange Order and served as a yeoman in 1798 along with his brother Charles and his son Nicholas.) Perhaps as many as two hundred terrified local people were incarcerated at Scullabogue, in the thatched barn itself and at the adjoining house (the property of a Captain Francis King), though not all of them died there. Tom Dunne, in his book *Rebellions* (2004), puts the number of those incinerated at 126; and among these victims were about eleven Catholics. The Catholics were taken solely because they worked for, or had dealings with, Protestants. The unspeakable episode invalidates the entire 'United Irish' ideology, and makes a mockery of Wolfe Tone.

The Scullabogue atrocity, depicted by George Cruikshank for W.H. Maxwell's *History of the Irish Rebellion* in 1798 (1845)

The two young Letts were lucky. There are several accounts of how they got away with their lives, but the one I prefer attributes their release from the barn to a couple of well-meaning and influential Catholics, Thomas Murphy of Park and a Mr Brien of Ballymorris. (It's cited by Charles Dickson in his book of 1955, *The Rising in Wexford in 1798*, when he quotes from a manuscript account of the atrocity written *c.*1871 by a Reverend Henry Lett, and dealing with the latter's grandfather's experience at the time.[4]) Another version of the story has Benjamin's sister Rebecca making a wild appeal to a priest and getting him to intervene to free her brother. And a disagreeable pamphlet with the lurid title *Murder Without Sin: The Rebellion of 1798*,[5] written by an Ogle Robert Gowan and first published in 1859, contains the following stark information about the Scullabogue prisoners: 'Out of the entire number, three only escaped, namely Richard Grandy, Loftus Frizzel and Benjamin Lett.' You can take your pick of the three scenarios. But whatever the truth of the matter, the Letts were safely away from the scene when the barn with its cargo of human flesh was set alight. It swiftly burned to the ground. A Quaker girl named Dinah Goff, whose home was located about two and half miles from Scullabogue, relates how 'I saw and smelled the smoke of its burning ... and cannot now forget the strong and dreadful effluvium which was wafted from it to our lawn.' The date was 5 June 1798. Four days later, on 9 June, the skeletons were cleared out of the barn and buried in a shallow hole with a covering of sods. As with other places of perdition – the Black Hole of Calcutta, or the Kenya Assemblies of God church at Kiambaa, where thirty-five Kikuyu were burnt alive on New Year's Day 2008 – Scullabogue and its horrors are etched into the landscape and into the subconsciousness of local people.

Scullabogue is burning, and at the same time, distraught Protestant families from all around Clonleigh and Carrickbyrne are piling their furniture and possessions on carts and heading for Enniscorthy, where some will find shelter in houses so crammed with their fellow citizens that no place remains for them to sleep but the bare deal boards. Others, not getting that far, spend nights on end in fields and ditches. The countryside is rife with horrors and rumours. Those refugees approaching the town are greeted with the flagrant warning noise of rebel drums beating to arms – and then they find that half the Protestant population of Enniscorthy has fled towards Wexford, many women in rags and tatters carrying children and trekking the whole fourteen miles on foot. Some, on the way, experience harassment from yeomen who take their dishevelled state to mean they are Catholics. But it was asking for death to stay at home. Dinah Goff, looking back from a distance of more than fifty years, laments the once-peaceful homes, 'abandoned in panic and destroyed in an orgy of incendiarism'.

The streets of Enniscorthy are burning too, as yeomen and Unitedmen butcher each other in droves. Genteel Protestant ladies, some never before confronted with death, step and stumble over a profusion of corpses as they head in desperation towards the Market House to put at least a solid door between themselves and the fighting in the streets. But there are no safe places. The whole town is a shambles, brimful of the noise and confusion of slaughter. Hopes for peace and prosperity, 'live-and-let-live', after gaining some ground in the course of the century, are once more dashed to pieces. A young insurgent, Thomas Cloney, looking on with horror, registers deep despair and records this emotion years later when he comes to write his *Personal Narrative of 1798* (published in 1832): 'This was my first time to behold the work of destruction performed by man against his fellow man.'

Thomas Cloney was twenty-five years old at the time, and, according to his later testimony, a reluctant rebel overtaken by the pressure of events (and by more immediate pressure from a band of his contemporaries, who turned up at his father's farmhouse 'and pressed me to proceed with them to Enniscorthy'). Of course, his *Narrative* is the work of a man in sober middle age, looking back; but Cloney makes out a good case for his youthful involvement in the insurgents' campaign, despite his many reservations. Things had fallen apart – and what could he do but make a stand against perceived abuses, with outlets for injustice proliferating in County Wexford of the 1790s? As a Catholic he lived his life in fear: fear of dispossession, fear of all the powers invested in 'a furious Orange ascendancy ... a bloodthirsty yeomanry, and a hireling magistracy', fear of going the way of his 'unoffending neighbours', whom he'd seen done to death and their property destroyed. ... Douglas Hyde, a century later, gives the picture in his 'Ballad of '98' (written under the name of *An Craoibhin Aoibhinn*):

> ... Their Captain's a fiend, from hell let loose,
> His men were the devil's crew,
> They burnt my gear; they burnt my house,
> My only son they slew.

The constant fear that gripped the Catholic population has its counterpart in stirred-up Protestant fears which come to a climax in the early months of 1798 – when everyone, it seems, Protestant and Catholic alike, is afraid to sleep at home and instead, at nightfall, makes tracks for the fields and woods where all of them will pass a troubled night. Any ditch or clump of brambles or 'friendly thorn tree' can do duty as a makeshift refuge – anywhere out of the reach of predatory neighbours intent on causing harm to neighbours. It's as if the whole of Wexford has turned into a vast open-air camp filled with cowering, frightened families trying to blend into the undergrowth, hearing any noise in the night as a portent of disaster. Most of these outdoor sleepers are women and children, men of a suitable age being occupied elsewhere – or no longer occupied. In one garden alone, it was said, thirty-two 'new-made widows' lay all night in the shelter of its rhododendron bushes. Neither faction has a monopoly on distress. And the psychological effect is ineradicable. A long way into the future, at the age of eighty-two, Mrs Barbara Lett of Killaligan, recalling the events of that dreadful year, comes out with a heartfelt imprecation: 'May we never more fall into the hands of our neighbours, who are more barbarous than any foreign enemy.'

People, neighbours, vying with one another to commit the bloodiest acts – yes, this is a part of the Wexford uprising as its purpose becomes distorted and brutality prevails. But a good many ordinary instances of humanity are on record too, some not too far away from Barbara Lett herself. At the time, she is twenty-one years old, the wife of a Mr Newton Lett – twenty-seven years her senior – and the mother of at least one infant son. She is connected in some way[6] to a Mr Joshua Lett of Ballybane House, Clonroche – who, though a man of nearly seventy, is a friend of the young rebel Thomas Cloney; and when Cloney accidentally shoots himself in the thigh and nearly bleeds to death, it's Joshua Lett who leaps on his horse and rides at high speed into Enniscorthy to fetch a surgeon, having first had the wounded Cloney 'conveyed' to Ballybane, and leaving him there in the care 'of his amiable daughters' (as Cloney describes them). (This shooting, horrifying though it must have been at the time, brings a relieving note of farce to the very fraught proceedings.)

Amid the awful spites and divisions in Wexford there were those who, like Mr Lett, refused to lead their lives in accordance with sectarian dictates. They had friends among 'the other sort', and among Mr Lett's was a Catholic schoolmaster named Walsh. At one point during the Rebellion, when it seems the insurgents have gained the upper hand, a rumour begins to circulate in the district to the effect that *all* Protestants, whether Orangemen or not, are about to be put to death. There's only one way they may save themselves – by assuming a spurious Catholic identity. So the schoolmaster Walsh, in deep anxiety about the danger facing his old Protestant friend, forces a moderately unwilling Mr Lett to sit down and undergo a crash course in Catholic theology. 'Never,' says Thomas Cloney, who is present at the scene, 'did any instructor labour more zealously for the improvement of his pupil than poor Walsh, and never did a pupil hang with more earnestness upon the dictates of his instructor than Mr Lett.' The effort of concentration required of the two old men has tears running down the faces of both. How will you feel, says the schoolteacher, if they come to pike you to death and all you have to do to save yourself is respond correctly to a question from the Catechism – and you fail to do it? But it isn't a bit of use. In the end, an exhausted Mr Lett declares roundly that even if his life were to be forfeit on account of it, he can't remember as much as a syllable of all the information so arduously imparted to him. Fortunately it doesn't come to that.

It doesn't come to that, but the danger was real. Bagenal Harvey (the rebel leader) at one point was heard lamenting to a friend that the war had become a war of religion, as certain misguided insurgents went about trying to ascertain people's denominational position – or, in the case of known Protestants, applying stringent proselytising tactics, as though an instantaneous conversion might be synonymous with a change of heart. While they thought they were carrying all before them – as in 1641 – the rank and file of Irish rebels jettisoned common sense, as well as common humanity. But sometimes they found themselves up against total defiance – and might even have been disarmed by it.

A relative of Joshua Lett's, a Richard Lett,[7] fell into rebel hands and wasn't having any of their bludgeoning and bluster. Asked if he was willing to embrace the doctrines of Rome, accompanied by a bit of jostling and threatening movement of pikes, he came back at his tormentors with the sturdy answer, 'Divil a bit'. Perhaps his candour was appreciated. At any rate, he escaped with his life; and for ever after the sobriquet, 'Divil a bit', stuck to him.

'The Letts, though belonging to the "gentry" class, were always a very broad-minded and liberal family.' This assertion comes from Katherine Lucy Lett's family history, written in 1925, and to back it up she cites the case of young James Lett, the only one of that name who fought on the rebel side in 1798. (I'll get to him in a minute.) We also have liberal Protestant Joshua, mentioned above. Other Letts, though – according to the Reverend Henry Lett, writing in 1871 – 'the descendants of men who had entered Ireland under Cromwell, who had suffered from O'Neill and Tyrconnell and James II, and who had been with Dutch William at Oldbridge, did not remain inactive during the rebellion ... [and] were found armed on the side of truth, law and order.' He means they were yeomen. Among them was Barbara Lett's husband Newton, and also Charles Lett (the Reverend Henry's grandfather), his brother William[8] and his nephew Nicholas.

When Barbara Lett succumbs to the panic-stricken mood of the day and leaves Killaligan with whatever she can carry, she gains a temporary shelter at the Enniscorthy home of a relative named Stephen. ... And here I have to attempt a bit of clarification concerning family relationships and allegiances. In the notes accompanying a recent book, *Protestant Women's Narratives of the Irish Rebellion of 1798*, edited by John D. Beatty, this particular Stephen Lett is confused with a different person of the same name: I don't know who exactly he was, but he wasn't Barbara Lett's brother-in-law Stephen. *That* Stephen, the older brother of Newton, had died in 1786, when his son James – the future rebel – was just one year old. His wife was a relative of Bagenal Harvey, and his family's sympathies were with the United Irishmen (see p. 88 below) – whereas the Stephen Lett of Duffry Gate, Enniscorthy, 'took an active part on the side of the loyalists', opening his doors to all manner of distressed Protestant refugees. And among them is Barbara, safe for the moment, though her arrival is not without its hazards, further shocks to the system. The house and its surroundings bear witness to the hellish disruption afflicting the town. In front of the house is the body of a dead rebel lying on his face beneath the parlour window. Go to the back, and, as a grisly counterpart, you find a dead yeoman lying on his face in the yard.

Further horrors are in the offing in these dark days. An elderly Protestant clergyman named Mr Hayden is piked to death by a local butcher (his trade as well as his nature), and the clergyman's body left lying 'on the steps of Mr Lett's Hall door'. Barbara Lett then adds a distressing detail: onlookers witness the corpse of poor Mr Hayden being eaten up by pigs. Couldn't someone have rescued it from this final indignity? Could it not have been dragged indoors? It seems a bit much, on top of the homicidal free-for-all and frantic debacle, to have carrion pigs roaming freely through the charnel streets.

A wounded yeoman is carried into the house of Mr Stephen Lett and tended by Barbara, who tears up a pillowcase to make a bandage for the gash in the yeoman's back. She may be thinking at the time of her own yeoman husband and hoping he will survive (he does). But this is a time when not only national, but family discords are brewing. Newton's brother Stephen, had he not been twelve years dead, would doubtless have found a different outlet for his civic consciousness; as it is, it's left to his thirteen-year-old son James to act the rebel part. James Lett makes himself conspicuous by his antics during the Battle of Ross, when he goes about waving a bannerette and egging on the pikemen. Wherever you look, you can't get away from confusion and inconsistency. Young James's cousin Benjamin Lett (the Scullabogue survivor), on the other hand, is supposed to have flaunted his Orange allegiance by festooning the bridles of the family's horses with orange and blue ribbons. I suppose these instances of juvenile bravado can be taken to represent an unthinking partisanship, a bid for top-dog status. But they take us as far as we can get from a non-sectarian blueprint, from the whole idea of an equitable society.

Reforms were needed, no one denies it, but a great divergence occurred between the Society of United Irishmen's grand revolutionary purpose, and what actually happened on the ground. Many people, historians and archivists and teachers, biographers and social commentators, have assessed the extent to which the Rising in Wexford was fuelled by United Irish principles. The inescapable conclusion is, not very much, as the green tree of liberty sprouted deplorable excrescences. In the main, the Rising broke out as a spontaneous local revolt against insupportable ills – though for some of the leaders, such as Bagenal Harvey, it was necessary action undertaken in a rightful cause.

How did the violation of the United Irishmen's anti-sectarian imperative come about? Well, perhaps Thomas Cloney has the answer – terrible social conditions, and masses of people recruited to the rebel cause who simply don't know any better. They can't differentiate between actual oppressors – i.e. the government in Dublin, the military presence, some magistrates and others in positions of authority – and their Protestant neighbours. They think they are being handed an opportunity to turn the tables on those they consider to be in the ascendant. They think they have a licence to burn and kill and maim and terrorise – and, inevitably, ferocity is matched with ferocity. A bloodbath ensues. And, when it's all over, the poor of Wexford are no better off than they were.

Barbara Lett has cause to sustain the bitterness that bedevils her even in old age. As well as Scullabogue on 5 June, another massacre of Protestants takes place on Wexford Bridge where prisoners are brought down in batches to be piked to death and thrown into the River Slaney. The date is 20 June 1798. Among the people murdered in this way is Barbara Lett's father William Daniel, who is forty-four years old at the time. (His home was a lovely eighteenth-century house, Fortview, near Wexford: now demolished by a local council to accommodate a link road.) 'Could anything be more atrocious or barbaric,' his daughter exclaims, shortly before her own death at ninety-one, 'than the cruelties inflicted at that time on innocent and inoffending persons?' To this rhetorical question we can only answer, no.

The same fate was nearly suffered by Charles Lett, also a prisoner in Wexford gaol and marked down for execution. What saved him was a band marching into the town playing 'Croppies Lie Down' at full volume, in celebration of the just-past rebel defeat at Vinegar Hill. ('At Vinegar Hill o'er the pleasant Slaney, / Our heroes vainly stood back to back ...'.) Charles manages to get out of the gaol in the ensuing confusion, and goes through Wexford broadcasting the good news – having first had the foresight to don an ill-fitting and ragged old army red coat, retrieved from a hook on a wall. Never mind how peculiar he looks, if he'd appeared in civilian garb he'd have run the risk of being shot as a rebel.

I don't know which of these Letts, if any, are among my actual forebears, so I am going to lay claim to all of them. The facts in my possession are as follows. My great-grandfather William Lett, the father of Emily Lett, was born at Clonleigh around 1841. *His* father was a Thomas Lett, to whom, logically, we can attribute a birth date at any time between 1810 and 1820. If the former, Thomas could be a son of Benjamin Lett or of the underage rebel the bold James Lett.[9] If, on the other hand, Thomas wasn't born until 1820, it's possible that his grandparents were Barbara and Newton Lett. (I'm not forgetting Charles Lett[10] and all the other Letts who crop up in connection with 1798, and their probable progeny. But, again, in the absence of documentary evidence, I've no resource but conjecture.) If the last should prove to be true – then my antecedents on both sides take on an alarming symmetry. On one side (my mother's) is an ancestor hanged by a mob outside Lord Aungier's castle in Longford for being a Protestant; and on the other side (my father's) is an ancestor done to death by a mob on Wexford Bridge for the same reason. And here's me – well, there I was, around 1960, daring to saunter down Sandy Row in Belfast with a tiny tricolour pinned to the lapel of my convent school blazer, and bringing no retribution down on my foolhardy head beyond some low-toned rumbles and growls from a gathering of elderly men outside a bookie's, whose ire is mildly aroused by the sight of the seditious emblem – what they call a 'wee fleg'.

When Thomas Cloney refers in his *Personal Narrative* to 'a furious Orange ascendancy', he, at least, unlike the rebel rank and file, holds in his mind a clear distinction between his Protestant friends and neighbours whom he cherishes, and the new Orange system which already seemed to embody all the worst excesses of bigotry, triumphalism and religious intemperance. Other accounts of the Wexford Rising single out the anti-popery brigade — the Orange Order — as a major trigger of explosive Catholic disaffection. Some would argue that rebel aggression was never meant to be directed against 'ordinary' Protestants, only against Orangemen — not, as we've seen, that this was of much benefit to the former, once all hell had broken loose.

If the Orange Order made a powerful focus for Catholic fear and detestation, it wasn't because the sentiments it purveyed were unprecedented. It was the organisation that was new, not the attitude. For at least twenty years, antagonistic factions had been active throughout the country, Protestant Peep o' Day Boys and Catholic Defenders — or whatever the equivalent local designations were, Shanavests or Caravats or Hearts of Steel, Whiteboys and Rightboys and Kick-the-Shite Boys (I've made the last one up) — all specialists in agrarian uproar. Periodic disturbances were a feature of everyday life in many rural areas, especially — and here the ubiquitous Tippings are about to re-enter the picture — in County Armagh.

It's true that some of these illegal societies didn't start by being overtly sectarian. Some, bands of tenant farmers, came into being to protest against increased tax demands and the current method of collecting tithes. Some were willing to jettison religious animosities in the interests of effective action against economic abuses. For example — the poet Art MacCooey (see p. 40 above) has among his works a ringing tribute to young Art O'Neill, last of the O'Neills of Glassdrummond, dead at twenty-six (in 1769). In his lament MacCooey refers to O'Neill's position as an elected captain in the Hearts of Oak, or Oakboys, a Protestant secret society whose members sported oak boughs in their hats and engaged in intimidatory pursuits by night. The fact that a Catholic O'Neill was selected from among scores of contenders to lead this illicit band suggests a state of *Protestant* disaffection so extreme as to render temporarily insignificant the 'natural hostility' between Planter and Gael.

But, gradually, the old sectarian bogey raised its poisonous tentacles again. By the 1790s, faction fights in County Armagh are taking place almost exclusively along denominational lines. When the Society of United Irishmen is founded in Belfast in 1791, its title has little meaning for those entrenched in their illiberalism. And Armagh in particular is getting a name for the bitterness of its conflicts.

And where in all this is the newly-Catholic Tipping family? We left the widow and sons of turncoat Henry in their new rented farmhouse at Ballynamoney in the late 1760s. Before this they were living in the mainly Protestant district of Roughan, and it may have been an increase in sectarian pressures that sent them scurrying across the Bann to the rather less riotously inclined townland of Ballynamoney. Or it may have been the latter's proximity to Lurgan, with its market for the finely-produced linen cloth in which the family specialised, that drew them in. Whatever the reason, they settled in north-east Armagh, where the widow Tipping's eldest son, another Henry (c.1746–1797), was chiefly responsible for running the farm and the linen-producing enterprise. Perhaps, as the Antrim weaver poet James Orr recorded, 'His thrifty wife and wise wee lasses span, / While warps and queels employed anither bairn'. Indeed, innumerable country families all over the North are employed in this way in the late eighteenth century, and Catholics, at last, are not excluded from the mild prosperity it brings.

Henry Tipping's second son James, progenitor of the direct line I'm more or less sticking to, was born at the Ballynamoney farm in 1770. Was he a sickly infant, with signs of the way his life would be curtailed apparent from the start? Or was he as robust as anyone, playing with his brothers in the fields and meadows round the farmhouse when he wasn't roped in to aid the family's finances, and loss of life only an unimaginable figment of the distant future? We can't know. But throughout his short life James must have been aware of troubles and tensions afflicting the neighbourhood – though perhaps not so aggressively as in other parts of County Armagh. One social commentator (John Byrne), writing in 1792, commends 'the peaceable inhabitants of Lurgan and its vicinity' for keeping a low profile while outbreaks of lawlessness proliferate elsewhere. Not one of them, he says, has been indicted for being a Defender or a Break o' Day man. (Can this be true?) If you headed southwards in the direction of Tandragee you'd find a very different class of carry-on. Horse-racing on narrow country roads, cock-fighting and private whiskey houses all contributing to the unruliness of the era. Coat-trailing and other provocations rampant. And underlying everything, the religious bigotry ready to flare up at the genuflection of a knee. 'Many Protestant gentlemen,' says the same John Byrne – I think he's using the word 'gentlemen' advisedly – 'lent arms to Papists' to enable them to safeguard themselves and their families against the fury of fanatics and madmen. But even so – like the people of Wexford a little later on – many Armagh

Catholics chose to abandon their homes at nightfall and sleep as best they could in little huts made of sods in the middle of a turf bog. And so it goes on.'Defenders' aren't backward in becoming aggressors, as in the case of the four arrested in Tandragee for smashing the windows of a constable's house in pursuit of some Peep o' Day Boys who had taken refuge there. And, as the '80s becomes the '90s and the Volunteer movement with its emphasis on *Protestant* nationalism begins to peter out – or at least to undergo certain crucial transformations – the way is open for putative unity to dissolve in a radical schism. As the historian A.T.Q. Stewart and others have pointed out, it was the Volunteer movement of Grattan and Flood that fostered the development of *both* the Society of United Irishmen and the Orange Society. Once again, we note the ways in which Irish history accommodates the strange and contradictory.

There is absolutely no evidence to link the Ballynamoney Tippings with any clandestine organisation or pursuit. It's tempting to place them in the middle of right action, as it would have appeared at the time, defensive action against bigotry and intimidation. These were things that were not to be endured or condoned. But no Tipping voice is raised in protest against abuses in County Armagh – and this does not accord with the activism of a few of their descendants when a different, but no less exorbitant, set of circumstances prevailed (as we shall see). How many of the Ballynamoney Tippings were there, who might have nurtured reasonable grievances in the 1790s? Our ancestor James had an older and a younger brother and a couple of sisters, Mary and Elizabeth; and their father Henry, still alive at the time, would have been of an age to hold forthright views and to influence his offspring. Perhaps he did influence them, to steer clear of trouble. In the absence of any information to the contrary, we have to envisage the lot of them sitting quietly at home, getting on with their hand-loom weaving and cultivation of crops, looking after their pig, cow and hens and keeping their noses clean.

Well – clean as far as factional intrigue is concerned. There are other areas, more productive perhaps, in which a spirit of waywardness or gumption may be asserted. Courtship, for example, or domestic life. By the time he is twenty – that is, in 1790 – James Tipping has married a local girl named Sarah Magee and is already the father of a son, another James. (Just to get the chronology straight in my head – that Sarah Magee was my grandmother Sarah Tipping's great-grandmother on her father's side. Whew!) There seems, as in several other instances, to have been some haste about the marriage. 'A high level of unlawful carnal knowledge' – in the sociologists' phrase – was maybe a thing to be acquired in the fields and byways of County Armagh. As with politics, sexual mores at the time could be said to hold out a prospect of liberation or repression – and we should be glad that James (if he did) subscribed to the former, since he didn't have long to enjoy any of the pleasures of the world. He was dead at twenty-eight, dead in that most significant year of the century, 1798 – though with nothing (again) to suggest his death was due to anything other than natural causes. It's just the date that makes conjecture irresistible. Perhaps James, fired by radical principles, shot up from his loom, retrieved a pike from the roof-space, and set off eastwards to join in the fighting under Henry Munro in turbulent County Down. Perhaps he died there, at Saintfield or Ballynahinch, at the hands of the York Fencibles or the Newtownards Yeomanry. But I think we'd know about it if he did. I think it's safer to blame tuberculosis, or some other common illness, for James's premature death.

Four years earlier, in 1794, James had moved his growing family (two other sons were born in 1792 and 1794, and there may have been a daughter as well) to a smallholding at Crossmacahilly in the parish of Seagoe. Going round in circles, we've now got back to Seagoe, where James's great-great-grandfather John Tipping is buried alongside his Blacker in-laws. (Keep that in mind: the Blackers are going to crop up again in a minute.) Crossmacahilly: the very name suggests an apex of uncouthness, just as the place itself proves the ultimate countrified locality. It sounds much better in the original Irish, *Crois Mhic Eachmhilidh*, McCaughley's Cross, as it was named after a prominent local sept. It's a townland of roughly two hundred and twenty acres, three miles south-west of Lurgan and about two miles from Portadown. In 1794, when James and Sarah Tipping arrived with their cartload of belongings to inhabit the smallholding, the whole area consisted of unreclaimed and worked-out bogland. The farmhouse and accompanying acreage of poor land was right on the verge of what contemporary maps call 'the Great Turf Bog', and one effect of the resulting perpetual miasma was a population particularly prone to tuberculosis – to which, as I've suggested, James Tipping may have succumbed, after four years of rigorous work to cultivate the land with constant deadly vapours circulating round his head. We can envisage him coughing and wheezing his way through the work of the farm, the children quickly learning not to aggravate him as his appearance grows gaunter and his temper worse. And then a coffin and candles and mourning dress. But not for being a pikeman.

Not a pikeman – but a republican spirit is infiltrating the family standpoint nevertheless. It is helped on by a marriage connection. In the 'trouble year', in the townland of Tamnaficarbet, three miles west of Lurgan town centre, in a two-room thatched cottage in the middle of a flood-plain, a fifteen- or sixteen-year-old boy named John Darragh is cheering on the rebels. Some years later, by now well versed himself in the ways of disaffection, John Darragh comes into the hands of the authorities. Charged with being 'an Irish rebel', he is tried at Antrim Assizes in 1809, and – after a spell in prison – transported on a convict ship to the penal colony at Port Jackson (Sydney) in Australia. A dark and horrible journey is ahead of him, but also, eventually, a new life far superior to the old one. When he sails from Cork in 1813, resentful, like Irish rebels before and since, of the convict status imposed on him, John Darragh leaves behind, in another townland of north Armagh, Tirsogue, a wife and six children. His wife, whom he'd have married around 1800 (the year of a more momentous union) was Mary, one of the Ballynamoney Tippings and the sister of dead James.

What was linen-weaver Darragh's actual offence? Alas, the records – along with many others – went up in smoke when the Four Courts was burnt. We've no resource, again, but surmise. Perhaps he was implicated in the stirring-up of trouble to coincide with Robert Emmet's planned uprising in Dublin in 1803 (see below, p. 76), and then evaded arrest for the next six years or so. 'On the run' is the stirring phrase suggesting spunk and danger and outwitting strategies. If John Darragh was on the run – or 'on his keeping' – no doubt many interconnected scions of Tipping and Darragh and Magee families all chipped in with shelter and sustenance and an eye out for danger. Like the Armagh rapparee Seamus Mac Murchaidh in the eighteenth-century song, John Darragh would have relied on his local knowledge to stay at large for as long as possible. Like Mac Murchaidh, he might have hankered after the woods of Dunreavy, or any closer woods where a fugitive might hole up. But the thing that would mostly have kept him going was the help of friends. And the shared protective mission, the sense of opposition to the way things were run in the country, would have strengthened (in particular) the Tipping commitment to Catholic Ireland. They'd only had a couple of generations to shed their Protestant colouring, and it would take another two or three generations before the republican ethic reached its fullest expression in the family. But the process was under way.

The 'Irish rebel' John Darragh, like the innocent Connerys in another popular Gaelic song, was deported to New South Wales, enduring foul conditions on the prison ship the *Archduke Charles*, and spending two years under the convict stigma, before being granted an 'Absolute Pardon' in 1815. Like many another ex-convict, Darragh then went on to prosper in his new surroundings. ... His son Felix Darragh, with wife and children, joined him in Australia in 1840. (Felix's wife was Alice Magee, a niece of the Sarah Magee who married James Tipping. ... I am sorry to cite all these convoluted connections, which are enough to make anyone's head spin; but I want to document, as far as possible, the influences impelling the stay-at-home Tippings towards full-blown republicanism, and the above information adds a detail to the picture.) ... When John died in 1858 Felix inherited the property at Figtree in the Illawarra on the south coast of New South Wales, and became a considerable landowner himself. These Darragh and Tipping descendants were thereby lost to the Irish cause. They made a new life for themselves and undoubtedly a better one, growing into their Australian identity. But John, remembering his Armagh origins and 'rebel' loyalties, called his farm at Figtree 'Tamnaficarbet'.

Tamnaficarbet, Crossmacahilly: it's a far cry from ancestral Carrickblacker House, where the teenage great-great-grandson of the William Blacker who fought at the Boyne is following manfully in his ancestor's footsteps. Once strong supporters of the House of Stuart (you remember), the Blackers turned Orange after the Siege of Derry. And in the younger William, born in 1777, the Orange affiliation reaches a kind of apex. Here he is in the mid 1790s, about to enrol at Trinity College Dublin and undergo an advantageous education – while at home in Armagh he is taking a vigorous interest in local unrest. Protestant uprightness is the bedrock of William's creed: he views the Protestants of County Armagh as an innocent people subjected to the vilest of unprovoked attacks and intimidation.

Or so the author of *For God and the King* would have it, in accord with his own opinion. In the eyes of J.S. Kane, the vicious sectarian outbreaks

A drawing of William Blacker in middle age, looking stouter of face and figure than in his rip-roaring days

infesting Armagh can be laid at the door of the Catholic population. He claims the Peep o' Day Boys came into being to defend themselves and their communities against the Defenders (most people would agree that it was the other way round).[11] He attributes a Catholic origin to almost every rampaging band provoking fear by night, oddly including the Protestant Hearts of Oak. When he gets to the famous Battle of the Diamond, he is unequivocally on the side of the victorious Protestant faction – and in all this young William Blacker of Carrickblacker takes the role of hero.

William Blacker, eighteen in 1795, is a boisterous advocate of Protestant defenderism. When Carrickblacker House gets a new roof, he commandeers the lead from the old one and sits up all night making bullets from it to aid the Protestant cause. In the early autumn of that year, after various skirmishes and outrages have made a large-scale armed confrontation inevitable, opposing forces muster at a place called the Diamond, at the junction of four highways (and only a couple of miles from Roughan, from which, we remember, James Tipping's grandmother, father and uncles had removed themselves in haste in the late 1760s). Hostilities break out on the morning of 21 September – and galloping towards the martial spot at a furious pace is young William Blacker leading 'a contingent of armed men', many of whom are workers on his father's estate. As he recalled the subsequent 'battle' later,

> The affair was of brief duration. The Defenders, completely entrapped, made off leaving a number killed and wounded on the spot ... from those whom I saw carried off on cars that day and from the bodies found afterwards by the reapers in the cornfields along the line of their flight, I am inclined to think that not less than thirty lost their lives.[12]

The jubilant Protestants, says J.S. Kane, 'had successfully driven off their oppressors [whew!] and had prevented the destruction of most of their homes and property'. William Blacker takes up the story again: immediately after the battle, he says, right on the field of action, 'measures were adopted for the formation of a defensive association of Protestants' – and thus the Orange Society came into being. Defensive: but what William Blacker fails to mention is that in the months succeeding the establishment of the first Orange Lodges, upwards of five thousand Armagh Catholics were driven from their homes.

William Blacker, whose presence adds a touch of gentry respectability to the loyalist proceedings, is right there in the thick of the hurriedly negotiated arrangements to impose a structure and an administrative system on the new society. From the start the Orange Order is composed of separate Lodges, one of which, No. 12, is quickly set up by workers on the Carrickblacker estate (the same workers who took part in the battle). 'Members of the Blacker family' – I'm quoting J.S. Kane again – 'were encouraged to join the fledgling Order and William's uncle George, recently appointed vicar of Seagoe parish ... became an enthusiastic member.'

There's a feature of the old-fashioned thriller, the 'had-I-but-known' syndrome, which provokes a sardonic response in readers of the present time. Had she, the witless Victorian heroine, but known ... that a would-be strangler or rapist lurked on the spot, she'd never have ventured into the lonely mansion, or graveyard, or oak wood at midnight, and no incident would have occurred to stimulate the plot and draw out the narrative indefinitely. I am now about to apply the 'had-I-but-known' principle to a few of those eighteenth-century Blackers and consequent implications for Orangeism in the North. Had William and his uncle George and his father the Reverend Stewart 'but known' that at nearby Crossmacahilly, in dismal circumstances, lived the stricken, industrious, Catholic James Tipping, a near-contemporary of William's and a blood relation of all of them. ... Had they but known this, would it have modified at all their Orange fervour and sense of utter moral rectitude? The dispiriting answer is, probably not. (I know I'm stretching the analogy here. One type of hidden factor has a bearing on an immediate action, the other on an attitude.)

The truth is, having got the Orange bit between his teeth and running with it at full tilt, William comes out against every egalitarian principle and aspect of enlightenment thinking that illumines the era. ... Here he is in his rooms at Trinity presiding over Orange assemblies, or holding forth to ever greater numbers of potential recruits at the Druid's Head Inn in South Great George's Street. Soon he is immersed in a full-scale 'war' against fellow students suspected of being United Irishmen. Among them is his contemporary Robert Emmet; and the rather older ex-students Wolfe Tone and Whitley Stokes (not to be confused with his grandson of the same name, the eminent Celtic philologist) can count themselves among his adversaries too. Trinity is in an uproar, between the Orange and Green contingents. The authorities find it difficult to curb the students' partisan intensity. Running battles take place along

Dame Street. Some of the 'rebel students' are described by William as 'low vulgar wretch[es] ... and probably ... Papist[s]', the ultimate slur. The University Yeomanry makes a further outlet for William's militant drive: here he is again, boldly enlisted in the 3rd Company of the College Corps. ... Back home in Armagh for the summer vacation, he throws himself into preparations for the first Orange parades to be organised since the founding of the Order (12 July, 1796); and a year later his Orange glory is consolidated when the title of Grand Master of the new Lodge at Portadown is conferred on him. He is still only twenty years old.

(Dear God, is there no end to the agitating revelations popping up like hybrid excrescences wherever I peer among the clustering branches of my chequered family tree! Where now are all my carefully cultivated liberal credentials? Not only do I have to take [ancestral] responsibility for fighting *against* Sir Phelim O'Neill in 1641, for allying myself with Cromwell in 1649, for defending Derry against the Irish troops of King James in 1689, for fighting under the standard of William at the Boyne, for ministering to wounded yeomen in 1798 ... but it seems I'm personally implicated in the founding and upholding of the Orange Order too. I'm joking.)

We haven't heard the last of the egregious William Blacker, but now it is time to consider events in the north of Ireland while Wexford went into its almighty convulsion. Those involved in fostering rebellion were frequently at cross-purposes, as we've seen. Some set out filled with oafish glee to turn the tables on their local enemies; while others, well-principled, held fast to an idea of social reform – reform much needed, with rising rents, leases unrenewed, unacceptable tithe demands, hearth money-collectors and excise officials making life difficult for everyone. Some, for these reasons and others, were driven to take up arms – but then came the news from Scullabogue, bringing despair to the hearts of Presbyterian Ulstermen and causing some of them to throw in the towel at this point. It must have seemed that the sectarian instinct in Ireland was endowed with an alarming tenacity – and for those committed to the union of Catholic, Protestant and Dissenter as a motivating principle, this was a considerable blow. Why bother, the argument might have gone, to fight for religious tolerance and an end to political abuses, when the country was coming down with sectarian diehards for whom 'patriotism' was cast in an inveterate and vicious form? The tree of liberty, that flourished in America and in France, had no chance of taking root in Ireland, it appeared, where blight had the upper hand. Where the immemorial struggle between tyranny and freedom was always adulterated by indigenous complications. Nevertheless, the Rising went ahead, more or less as the leaders – visionaries – had planned it. Two weeks after Wexford erupted, on the morning of 7 June 1798, thousands of United Irishmen assembled at Donegore Hill on the outskirts of Antrim, ready to march on the town; and two days later, battalions of insurgents from north Down joined in the action. Once more, the game was afoot.

... And it was quickly quelled. The story has been well told, by Charles Dickson and A.T.Q. Stewart among others; and I won't repeat it here. When it was all over and the leaders executed, myth, romance, all the glamour of enlightened dissent began to gather round the stark event, the United Irish defeat. 'Well, they fought for poor old Ireland, and full bitter was their fate ...': this is one expression of the popular nationalist view. But however you look at it – a resounding moment, a great endeavour, a bloody rebellion – 1798 carries the strongest possible charge of fatefulness and exhilaration.

In Presbyterian folk memory, the year – 'the trouble year' – came to be viewed as a highly consequential time when ordinary people, the opposite of hotheads, left their farms and businesses in a spirit of revolt against unutterable injustice.

> ... Us ones quet from mindin' the farms.
> Let them take what we gave wi' the weight o' our arms,
> From Saintfield to Kilkeel.

I'm quoting these lines from Florence M. Wilson's sterling ballad 'The Man From God-Knows-Where', a party-piece in the North but more than that, a reminder of the Presbyterian heritage of high-minded revolt. It was written in 1918, and its subject is Thomas Russell, librarian of the Linen Hall Library in Belfast, United Irishman and close friend of Henry Joy McCracken and his sister Mary Anne. Russell was arrested in the run-up to the Rising and seethed in a Dublin prison, unable to take part. When he got out, he returned to the North, and to his seditious ways. He was destined to go the way of his friends, McCracken and Wolfe Tone, only a few years later. A new century had arrived and with it, the Union of Great Britain and Ireland, but parts of Ireland remained unpacified, even if the end of the Rising had, for the moment, knocked the spirit out of them. Thomas Russell had hoped to stir things again towards a new revolutionary enterprise, but nothing came of it. The mood in the country was utterly changed, and revolution – rebellion – was viewed with horror, not optimism. Instead of mustering a northern contingent, Russell was arrested again and executed at Downpatrick gaol in 1803, following his forlorn attempt to rally the North in support of Robert Emmet's Dublin affray. The ballad by Florence Wilson covers the years between 1796 and 1803, and as Charles Dickson says in his book *Revolt in the North*, it expresses 'admirably the spirit of the United Irishmen in County Down'. It's a *Presbyterian* spirit it expresses, indeed, with its emphasis on everyday dealings and a slow-burning anger and bitterness.

> Well 'twas gettin' on past the heat o' the year
> When I rode to Newtown fair:
> I sold as I could (the dealers were near –
> Only three-pound-eight for the Innis steer,
> An' nothin' at all for the mare!)
> I met M'Kee in the throng o' the street,
> Says he, 'The grass has grown under our feet
> Since they hanged young Warwick here.'

Hanging is the end of the road for many of the rebels, as all the bright hopes for social amelioration come to nothing. Among those who died in this manner was Henry Munro, a linen draper from Lisburn and chief commander of the County Down insurgents at Saintfield and Ballynahinch. (Here we have another instance of things coming round full circle. Henry Munro could claim collateral descent from the Colonel Robert Munro who, with his army of Covenanters, had landed at Carrickfergus in 1642 and assumed command of all the Scottish and English forces in Ulster, whose mission was to subdue the natives.)

When Munro stepped out to meet his death on a gallows set up in Lisburn's Market Square, the person appointed to carry out the execution was so incompetent that the thing was bungled and the unfortunate insurgent left half-dead. ... And here comes William Blacker again bristling with loyalist heave-ho, rushing up to lend the hangman a hand. Whether an impulse of humanity or vengefulness dictated this action, I cannot say. It was due to Blacker's Seagoe Yeomanry that Henry Munro was captured, and William was designated 'Officer of the Day' for the execution. ('He with his loyal Orangemen united to the king/While other haughty rebels in a halter they will swing,' goes a couplet from a makeshift contemporary ballad, not one by William himself.) Years later, however, he described Henry Munro as 'shrewd, brave and active' and commended his leadership, arguing that his plan of attack might well have succeeded, had it actually been carried out. That it wasn't, he speculated, might have been because 'the Popish portion of the rebels disliked going under the command of a Presbyterian ...'. (Actually, Henry Munro was an Episcopalian, but the point remains.) So there you have the 'Popish portion' in the Blacker view: sectarian, pig-headed and inept.

Why did Armagh stay out of the Rising of 1798? For some not very creditable reasons. When the Society of United Irishmen was founded in 1791 (in Belfast, by William Drennan), its ideals and objectives were somewhat at odds with the way things were managed in County Armagh. That part of the North was saturated in ancient enmities, and a popular means of expressing hostility and resentment already existed there for young malcontents on both sides – the notorious faction fights. 'Unity' on the whole was not an option in the county while factional imperatives predominated. Though some Defenders did merge with United Irishmen, you weren't, by and large, about to see Defenders and Peep o' Day Boys sink their traditional differences in the interests of a French- or American-inspired egalitarianism. In a version of what happened in Wexford, Armagh men stuck to their sectarian guns – and without the overlying ideological gloss that gained Wexford a place in the nationalist pantheon. And when the new loyalism began to be consolidated, it was a natural progression for Peep o' Day Boys to become full-blooded Orangemen.

And now we reach a reversal of the set-piece exodus of desperate Protestants all over Ireland running for their lives (a compelling image for me, now I've discovered that so many of my ancestors were among them). In her magisterial history, *The Catholics of Ulster* (2000), Marianne Elliott quotes a set of verses written in County Armagh in the 1790s:

> The jails they are filled with your nearest relations,
> Your wives and your children are sorely oppressed,

Your houses are burned, your lands desolated,
By a band of ruffians with Orange cockades.

She goes on: 'When threatening notices signed "Oliver Cromwell" were affixed to Catholics' homes, ordering them to quit or be burnt out, most chose to leave without question.' They scattered in all directions, into County Down, southwards to Tipperary, north-west towards Donegal: any locality, however remote, in which it seemed a life free of intimidation might be a possibility. The apocryphal Cromwellian dictum, 'to hell or Connacht', took on a horrendous contemporary reality.

Some of these refugees made their way to Connemara, where they arrived in a desperate state. Help was at hand: they were taken under the wing of Richard Martin of Ballynahinch and his wife Harriet, who supplied food, accommodation, and sympathy for the Northerners' plight. Martin – 'Humanity Dick'[13] – was a substantial landowner who presided over what the author Tim Robinson calls 'a kingdom within a kingdom': a place of 'equivocal allure' due to Martin's scant regard for law, and other exorbitant qualities.[14] By providing succour for some of the people exiled from Armagh, he gained a position on the extreme edge of the Ulster story, and placed himself on the side of the angels as far as northern memories of persecution are concerned. The opposite of 'Cromwell' in every respect.

(Incidentally, Oliver Cromwell has much to answer for in Ireland, but making him a scapegoat for *every* atrocity that occurred is really going too far. I'm thinking here of Scullabogue, and how it gradually got transformed in one section of the popular mind – a mind reluctant to admit even the possibility of sectarian wrongdoing on the Catholic side. Tom Dunne, in *Rebellions*, mentions passing the site of the barn in the company of an elderly relative and being told by him in all sincerity: 'That's the place where Cromwell burned the Catholics.')

In the midst of all the alarms and instability and night frights besetting County Armagh, the Tippings stuck it out. They weren't among the thousands of Catholics forced to abandon their homes and livelihoods in the last decade of the eighteenth century. The last of the Crossmacahilly clan was still inhabiting the same ramshackle house as late as 1944. But, for many reasons, life must have lacked overwhelmingly congenial elements for struggling cottiers, subsistence farmers and hand-loom weavers, battling to scrape a living while coping, day in, day out, with neighbourly hostility. (I know that sounds like an oxymoron, but there it is.) This was a time of exorbitant sabre-rattling in County Armagh, of brawlers, fanatics, hangmen, outrages, flames from burning houses lighting up the night sky, unnerving encounters along secluded lanes. 'And neighbours on the roads at night with guns.'[15]

One's heart goes out to young Sarah Magee in the middle of it all – newly widowed, with four or five children under the age of ten, a farm to run, home-based weaving to carry on, day-to-day living with all its exertions and vexations to oversee. And no prospect before her but the fields and meadows stretching away into the distance, and beyond them the bog, and so on to infinity. How she managed in the circumstances I do not know, but manage she did. Like her great-granddaughter (my grandmother, another Sarah Tipping), who found herself similarly bereaved in 1915, James Tipping's widow showed her mettle by not falling to pieces, by acting out a dogged determination to make a go of things. Possibly, again like my grandmother, she had friends and relations at hand to ease the worst of the burdens, practical or financial or psychological as the case may have been. The rent was paid, the farm kept up, the children reared. In 1812, when the oldest son James comes of age, his mother gets him to take out a lease on the farm, which gains the family an enhanced security.

Ancestral houses. I never set eyes on the Crossmacahilly farm until it was nothing but a rickety survival fast returning to the clay. It had dwindled to a store for cattle-feed, in the middle of a morass. It was stuck at the end of a *bothairin*, or loanen, or whatever you like to call it, and approachable only by means of this swamp-like footway through which you had to struggle and squelch. The winter sky is overcast, the surrounding mud is prodigious, and the emptiness of the fields all around strikes a desolate note. You feel you might have stepped back into the early nineteenth century – only then, of course, the house and land, on the estate of the absentee Duke of Manchester, would have had a kempt appearance. I won't go as far as roses round the door, but the house and its adjunct, a smaller building at a right angle to the main dwelling, would then have been neatly thatched and the garden cultivated. Indoors, sugan chairs, settle beds, creepie stools, deal tables, a turf fire blazing in the open fireplace ... all the fixtures of a farmer-weaver's living quarters would be in place. Perhaps a dog and a cat made their home here too. A degree of order and diligence would have prevailed.

Hard to reconcile all that with the tumbledown wreck now standing – barely – on a byroad somewhere in the wilds between Lurgan and the recent town of Craigavon. Due to a quirk of temperament, I have always been enthralled by historic buildings and the associations they encompass – but Crossmacahilly is too far gone, too wretched looking, to chime with any invigorating sense of the past. It requires a tremendous act of the imagination to restore to it any form or substance whatever. Carrickblacker, on the other hand ... well, that's a handsome pile I'd have taken great delight in. I like, as I say, to savour a house with a history, and the denser the history, the more enraptured my responses. My actual claim to a share in Carrickblacker may be genetically exiguous, but it stands up well in terms of affinity (aesthetic affinity, that is, *not* fellow-feeling for its Orange ambience). Alas, the great house was wiped out of existence before I ever heard tell of it. It and I overlapped by about thirteen years, not long enough for it to impinge on my antiquarian consciousness. I know it only from photographs.

Robert M. Young, writing in 1909, describes Carrickblacker as 'an ancient battlemented mansion', standing in 250 acres, with the River Bann flowing through the grounds before it merges with the Newry canal about a mile away. Like the even more resonant Springhill at Moneymore, Carrickblacker was a rare Northern Irish architectural treasure from the seventeenth century. Unlike Springhill, it was considered dispensable. In the inter-war period, when the role of military grandees in Portadown was failing somewhat, the current Lieutenant-Colonel Blacker moved his family to Devon and sold the house to people named Atkinson, who in turn allowed it to come into the disrespectful hands of the golf club mentioned above. And that was the end of it and its vivid narrative, its venerable interior and ethical heritage attached not to Ireland and liberalism, but to Protestant conservatism and soldierly integrity. Its heavy old chimney-pieces, oak panelling, yew bannisters, Jacobean furniture, equestrian portraits lining its stately walls ... all dispersed or destroyed.

And so to Clonleigh. This was a sturdy, prosperous, two-storey Wexford farmhouse, built in the eighteenth century. Containing at least six rooms indoors, it had plentiful outbuildings and farm offices besides. It included stables, a dairy and a piggery. Five plain sash windows gleamed in sunlight at the front of the house: one on each side of the

Carrickblacker House in its heyday

door and three above, like a house on a child's embroidery sampler. In
the garden were flower beds and a vegetable patch. A high, dry-stone
wall surrounded it, and an iron gate was hung between a couple of those
characteristic round white gateposts, which feature so prominently in
the Irish countryside. Some horses lived there, and a donkey was kept to
draw a small cart. There were mongrel sheepdogs everywhere. And hens.
And fuchsia bushes. And the view from the front windows included a
low range of blue enticing Wexford hills. And some miles to the south,
beyond another hill, Carrickbyrne, lay Scullabogue.

The farmhouse survived the turbulent events of 1798, but, as we've
seen, the house and its neighbourhood weren't untouched by them. Then,
as far as we can tell, came years and years of obscurity and repose. More
than a century and a half went by with nothing happening in this part
of rural Wexford but the routines of farming and daily life. (Well, with
one or two exceptions which I'll touch on later.) My great-grandfather
William Lett was born at Clonleigh in 1841 and when he died in the
same place in 1932 he left the farm and everything in it to his second
daughter Miss Annie Tennant Lett. My grandmother, Emily Anne Craig,
received a legacy of £50 from her father, and the same amount went
to one of William's Wexford granddaughters. There was a son, Thomas,
who was due to receive £200 according to the terms of an earlier will,

but this legacy was revoked in a codicil. Having provided for Thomas during his lifetime, William announced, he was damned if he was going to go on doing so after his death. (Or words to that effect.) Let Thomas fend for himself – not before time. So we gain an impression of twice-widowed William Lett as a forthright and doughty old farmer, a person who knew his own mind and never hesitated to assert his authority as head of the household.

I went to Clonleigh once, when I was twenty-something. It would have been about 1972. My grandmother's half-sister, Aunt Annie, was on her deathbed. My father drove us – his mother, his sister Ruby, my mother and myself – all the way from Belfast to the South. Emily and Ruby Craig stayed overnight at the farm, while the rest of us had booked into a small hotel not far away – probably in New Ross. There was nothing sombre or funereal about this excursion: we were all in high spirits. It was the summer holidays, and I was home from London. The drive was exhilarating, through the different landscapes of Down and Armagh and Louth and Wicklow. Whenever I opened my mouth, the car rang with nervous laughter; I seemed to have this effect on my relatives, with the simplest statement – 'Oh look at that lovely old house over there, among the trees' – causing an outbreak of hilarity. They never quite knew what to make of me. Their incomprehension was mostly benign, though an acerbic edge to it wasn't unknown. It could go from, wonderingly, 'She's not like a Belfast girl at all', to 'Sure who's like her since Leather-arse died', pronounced with a dry intonation. It was at its peak, I suppose, when I was around twenty; thereafter my supposed eccentricities were toned down at family gatherings as I learned to fit in. Well, up to a point. A faint unease persisted on the part of some relations – not all – perhaps caused by my 1920s dresses and other London crotchets. These might have been viewed as an extension of oddities apparent almost from the word go. (The commonplace, 'Nose stuck in a book', among them.) I belonged to the family, no doubt about it, but I'd never quite conformed to family expectations. There was always something that set me apart – but if this was liable to provoke an unadmiring response, it would never have done so in my mother's presence. For all her amiability and social know-how, my mother would have made it clear that the smallest critical assessment relating to me was absolutely off-limits.

And now I was going to meet some totally unknown relations. Three women lived in Aunt Annie's farmhouse: herself, and the two

PC's great-aunt Miss Annie Tennant Lett, c.1920

elderly nieces whose role was to minister to her needs. (Aunt Annie would have been well over ninety at this time.) Bessie and Dolly. These were a pair of stout Wexford women, probably in their late sixties. Their mother, long dead as far as I know, was Annie's older sister. They, just to clarify these family relationships, were my father's cousins. I don't think my mother and I would have made the slightest impression on them. We were visitors, no more, to be offered hospitality in the kitchen-cum-dining-room with its autumn-leaf wallpaper and old-fashioned accoutrements. I don't know if we ever got upstairs in the house – though I know about the four-poster beds in every bedroom, so perhaps we did. They, the nieces, in my brief view of them, showed a surface jocularity which overlay their countrywoman's toughness and tenacity. They had handsome battered faces surrounded by wiry grey-brown hair, and their clothes were protected by patterned overalls. They looked well able to transact all the business of the farm, with only a hired hand named Danny for the rougher jobs. A capacity for hard work was all the nieces had in common with their aunt, my grandmother, as far as I could judge. She did not have a strong personality or any instinct for intrigue. She liked things to be blithe and uncontentious. She left opinions to others. I believe she was a dab hand at a pigeon pie, but if any such carnivorous cooking had taken place in my presence, no doubt I'd have run out of the room screaming.

The point about Bessie and Dolly is that their name was Hornick. The Hornicks were of German Palatine descent, having originally arrived with other refugees from the Rhine Palatinate to settle near Old Ross in the early part of the eighteenth century. These Continental immigrants were, of course, Protestant, and what they were fleeing from in many instances was 'Popish' persecution. Like the Huguenots before them, they threw in their lot with the Irish Protestant community – which made them doubly vulnerable, as outsiders with odd names and conspicuous non-Catholics to boot, when the 1798 Rebellion went awry. A Philip Hornick was burned with the other victims at Scullabogue and his bones shovelled into the shallow grave by the side of the barn.

So – the ancestral web I'm constructing reaches a point of thickening and darkening, with more of my family connections (if only by marriage) leading back and back to Scullabogue. And it doesn't end with the Hornicks. It recently emerged that Bessie Hornick had been married at some time, though – whatever went wrong – this was a circumstance she kept very quiet. Many of the Craigs and other cousins were unaware of it, taking both sisters to be spinsters. But married she was, and her married name was Parslow. It's a name, like Hornick, with a devastating resonance. Two among the dead of Scullabogue were also named Parslow.

I didn't have Scullabogue in mind at all when I went to Wexford in the summer of 1972, and I'm certain no one else did either. These particular relations, to the best of my knowledge, were not history-minded. I'm sure our 'Catholic' orientation, my mother's and mine, wasn't held against us. We wouldn't have been blamed for Scullabogue, if Scullabogue had had any currency at the time. But I doubt that it did. It was just – if, indeed, it was known at all – a fragment of a desolate past, a shadowy horror and indisputable wrong. Nearly two centuries after it happened, Scullabogue had no place in the validating of local renown. It was best obliterated. Catholics weren't about to assume ancestral guilt and go about beating their breasts, and Protestants had no wish to dwell on their victimhood, even long-ago victimhood. The years of peace, relative peace, counted for more than ancient and hellish pandemoniums. The heartfelt cry of Barbara Lett against 'barbarous' neighbours held not the slightest relevance for farming families in the middle of the twentieth century, when neighbourly cooperation and civility cut across religious barriers.

And yet. A little Protestant enclave survived in Catholic Wexford, composed of people with names like Lett, Parslow and Hornick. Belonging to the Church of Ireland was the thing that bound them together. They had their rituals: church, Sunday best, high tea, evensong, excursions to nearby coastal resorts such as Fethard-on-Sea, business and social dealings with one another. It all seems very distant and decorous, and unequipped to persist into the present. Modern life eventually caught up with it. What happened – well, what happened to Clonleigh in particular? Aunt Annie died, the nieces inherited, the old house was abandoned, a new dwelling appeared – one of those bungalows of horrid aspect that erupted like boils all over the countryside as Ireland got into the grip of a rage for modernisation. ... In due course, the bicentenary of 1798 occurred and gave rise to a lot of commemorative edifices and activities, including a good many specially built Heritage Centres and a Vinegar Hill Day. And Scullabogue? If it couldn't be entirely ignored, it wasn't highlighted. The atrocity is commemorated as a 'tragic departure' from United Irish ideals, in a rather uninformative inscription on a stone positioned in a corner of the little Church of Ireland churchyard at Old Ross. No mention of Protestants or pogroms. There, in the graveyard, the Scullabogue stone stands – a blip in the middle of all the nationalist brouhaha.

At this time too, a rash of plaques went up on walls connected with

1798 and its legends, and one of these of particular interest to me is situated at Newcastle House, Cleariestown, where the children of Stephen Lett (brother-in-law of Barbara) grew up and devoted themselves to the thrilling rebel cause. Yes, here comes that valiant boy James Lett again:

> When Erin gives due honour
> To those who fought and fell
> Beneath her flashing banner,
> 'Mid roundshot, grape and shell,
> Upon the scroll of glory,
> Historian, don't forget
> To write the name and story
> Of brave young Master Lett.

James is commemorated at Newcastle House along with his equally valiant sisters, on whom the sobriquet 'the Rebel Angels' was conferred, as a consequence of their skill in embroidering banners proclaiming a subversive allegiance. The inscription on the children's plaque reads: 'In memory of young James Moore Lett and his sisters Mary, Dora, Frances and Sarah, who courageously played their part in the cause of Irish freedom in 1798.' Then comes a line in Irish: '*Go ndeanfaidh Dia trocaire orthu go leir.*'[16]

Well! I now have to backtrack, to say that – via those distant Letts – I can after all claim an ancestral connection to the 1798 Rebellion on the romantic-Irish side – and to Scullabogue, and to the loyalists of Enniscorthy, and to Cromwell's massacres, and to centuries of high and low deeds, all rolled into one. If adolescent James Lett's[17] behaviour on the field of battle – as I now learn – secured for his family name 'an immortality in the annals of Irish patriotism' (I'm quoting from an old newspaper article about a hundred years after the event), where does that leave his Aunt Barbara (to whom his mother and sisters weren't very nice, at the height of the turmoil), his Uncle Newton and all the other 'loyalist' relatives? In a blurred or blended, murky, complex and inconsistent genetic mould along with all the rest of us, that's where.

Scullabogue. When all those patriotic poems were surging into my highly receptive head, when my green-white-and-orange immersion was absolute, it might have surprised me to learn that another perspective was available, that a whole different set of circumstances existed, to which

I might have had access if I'd taken the trouble. (Had I but known ...). I chose not to envisage more than one kind of trigger for retrospective outrage. I ignored the possibility of putting the complex into the simple – as William Empson has it, in a different context – but simple-mindedly cried up every bit of family lore confirming an Irish identity, and blotted out the rest. I mean, I knew my attachment-by-breeding to Irish-Ireland was never going to be as secure as I'd have liked, but I was happily ignorant of just how much of a nonsense it was.

CHAPTER 4
BARDS OF ARMAGH

... I hear an old sombre tide awash in the headboard:
Unpathetic och ochs and och hohs, the long bedtime
Anthems of Ulster, unwilling, unbeaten,

Protestant, Catholic, the Bible, the beads,
Long talks at gables by moonlight, boots on the hearth,
The small hours chimed sweetly away ...

Seamus Heaney, from 'The Settle Bed'

My mother's well-stocked mind contained a lot of songs and recitations. Sometimes she had to laugh at the things that swept into her head: comically sad verses, absurd-Irish doggerel. She didn't choose to repeat these things, either silently or out loud, but they simply wouldn't leave her alone: 'Poor Pinch and Caoch O'Leary'; 'The woman was old and feeble and grey'; 'The Garden where the Praties Grow'. Her repertoire was prodigious. 'The Old Bog Road' was a feature of her mental landscape, along with 'The Deserted Village'. 'Barbara Fretchie' was in it, rubbing shoulders with 'Wee Hughie'. These and many other items of bromide were a permanent acquisition of her brain. Some party pieces, and other more serious lyrics and stanzas, were a legacy of her Catholic primary school in Lurgan, where a class of seven-, eight- and nine-year-olds sat undergoing a programme of rote-learning, with a variable outcome. It was the 1920s, a doleful decade. Some pupils – 'scholars', as they were called – were hopeless from the start, big ungainly girls with vacant expressions, or sharp-featured little oddities undone by poverty. But not my mother. My mother is destined for better things, including an education unimaginable to the bulk of her early classmates. She is singled out on account of her quick responses and her retentive memory. This is a girl, a little half-orphan from a poor background, who is clearly *not* mill-fodder. Before she's thirteen, my mother is enrolled at a swanky new fee-paying convent school on top of a hill called Mount St Michael's, to which she hastens every morning, bursting with pride in her second-hand navy school uniform, carrying a leather satchel filled with books and a hockey stick as a symbol of her new status. She is walking on air.

She's got to Mount St Michael's on a scholarship, of course, and a succession of scholarships will see her through to her eventual BA degree from Queen's University in Belfast. It's an exhilarating time for her: she loves everything about the school, the nuns, the lessons, the atmosphere, new friendships formed and consolidated, her own prime position in the class, the sense of possibilities opening for the future. And, although her attributes (like mine) don't include a good singing voice, she has, as ever, no bother with the words of songs and poems (and passages from Shakespeare). A high proportion of the songs she learns are Irish-orientated – though a long way from *sean-nos*: a local anthem is more likely to begin, 'By Lough Neagh's shores where the fisherman strays ...' than '*Ag Ur-Chill a' Chreggan 'se codhail me 'reir faoi bhron ...*'. The great revival of interest in traditional Irish singing hasn't yet happened, and when it does happen it's too late for my mother to be affected by it. For her, the store of national, and nationalist, songs is confined to ballads and folk songs in the English language of varying degrees of authenticity. Some have authentic airs and new words – 'She Moved Through the Fair', 'Boulevogue', 'Down by the Salley Gardens' – and some are entirely new: 'The Kerry Dancers', 'The Rose of Tralee'. Most are pleasant and soporific and supposedly enshrine a devotion to Ireland even if they lack the genuine, austere or plangent note of a complex Gaelic folk tradition. One of them, 'Bold Phelim Brady, the Bard of Armagh', is a particular favourite of my mother's despite its shillelagh and brogues-bound-with-straw motif.

Well, it's understandable: was she not herself a Brady of Armagh

(County Armagh, at any rate)? I am sure she envisaged a kinship with this bold Phelim, whoever he was (actually I think the original of the song was an eighteenth-century Gaelic poet, though the English lyrics cast 'the poor Irish harper' in an unduly sweet-and-bland patriotic mode). That song – never mind its trite emblematic overload ('the shamrock', 'the Saxon lion's paw', etc.) – its heart was in the right place. It was embedded in its ancient harpist's dear native land. And that Phelim Brady was the goods, in my mother's view. He had exclusive rights to the designation 'the Bard of Armagh'.

The original Brady sept belonged to Cavan, but some of its members, like the bold Phelim, must have migrated north-eastwards through Monaghan and into Armagh and Down. At any rate, the first of my known, or unknown, Brady forebears turns up in nineteenth-century Newry. What he was doing there, or what his occupation was, I have no idea. His name was Bernard, and I think he had married a Miss McManus. (I'm basing this supposition on the fact that three maiden aunts named McManus turn up at the Lurgan home of Bernard's son Terence in the census of 1901.) Did he keep moving backwards and forwards? According to the 1911 census, the birthplace of Terence (1859–1915) was County Cavan. But Terence and his brother Michael grew up in Lurgan town. Terence became a tailor and married a local dressmaker named Catherine Harland. Their oldest son, William Brady (1881–1915), in due course married a girl from nearby John Street, Sarah Tipping. (William's cousin David Brady, a son of Michael, had already married Sarah's sister Ellen … but that's another story.) Hence my mother Nora Brady, and then me. So I suppose I can claim a miniscule line of descent from the 'illustrious' Mac Bradaigh sept of Cavan mentioned in the seventeenth-century *Annals of the Four Masters* (so can nearly every Irish person called Brady, for that matter …).

My mother was proud of her Irish name and its nationalist associations. She was happy to share a surname with the Bard of Armagh. … Would it also have pleased her to learn of a rival 'Bard of Armagh' to whom she really was obliquely related? Not likely, since the second so-called bard was the redoubtable William Blacker (also known as 'the Orange Minstrel'). He'd acquired the title on account of his Orange songs, in one of which occurs the alarming line, 'But put your trust in God, my boys, and keep your powder dry.' In full flow, with Williamite triumphalism firing his imagination, this scion of the Blacker dynasty goes on to compose the definitive Orange anthem, 'No Surrender':

> And Derry's sons alike defy
> Pope, traitor or pretender,
> And peal to heaven their 'prentice cry,
> Their patriot, 'No Surrender'.

This is partisan history with a vengeance (but note that it's Derry throughout, never Londonderry). We can picture William Blacker in the early years of the nineteenth century, stouter of face and figure than in his uproarious Trinity days, sitting at home in his study at Carrickblacker and cheerfully giving vent to an impassioned illiberalism. He is Protestant through and through – and Protestant unity, he holds, is the best defence against a bugbear of the times, a creeping Catholicism:

> Let the Presbyter strike by the Prelatist's side,
> And stem, in strong union, fell Popery's tide.

We have to wonder what made him so implacably anti-Catholic – and wonder even more what he means by statements like the following: 'But Popish power, in evil hour, / Has o'er us flung its galling chain.' Popish power has done nothing of the sort. Popish power is non-existent in Ireland, especially in the years before Catholic Emancipation.

Protestantism didn't have to be so venomous and melodramatic. Many upholders of the Protestant faith were also subscribers to the liberal ethic. A supreme example here, I suppose, is Dr William Drennan (the actual founder of the Society of United Irishmen, back in 1791). Drennan is responsible for inventing the phrase 'the Emerald Isle' – but his verse in general provokes a lot more admiration than William Blacker's, and not only because it's written from a different standpoint. While Blacker urges, 'On, on, gallant hearts, for the Bible and Crown', Drennan is more concerned to 'drive the demon of Bigotry home to his den'. As with many reasonable people before and since, the demon of bigotry is, for him, a cause of the utmost despair. ... At one point, reviewing in verse for the Belfast Monthly Magazine a long topographical poem called 'The Giant's Causeway' by the Reverend Hamilton Drummond, Dr Drennan delivers to his readers an unabashed injunction: 'Avaunt his verses be they ne'er so fine, / Who for the Catholics – REFUSED TO

SIGN!' The immediate cause of his ire (the year is 1811) is a past refusal by Drummond to add his name to a petition in support of Catholic Emancipation. But reading the Reverend Drummond's lines about the recent Act of Union – 'No more fell faction hurls her flaming brand, / But smiling concord waves her olive wand', and so on, and on, florally and obsequiously – you can see why the whole drift of the poem would get up the nose of an old Irish separatist like Dr Drennan.

It was not a good time for principled dissent. The Reverend Drummond is at one with William Blacker in his adulation of the English connection, and consequently his historical references fall within a tradition of unionist orthodoxy: 'Boyne foams with blood – a coward monarch flies, / War sheathes his gory blade – Rebellion dies' (the coward monarch, of course, being the unfortunate James II). It's likely that Drummond had a more recent rebellion in mind when he wrote these lines; and indeed, at this reactionary moment (the early years of the nineteenth century) 'rebellion' was discredited as a means of effecting social change, and not only among those of a conservative bent. The weaver poet James Orr, for example – author of the wry and disabused poem 'Donegore Hill' – never relinquished his hopes for a true democracy in Ireland. But after 1798, when he'd witnessed the inadequacy of republicanism in action, he attached these hopes to a different system: reformist rather than revolutionary.

Orr, as an ex-rebel, one-time contributor to the radical newspaper the *Northern Star*, and ultimate pragmatist, exemplifies the attitudes prevailing one after the other among the Presbyterians of the North. At one moment, it seemed, the republicanism of Wolfe Tone, Henry Joy McCracken and others was an impeccable doctrine, and the next moment it wasn't. It was impeccable while it grew apace in opposition to misgovernment; but lost repute when it began to be viewed solely as a disruptive force. Events were taking some complicated turns, and among them arrived a hesitancy, even among liberals, in relation to the kind of anti-Catholicism purveyed by Blacker and others. This was still to be deplored – but deplored, perhaps, with reservations. The anti-sectarian instinct had a strong foundation in the North, and the thing that chiefly got it up in arms was the treatment of Catholics. But at times it looked as if any such benevolent instinct might not weather an absence of democratic principles among Catholics themselves, whenever this absence became apparent – as it did, for example, in Wexford during the Rebellion, and again at the height of the Emancipation struggle. Catholic smugness or xenophobia is as much to be regretted as any other sort.

Those Protestant 'United Irish' advocates of tolerance, though, who lived on into the nineteenth century, continued to speak out on behalf of Catholic Emancipation – even though it's unlikely that Daniel O'Connell, with all his magniloquence and southern showmanship, would have held much personal appeal for them. It's true that both James Orr and William Drennan had died (in 1816 and 1820 respectively) before O'Connell's Catholic campaign reached its zenith in the 1820s, and thereby evaded a possible erosion of their sympathies. They retained their liberal values to the end. Drennan's famous directive with regard to his funeral arrangements shows a wit and a kind of enshrinement of his lifelong concerns. He left instructions that his coffin should be carried to its final resting place in Clifton Cemetery, Belfast, by an equal number of Protestants and Catholics – six of one and half a dozen of the other.

Daniel O'Connell's 'Catholic Rent' – the scheme by which a penny a month was subscribed by individual Catholics to a pro-Emancipation fund – this scheme was embraced less vigorously in Ulster than in other parts of the country. Poverty was the reason: many poor northern Catholics lacked even so small a surplus income as the Catholic Rent required. They found themselves 'overwhelmingly confined to the lowest rungs of the social ladder', the historian Jonathan Bardon says. The most prosperous members of the Catholic population, and it was only a very limited prosperity, were 'the farmer-weavers of the Linen Triangle'. Among them, I think, we may place the Crossmacahilly Tippings, who probably would have contributed their penny-a-month as the idea of a Catholic nation took hold among the disaffected. Was 'Popish power', at last, actually becoming a possibility? If so, it was a glorious prospect for the downtrodden and something to be encouraged at all costs.

At this time, the 1820s, the Tipping farm is home to the brothers James, John and Matthew, and possibly their mother Sarah (née Magee) is still alive and living there as well – though by 1833 it seems she isn't, since her name has disappeared from the records. Within the next ten years the youngest son Matthew has vanished too, maybe dead of whatever it was that had killed his father, when he (Matthew) was only four. That leaves James and John. By the mid 1820s both were married and occupied adjoining farmhouses, the smaller forming a right angle with the larger.

At this time, it is possible that Matthew was employed by his brothers as a labourer. And, if the Catholic Rent was paid by anyone in the family it was undoubtedly James who paid it, as the oldest and steadiest of the brothers and the one most strongly endowed with Tipping gumption.

James might have relished the sense of a growing Catholic solidarity not tied up with what he already knew only too well, the deadly and ruinous faction fights still bedevilling the Armagh countryside. The old Defenders and their Peep o' Day antagonists hadn't died out, they hadn't gone away, and neither of them had absorbed a jot of United Irish idealism. Under the new names of Ribbonmen and Orangemen they went on implementing their complementary programmes of cruelty, blackguardism and intimidation. ... I don't know if any of the Catholic Tippings were caught up in Ribbon activity, but I think it unlikely: at least, I hope I needn't add arson and attacks on innocent Protestant *cattle* to the list of ancestral (or quasi-ancestral) enormities I'm contemplating with alarm.

A Ribbon/Orange confrontation which later gained a magnified status had taken place in County Derry in 1813. It became known as 'The Battle of Garvagh', after the title of an anonymous ballad which began to circulate shortly after the event:

> The day before the July fair
> The Ribbonmen they did prepare
> For three miles round to wreck and tear
> And burn the town of Garvagh.

Needless to say, their terrible plan of action was foiled by the Orange Boys of Garvagh, who shot dead one Ribbonman and wounded others. This, along with many other similar incidents, didn't have a calming effect on denominational excitability. Finally, local and national authorities could stand no more of it, and by 1823 both Ribbon and Orange societies were proscribed organisations under an Unlawful Oaths Act passed in that year. This piece of 'anti-Orange legislation' – I'm quoting the useful J.S. Kane again, in his Blacker family history – was followed by the Unlawful Associations Act of 1825, which to Kane's indignation clamped down on the Orange Order, and even (God save us) on the Freemasons, 'neither of which was in any way unlawful'. Well! As a consequence, he adds, 'the Grand Orange Lodge of Ireland dissolved itself in March 1825'.

But unholy passions continue to be exacerbated. Picture a scene in Lurgan town, in May 1828, when hundreds of anti-Emancipationists take to the streets armed with sticks and cudgels in an episode of organised violence against Catholics. ... There they run, in an access of roaring hostility. Papist doors and windows succumb to their blows, driving them on in a triumph of rage to further acts of destruction. And here comes John Hancock, Protestant magistrate and agent to Charles Brownlow, riding up on his chestnut horse to read out the Riot Act, confident in his position as law-enforcer. Well, he can read it out till he's blue in the face but no one takes a bit of notice. Restraint is not imposed on the Lurgan berserkers, whose number includes members of a local yeomanry corps. Far from helping to round up the rioters, these yeomen are running pell-mell with the worst of them, yelling and bawling and wrecking all before them. At the same time, their overexcited sergeant heaps abuse on the head of John Hancock for his 'Papist' pusillanimity.

In the end, only nine of the rioters are arrested and dispatched to Portadown gaol. The others get off scot-free, dispersing themselves among alleyways and back streets known only to local residents. On the way to the gaol, passing along Edward Street in Lurgan – location of the magistrate's substantial home – the caught miscreants are accompanied by an Orange band blaring out 'The Boyne Water', 'No Surrender', 'Croppies Lie Down' and anything else guaranteed to cause offence to any Papist ears in the vicinity. A hastily composed ballad attacking the Protestant magistrate Hancock hits the streets a few days later:

> Oh, Lurgan town's an altered town,
> Since Papish Hancock he came to it.
> If ye walk out upon the Twelfth,
> You may depend he'll make you rue it.
> And if you sing an Orange song,
> You'll be jailed for eight and forty hours;
> Fresh orders he gave the police,
> To make prisoners of none but ours.

That's Lurgan for you: a town of bitter enmities, where 'the residents of Ballyblough and the Pound River are for ever stoning and fighting'. At this date, the late 1820s, the Orange Order is still an illegal body, and rumbles among disbanded Orangemen deprived of their July shenanigans finally come to a head in 1835, when, from all over County Armagh, they converge on Carrickblacker House and assemble on the lawn (an awesome twenty thousand of them, according to a contemporary newspaper report, 'of all ages and sexes'), thereby involving the upright Colonel Blacker in an inadvertent act of law-breaking. He rises to the occasion, however, addressing the crowd like a Dutch uncle and prevailing upon the lot of them to go home in a peaceable spirit (as reported, again, in the *Evening Packet*), never deigning to notice any Ribbon provocation they might encounter along the way. (The leaders of this demonstration were, nevertheless, brought to justice by the aforementioned John Hancock, an action creating strong ill-feeling between him and William Blacker.) The colonel's lady, Mrs Blacker, makes a rare appearance on the same crowded lawn, causing questions to arise: how did she fit in among that vast assembly? Wasn't she intimidated by the masses of Orange hoi polloi? It would seem not – for here she is, wearing an orange dress to proclaim her enthusiasm for the Protestant cause. And, for good measure, in festive exuberance, Carrickblacker servants are milling about the place with orange lilies entwined in their hair.

(I think of my grandmother Tipping's pronunciation of the word 'orange' which she reduces to a single syllable, articulated with a growl: ornge. 'Them oul ornge bigots'. And again, I think of the field at Edenderry in the twentieth century, with daft middle-aged women draped in Union Jacks weaving drunkenly through the thickets of Orange celebrants.)

Crossmacahilly, 1830s. The place is coming down with children, the offspring of James (eight born between 1826 and 1839) and John (father to at least four). We can visualise them tumbling about the stone-floored kitchen, boys and girls alike wearing woollen petticoats, and applaud the adults' unremitting efforts to maintain a certain standard of comfort and hygiene. (I'm taking this to be true, because it was a ferocious preoccupation with all of their descendants. Woe betide the speck of dirt that would show its face in any Tipping or Tipping-related household.) If it's summer, we might see homespun blankets spread over hedges drying in the sun; or the same lumps of children foraging for wild strawberries and mushrooms in the fields (and maybe exchanging insults with infantile Protestant neighbours: 'Proddy gets'; 'Papist pigs'). Cold damp winters might bring running noses and chilblains (a common Tipping affliction).

And always, there are chores to perform: water to be fetched for cooking and washing, floors to be swept, the kitchen 'redd'. By this stage it's likely that the linen-weaving enterprise is merely a sideline, as the growing number of flax mills and factories signals an end to home production. Farming would be the main source of income for households like the Tippings', with all its drawbacks of incessant labour and uncertainty of outcome.

Crossmacahilly. I'd like to think the place provided scope for seasonal pleasures too, with ancient customs like the Cutting of the Calliagh still going strong. 'The calliagh' was the last sheaf of corn left standing after the rest had been harvested. Separated into three strands where it grew, and plaited by one of the women working in the fields, it was then cut down by having a sickle thrown at it. 'Cut her down, cut her down,' the reapers would cry, and afterwards raise a cheer when the deed was done. A celebratory meal – the calliagh feast – would then take place in a farm kitchen, with perhaps dancing and singing until well into the night. Though the purpose of this ritual would largely have been forgotten, even in the nineteenth century, it had something to do with an idea that 'the spirit of the corn' resided in the last sheaf, and that the actions connected with the calliagh would ensure a good future harvest.

There were other rituals, to be enacted at due seasons. 'Above my door the rushy cross', John Hewitt wrote,

> The turf upon my hearth,
> For I am of the Irishry,
> By nurture and by birth.

The 'rushy cross', St Brigid's cross, placed above the door to protect the home, was traditionally fashioned from rushes gathered on the last day of January – they had to be plucked, not cut, and carried indoors after sunset, whereupon the work of shaping them into crosses would begin, accompanied by a meal of pancakes or apple potato bread. Rushes grew in abundance around the Crossmacahilly bogs, and no doubt generations of Tipping children were sent out to collect them, with instructions not to get their feet wet or their clothes destroyed. Like other country families the Tippings would have been dutiful towards immemorial customs, I think, and wishful not to neglect any time-honoured means of drawing good fortune to themselves.

But even in towns and cities the custom of making Brigid's crosses persisted until well into the twentieth century. I was shown how to do it myself, instructed by the nuns of my primary school Aquinas Hall in Windsor Park, Belfast, in the 1950s. It made a welcome respite from the usual classroom ennui (geography or elocution lessons – ugh!), and it was satisfying to view the finished article you'd knocked together with your own hands, once you'd grasped the technique of folding the rushes one on top of the other into a swastika-like shape. The crosses we turned out each year on 1 February made a pretext for a lecture on our religious heritage. We sat at our desks wearing royal blue gym-slips over grey winter blouses, hair neatly plaited or cropped and curled, and learned that Brigid was one of Ireland's holy trinity of ancient saints, along with Patrick and Columcille – but not that the abbey over which she presided at Kildare was a 'mixed house' (i.e. one in which monks and nuns were at liberty to marry, if they chose); or that Brigid herself was ordained a bishop, in a society that placed few restrictions on women's advancement. These facts would not have been considered suitable for our infant ears. Neither was the fusion of pagan and Christian customs dwelt on. This was the 1950s: Irish Roman Catholicism reigned supreme and nuns' power over their charges was absolute.

At Crossmacahilly there are good years and bad years, and through it all it's James who shoulders the heaviest burdens of both families, his own and his brother's; James the good manager, the cautious risk-taker, the one blessed with foresight; James my grandmother's grandfather. James pays the whole of the Crossmacahilly rent to the Duke of Manchester's agent Henry John Porter (John repaying his share whenever he can). James borrows money from the Tandragee Castle Loan Fund – set up by the same agent – to buy lime, rye grass, turnip and parsnip seeds, making regular repayments to the fund. John borrows too, for clothes as well as seeds and crops, but, unlike his brother, he gets into difficulties and has to appeal to James to settle his debts (which he does). James takes advantage of a drainage scheme which improves the land and increases the yield of farm produce. It is all carefully thought out – and when he dies in 1853, James leaves no debts for his heirs to grapple with. All his borrowing is repaid to the last farthing. It's a lesson in good husbandry, confounding the implications of indolence and fecklessness attached to the letter 'R' – 'R' for Romanist – which appears beside the names of the Tipping brothers in the estate rentals. In the townland of Crossmacahilly there are only eight Catholic families, alongside forty Protestant.

'Romanist' or not, throughout his industrious life, James would have had more pressing worries than the state of his soul. The Tippings and their neighbours lived with constant fears, fear of sectarian harassment, fear of bad weather, fear of hard times. Praying is a resource though, especially when it seems apocalyptic anticipations are about to be realised. There comes a night in January 1839 when, through sheer expedience, the entire townland would likely have been down on its knees asking God for deliverance from a raging storm: the Night of the Big Wind, as it's gone down in folk memory. This was the night when roofs were lifted clean off houses and hurled through the air, when trees toppled like a deck of cards, when the 184-foot chimney of Mulholland's flax mill in Belfast crashed to the ground. To those of a religious turn of mind, it looked as though the end of the world had come. One consternated cleric, the Reverend William Boyce of High Street, Belfast, could hardly take in the extent of the destruction being wrought around him, and later recorded his impressions of that wild night in an awestruck outburst.[1]

> How dreadful raged that storm o'er Erin's face!
> And who may tell t'effect on Land, in part?
> Chimneys, tiles, and slates, gas lamps, and spinning mills,
> Demolished windows, houses, roofs, huge funnels tall,
> Factories, walls, mill-chimnies, prostrate laid;
> A watchman killed by Falls-road mill's descent! ...
> The wings of Windmills, canvas, rails, and nails,
> Completely torn asunder! ...

So it goes on, page after page of heartfelt unrestrained verse commentary: 'Then yelled the tempest furious through Portrush'; 'It rushed through Aghalee, by Finaghy, / By Lurgan, Markethill, the Middleton, Pointzpass.' 'It broke huge elms, / and oaks,' so it did, while going about the fearsome work of 'smashing ships, trees, towers, and men'. No portion of the North escaped its fury. Even at supposedly unassailable Carrickblacker, alarmed inhabitants felt the great house shake to its foundations, they heard hundreds of tiles erupting from the roof, and then the tremendous noise of trees uprooted in the demesne. The following day, the damage was contemplated with awe and disbelief. Hundreds of Carrickblacker elms lay strewn about the estate like fallen participants in some mythical battle.

But it wasn't all despair and ruin. A future prosperity was in store for local carpenters who rushed to buy up the sudden glut of wood. (Just as the income of glaziers was substantially increased during the Troubles of the late twentieth century.) One uprooted elm, however, carefully selected by William Blacker himself, was set aside and earmarked for his coffin. Duly constructed and stored in an outhouse, the coffin sat awaiting its future occupant who wandered out every now and then to take a look at it – not a morbid procedure at all, he said, just a practical acknowledgement of his ultimate end.

I believe I have a slight understanding of what the population of Ireland went through on that January night in 1839, having experienced the great English storm of 1987, when my husband and I lay huddled together on the top floor of a tall house in Blackheath waiting for the roof to blow off or the chimney to crash down on top of us. ('Terrific howled the hurricane around,' as Boyce might have put it.) Earlier, we had listened to the wind increasing in volume and were shocked by the sudden extinguishing of all the lights of south London as the power supply went kaput. Plunged into total blackness, we twentieth-century sceptics were braced for a moment to undergo an apocalyptic outcome. And indeed the morning's devastation didn't seem to fall far short of it. Though it wasn't on the scale of *Oidhche na Gaoithe Moire,* the Night of the Big Wind, enough havoc was caused by the 1987 storm to etch it into the remembrance of everyone who endured it. As for me – I'm exhilarated by most extremes of weather, cold, rain, snow: but not wind. My anxiety level rises with every blast of rising wind.

So I can all too easily enter into the state of mind of the Crossmacahilly family hunkered round the fire – to borrow an image from Richard Rowley's *Tales of Mourne* – 'waitin' every minute for the walls to blow in on top o' them'. Did one of them, again like Rowley's narrator, see himself in desperation 'houldin' on the thatch wi' my finger-nails ... afore mornin'? However the thatch was held on – perhaps weighted down with ropes and stones before the worst of the weather struck – it seems to have stayed in place; at least, there are no reports of the farm or outbuildings being whirled away into oblivion. But appalling sights met the eyes of people creeping out at daybreak to begin the work of salvage. Dead birds and animals, fields churned up, hedges flattened. A yellow, overladen sky and an ominous atmosphere. And in the battered towns of Lurgan and Portadown, where people gathered in the streets to view the wreckage left by the storm, the dishevelled houses and shops, the broken-down factory chimneys, the fallen spires of different churches, all crushed alike by a force of nature.

Tenant farmers gritted their teeth, in the wake of the storm, and got on with the next thing. But the nineteenth century has further catastrophes up its sleeve for the Irish nation. Some years after the Big Wind comes the first potato-crop failure. The ensuing Famine provides a standard against which all subsequent calamities may be measured. Nothing – the reaction to some later scourge might go – nothing has bred so much consternation in the townland since the wee boy came running into the farm kitchen bearing news of a terrible smell in the potato fields.

He might have been my great-grandfather Matthew Tipping, that archetypal small boy, Matthew the third son of diligent James and one of a clatter of weans – that's the word they'd have used, weans or the equally expressive 'childer' – growing up on the edge of a bog, all imbued with a strong sense of kinship and thoroughly schooled in argument and assertion. (Remember those forty Protestant families occupying the same small area.) All of us there. What kind of people were they? Even if the world they inhabited is essentially unknowable, faded away to nothing like a badly preserved sampler, there are clues to be picked up about the way they viewed it and each other, and how particular traits were evolving within the family, distinguishing each individual member from all the rest. I think I'm right, for example, in attributing a certain headstrong quality to Matthew, a kicking-over-the-traces predilection. I'll come back to this – but in the meantime the overwhelming consideration is the rotting potato crop of 1845 and subsequent years.

No one died of starvation on the Tipping farm and this was probably due to James and his turnip- and parsnip-sowing, his continuing production of flax and whatever oats could be salvaged from a lesser but not insignificant blight, concurrent with the potato blight. None of the family died of actual hunger, but the Famine claimed its Tipping victim nevertheless. In December 1848, James Tipping's younger brother John, the one continually in need of propping up, is admitted to the Lurgan Union Workhouse suffering from typhoid fever. It kills him within a couple of weeks. Fifty-seven years old and long a widower, John Tipping already had the disease – the dreaded famine fever – before he went in, but conditions in the workhouse made it a place to die, not a centre of proper medical treatment. ... There John lies among the destitute poor, perhaps on a damp and insanitary cot, bedlam around him, until he simply gives up the ghost. He is hastily buried on the following day, taken from this place of doom and wretchedness in a makeshift coffin, over which not a single funeral offering is made (according to the Seagoe Catholic parish church records). The previous horrendous year, Black '47, had depleted all the meagre Tipping resources. James at least must have suffered bitterness and mortification at the failure to do things properly, to arrange a respectable exit for his brother John, but circumstances were against him. For all his frugality and astuteness, he was overtaken by events. And he could point with some pride to what he *had* achieved: a tribe of children pulled through the crisis. All of them, on their shaky smallholding, were lucky indeed not to go the way of John.

The Lurgan Union Workhouse – hmn. Who is chairman of its board of guardians at this fraught time? Stiff-necked, high-principled William Blacker, that's who. While John Tipping lies approaching his appalling end, we might find Colonel Blacker journeying abroad on one of his holiday trips to Frankfurt, Paris, Brussels or London, avoiding the chills of an Armagh winter and the countryside heaving with disease and distress. Driving in a carriage around Belgian boulevards might be on the cards for the Blacker party, or elaborate dinners attended by glittering guests. At Cheltenham, another favourite holiday destination, Ulster grandees away from home, including Charlotte Lennox-Conyngham of Springhill, play host to one another or gather to applaud Colonel Blacker's speechifying at a Conservative dinner. A lavish, assured and highly organised life – and with all these divertissements to absorb his attention, a dying Catholic workhouse inmate, one among hundreds, would be the least of William Blacker's concerns.

Don't worry, I'm not making a facile point here about heartless gentry and suffering peasantry (though there's scope enough for it). I don't mean to do down William Blacker and his lord-of-the-manor hauteur (well, not really). His views on social responsibility are in line with the mores of the day. He is deputy vice-treasurer of Ireland. He's a great committee-man, militiaman and occasional host at Carrickblacker to the 'cream' of the Protestant ruling elite. And if it's a world away from the scrabbling, swarming underclass of tenant farmers and tramps and artisans – well, no one can blame Colonel Blacker for making the most of his fortunate position in the world. Nothing happens in his life to topple his landowner's certainties. But – here comes another instance of 'had-he-but-known' – there were reasons why this particular stricken subsistence farmer John Tipping might have impinged on the aloof Blacker consciousness. Though neither was aware of it, both the gentleman and the famine victim had a common ancestor, in the direct line, in the Royalist officer Valentine Blacker who built the manor house known as Blacker's Bawn and restored the seventeenth-century Seagoe parish church. It's the genealogical irony that snares my attention here.

But let us consider young Matthew growing up in the wilds of Crossmacahilly, living through the years of Famine with all the frantic expedients to stay alive, and perhaps already fixing his sights on better things. Matthew is the fourth child and third son of farmer/weaver James, and himself an eventual father of twelve – whose lives, bar two, I don't propose to examine in detail (Whew! I hear you go). The exceptions are Matthew's youngest child, my grandmother Sarah, and to a lesser extent her half-brother Henry, twenty-five years her senior, who frightened her under the kitchen table with his impassioned rendering of the patriotic ballad 'Fontenoy' when she was two years old; but as yet, these are only figments of a shadowy future.

Matthew gets round to begetting early on. Like his grandfather James (perhaps), he doesn't curb, indeed I imagine he flaunts, his erotic drive; and it's possible that more than one local girl is warned to consider him a danger and affront to good Catholic chastity. One girl at least pays no heed to the voices of prudence, however: Eliza O'Hara from nearby Legahorry, who bears Matthew a daughter long before the pair of them are out of their teens. Is agitation engendered by this event? Or is a shrug and a grimace more in keeping with contemporary country attitudes? You can't stop nature taking its course, any more than the effects of the potato-crop failure can be reversed, or the howling wind be stopped in its tracks. And here's Helena Tipping to prove it, a babe in arms when her parents finally stand before the parish priest of Seagoe to take their marriage vows. What took them so long? Was it reluctance on the part of one or the other? Perhaps Eliza O'Hara was gifted with foresight and jibbed at the state of almost continuous pregnancy looming in front of her like a wrecking ball. It would finish her off before her time, she might have feared – and it did. Or maybe it's simply a question of space, the marriage-delaying factor, with the Crossmacahilly farmhouse so crammed with inhabitants that absolutely no further bodies can be squeezed in.

Be that as it may, Matthew the married man installs his wife and daughter in his parents' home, and swiftly increases the congestion on the spot by begetting another six young Tippings. (Inadequate accommodation, caused by too much procreation, is just one of the scourges the nineteenth-century poor have to put up with.) Before the first new infant arrives, however, Matthew's father James has bowed out of the proceedings, creating a bit of space by dying in 1853 at the age of sixty-odd years. ... No doubt James Tipping's funeral is an altogether more seemly affair than his poor brother John's. But for a real showpiece Armagh interment we need to look higher up the social scale. And here it comes. Two years after the death of James, in November 1855, his distant kinsman William Blacker's long and punctilious existence reaches an end. The elmwood coffin from the Night of the Big Wind gets its rightful occupant at last. At twelve noon on the last day of November Colonel Blacker's funeral cortège leaves Carrickblacker House for old Seagoe Church, 'headed by the children of the schools which William Blacker had done so much to encourage over the years'. A long line of respectable gentry follows, J.S. Kane goes on; and next come high-up representatives of all denominations: Church of Ireland, Presbyterian, Roman Catholic,[2] Quaker. Also present are 'William's most trusted Orange colleagues' (well, they would be there, wouldn't they), his nephew and heir Stewart Blacker, members of parliament and peers of the realm. (Kane is careful to specify the peers of the realm.) And lining the funeral route along the Gilford Road are rows of tenant farmers and weavers come to pay their last respects and suitably chastened, no doubt, by the solemn appearance of the six black horses festooned with black ostrich feather plumes, the hearse with its black-clad coachman, the mourning coaches, the slow procession of dignitaries following after. I don't think you'd have found any deferential Tippings, though, standing with bowed bared heads along the roadway, even though the stately cortège was making its way towards the very spot where an ancestor of theirs, the seventeenth-century John Tipping, lay buried with his in-laws in the Blacker family mausoleum.

Eighteen-forty-eight, the year of the later John Tipping's death from famine fever, was also the year in which the planned 'Young Ireland' uprising failed to come to fruition. In March, Charles Gavin Duffy of *The Nation* had announced that 'Ireland's opportunity, thank God and France, has come at last'; but his rhetorical gratitude turned out to be without foundation. Neither he nor his colleague the Banbridge Presbyterian solicitor John Mitchel was able to drum up sufficient fervour in the North to get any kind of revolutionary enterprise going. The reason isn't hard to find: 'a starving people,' comments Jonathan Bardon drily in his *History of Ulster*, '... had no interest in insurrection.'

No interest, but in households like the Tippings', nevertheless, there'd be talk of misgovernment, and of ways to engage in nationalist dissent. In the parishes of Shankill, Seagoe, Tartaraghan, people were dying of hunger and disease until it seemed the whole of society was collapsing in on itself, its day-to-day enactments driven by fear and distress. A world was being unravelled, and then, at some point, it would have to be put back together again, as survivors like the Tippings were left to pick up the pieces. It was a defining moment. Protestants had died – indeed, in north Armagh, more Protestants than Catholics were counted among the famine victims – but for Catholics and nationalists, the potato famine was tied up with cruelty and exploitation of the whole population of Ireland. Starving people standing on a quayside, silently watching as tons of provisions are shipped elsewhere, 'relief work' consisting of roads going nowhere, soup kitchens, derelict townlands, mass graves, coffin ships: these images are entering into the nationalist mythology, as a powerful opposition to all representatives of a ruling elite takes hold. Being '"agin" the government' is coming to constitute a way of life.

Another image from those years comes to mind. It was relayed to me by my mother, who got it from her grandmother, who figures in it. Ellen Jordan was a young child when the Famine struck north Armagh, and among her sharpest memories was one of herself, wrapped in a shawl, being carried by *her* mother, Susan McCorry from Moyraverty, to a soup kitchen hastily set up to aid the starving poor. She recalled the sense of desperation felt by many in the blighted countryside as their livelihood, and indeed their lives, were put in jeopardy. There is utter subjugation in the air. ... And here's another anomaly of my up-and-down ancestry. These Jordans may have been poor (how poor I don't know), but some of their relations were, on the other hand, well placed to savour the benefits of a provincial affluence.

Ellen's father is Edward Jordan, and Edward's cousin Thomas is the founder and managing director of the Lurgan linen-handkerchief-manufacturing firm of T. Jordan & Sons. They are business people with a steady income and highly developed sense of their own importance. Thomas has arranged matters so that his wife and children will rise to their feet when he enters the breakfast room of their Lurgan home, and has them call him 'Sir'. 'Good morning, Sir'; 'More toast, Sir?' And this in plebeian Lurgan with its adept deflating tactics! (Actually, of course, this kind of paterfamilias formality was a commonplace of the era, and I shouldn't make too much of it – it's just hard to resist a soupçon of mockery at mercantile Thomas Jordan and his pretensions. ...)

The prospering Thomas Jordans will eventually take over the former home of Lord Brownlow's agent John Hancock in the centre of the town, the manor house at the bottom of Edward Street. By this time, though – the late Victorian era – the Jordan sons have probably succeeded the autocratic father. They may have been equally full of themselves, for all I know. I only mention this pompous branch of the Jordan family, my great-grandmother's relations, to show an unprecedented type of life evolving in post-Famine County Armagh. These factory owners and large-scale employers may be taken to represent a new rising class, the Catholic middle class despised by W.B. Yeats for its go-getting drive and philistine orientation. It had gained a foothold once Emancipation was secured, and now nothing was going to stop its progress. (It pleases me to think of these uppish Jordans in their grand town house being disgraced by the presence of huckster relations just round the corner in lowly John Street. ... and how the latter came to be there I'll relate in a minute.)

The Lurgan of those days in the nineteenth century has a reputation for discord. Rioting in its streets is a feature of the times. Fury and resentment are in the air it breathes. And anyone may get caught up in its shindigs.

Take the elderly John Hancock – still the owner of the Manor House – who, driving home in his carriage one day along Edward Street, is attacked by a stone-throwing mob assembled at the corner of Shankill Street (though it seems their main targets are members of the police force and I don't think Hancock is hit, though no doubt he is shaken and his horses frightened). One of the attackers caught and arrested on a charge of riotous behaviour is a young James Tipping, a son – one of many – of Matthew and his wife Eliza O'Hara. James, unable to pay a fine of 16s 6d, is sentenced to fourteen days in gaol.

A twisted pattern begins to take shape around this incident. Hancock, in fact, is at one with the young stone-throwers in being a major opponent of the Orange Order – a circumstance which, in the past, has got him into very bad odour with Colonel Blacker in particular. Blacker, as a matter of principle, opposes every suggestion put forward by Hancock when both are serving on the Lurgan Union Workhouse board of guardians. The aversion felt by this pair towards one another goes back to the Orange demonstration in the grounds of Carrickblacker House in 1835 and subsequent arrest of some of the demonstrators by the then young magistrate Hancock. ... Had the 1870s rioters been apprised of this fact, would they have held their fire while Hancock and his son drove by? Or, for the young male Lurgan poor and derided with stones in their hands, is *any* carriage-owning person fair game? The spirited thing is to be for ever trying to get your own back for the miserable circumstances fate has dumped you in, to achieve social or tribal recompense in any way available.

So here is Matthew's son James, the first and most heedless of the tearaway Tippings, perhaps, immersed to the full in games of defiance and 'Fenian' assertion and ignorant to the same degree of his own oblique family connection with the topmost Orange dynasty of them all, the bigwig Blackers. And here's John Hancock, whose effigy was once burned by Orangemen, now a target for the other lot and similarly unaware that one of his would-be assailants possesses a modicum of the dread Blacker blood – or indeed that his own well-appointed home will be taken over in due course by people related to the same young stone-thrower through his stepmother Ellen Jordan. Ah, hindsight.

James Tipping was ten years old when his father Matthew uprooted his family from Crossmacahilly and its bogs and trundled them into nearby

Lurgan town on a cart; wife, seven children, belongings and all. We can picture the weariness, the squabbling youngsters, the put-upon wife and exasperated father, as they finally reached their destination, a recently constructed terrace house in James Street, and set about obtaining a bit of order. The year is 1869, and along with its meagre possessions the family comes carrying its strong convictions to a town already vehemently divided along sectarian lines. Two years previously, in the wider world of Irish politics, the Fenian uprising was quelled by the Irish constabulary, aided by 'a great fall of snow' which scattered the insurgents. Jubilation among Orange Lurganites, and concomitant nationalist bitterness, ensued.

The Irish Republican Brotherhood, better known as the Fenian movement, was founded in 1858 by the veteran revolutionary James Stephens; and although it never really took hold in the North, its progress would have been carefully monitored by Catholics and proto-nationalists such as the Tippings. Major events of the time such as the attempted rescue of Fenian prisoners in Manchester and subsequent execution of three of those involved (the Manchester Martyrs), and the explosion at Clerkenwell in London which killed twelve people in the same year, 1867 – these would have had a tremendous impact on ordinary families all over Ireland primed to come down with ferocity on one side or the other. I don't know what degree of literacy prevailed among the nineteenth-century Tippings, but I believe at least some of them would have had sufficient reading skills to get to grips with a newspaper. And certainly, after about 1850, you had local and provincial papers circulating even among the poorest of the population. Even the illiterate had a resource. In every townland there were special houses where groups could gather to hear one person read out the burning news of the day, after which a heated discussion would be set going. (The Tipping farm at Crossmacahilly was one such gathering place in its later days; see p. 116 below.)

'... a deep fall of snow'. This phrase, which I misquoted above, comes from Alice Milligan's best-known and most beguiling poem, 'When I Was a Little Girl'. When she was a little middle-class girl in Omagh, County Tyrone, in the 1870s, the Fenians had acquired an extraneous role. The name was uttered with fear and drama as a topical bugbear, like Bonaparte earlier in the century, to scare small Protestants into instantaneous obedience: 'Come in! or when it's dark / The Fenians will get ye.' The old nurse's nightly threat has an immediate effect on all the little Milligans who scuttle indoors squealing – all bar one.

> But one little rebel there,
> Watching all with laughter,
> Thought 'When the Fenians come
> I'll rise and go after.'
>
> Wished she had been a boy
> And a good deal older –
> Able to walk for miles
> With a gun on her shoulder ...

Thus was the family rebel shaping up to be an Irish nationalist of the future. Even when the Milligans had moved to Belfast, where Alice found herself 'submerged amid an Orange population' (going to school at the Methodist College), the convictions she'd acquired at an early stage didn't undergo the smallest modification.

It was a cause of annoyance to Alice Milligan that anyone should be considered less of an Irishwoman through being born a Protestant. A strong tradition of Protestant nationalism, from Grattan onwards, reinforced her own particular attachment to Ireland's cause. Among her antecedents, she could point to a great-grandfather who, with his sons, had marched on Antrim with the insurgents of 1798. ... Her attitude in this respect, perhaps inevitably, provoked a degree of estrangement from at least one sibling, her sister Edith who was married to a unionist; but on the credit side it brought Alice many dazzling friendships. She conducted Yeats on an excursion up the Cave Hill when he visited Belfast, and accompanied Roger Casement to a feis at Toomebridge. And among her neighbours on the Antrim Road she found a kindred spirit and fellow poet in Anna Johnston ('Ethna Carbery'). The two young women, one Protestant and one Catholic, joined forces in Belfast, in the late 1890s, to edit a nationalist newspaper, the *Shan Van Vocht*.

James Connolly, who believed the working classes were 'the incorruptible inheritors of the fight for freedom' in Ireland, was a regular contributor; and the name of Miss Maud Gunne (sic) occurs in more than one issue. (But not Constance Markievicz, whose peculiar gardening notes were reserved for the slightly later *Bean na hÉireann*. She advised her readers to look on the English in Ireland in exactly the same light as slugs in a lettuce bed – a view which would have found favour with the *Shan Van Vocht* clientele.) Poets in droves came up with verse for the magazine whose dominant motifs – the heathery hill, the spinning wheel, the milk churn, the holy well, the misty glen, the little green linnet, the black, black wind from northern hills – are full of potent associations for the romantic nationalist. I know, because I lapped them up at an appropriate age, while I was undergoing a sentimental education.

Some of them I encountered for the first time in a small thick notebook, four inches by six and a half, carefully covered in brown paper, into which my mother, as a sixth-former at Mount St Michael's, Lurgan, and later as a student at Queen's University, had transcribed her favourite poems. Yeats was there, and Wilfred Owen, and Hardy and James Stephens and Padraig Pearse and Helen Lanyon. Ethna Carbery and Alice Milligan were well represented in this personal anthology. Their verses struck a chord with me too, when I was sixteen and believed the essence of Irishness resided in some mystical locality of the unadulterated West. Mary O'Hara, Donal of the Rosses, mirth and song, windswept heather ... all these denoted an indigenous exquisiteness far removed from the cinema-going, coffee-drinking, fashion-conscious populations of towns and cities that was our milieu. And by extolling the West, we thought we might aspire to a touch of that aboriginal integrity.

When Alice Milligan's *Hero Lays* was about to be published in 1908, she didn't want the poem 'When I Was a Little Girl' included in the collection. She thought its spirited pro-Fenian stance might offend the Catholic clergy (who had proscribed the movement), or aggravate readers averse to infant militarism. Fortunately George Russell, AE, who edited *Hero Lays* for the publishers Maunsel & Co. in Dublin, told her to catch herself on (or words to that effect). 'The story of your little night-dressed Fenian has put fire in me and in the name of that child I confront you and defy you.' The appeal was irresistible. The poem went in.

Though he regarded himself as a Dubliner, George Russell was actually born in Lurgan (in 1867) and spent his first ten years in the town, attending the non-denominational Lurgan Model School along with his brother and sister. The Russells lived in William Street at the time of his birth, before taking up residence in a gate lodge inside the North Street entrance to Lord Lurgan's demesne. Their circumstances were undoubtedly a lot more comfortable than those available to the incoming Tippings; but, since the town was not large in the 1870s, the younger members of both families must at least have passed one another in the street. Were catcalls exchanged? The insults-and-fisticuffs atmosphere of the Lurgan streets was anathema to the future poet and mystic – and once the Russells had bettered their prospects by moving to Dublin, George never ceased to give thanks 'to Providence for the mercy shown to me in removing me from Ulster'. '[T]hough I like the people,' he goes on, 'I cannot breathe the political and religious atmosphere of the North-East Corner of Ireland.' However, he continued to spend long childhood holidays with his maternal grandparents in County Armagh, staunch Church of Ireland people whose parish church was the one at Seagoe originally restored by Valentine Blacker in the seventeenth century.

The James Street lodging was only a temporary resting place for Valentine Blacker's disreputable descendants, Matthew Tipping and his brood. Before long we find the family installed in another terrace house, this time at 3 John Street,[3] which becomes a permanent residence for some of them. Matthew has his trade as a cambric weaver, whether he engages in it at home, or in one of the numerous factories and spinning mills springing up all over Lurgan in response to the increased demand for linen cloth. (It was probably at home; my grandmother remembered an enormous loom taking up half the meagre ground-floor space in the house during her childhood in the 1880s.) To supplement the family income he also sells foodstuffs such as buttermilk and vegetables, obtained from his relations left behind in Crossmacahilly. His outlet for this produce is either an improvised huckster's shop set up in another tiny portion of the John Street house (a common expedient at the time, and later), or a barrow in the market, I am not sure which.

Six years after the move to Lurgan, in 1875, Matthew Tipping's wife Eliza dies in childbirth and is buried in Dougher Cemetery. She is forty years old. She bequeaths to her husband a houseful of children, ranging from Helena (aged twenty-four) down to newly born Peter. Both of these, too, will be dead within a few years, one a victim of tuberculosis and the other uncared for in the immediate aftermath of his mother's death.

As well as sickly Helena, the disrupted household contains two girls

PC's great-grandmother Ellen Tipping – née Jordan – in her Victorian finery

aged eight and five, but the others are all boys and probably not attuned to domestic management. Something needs to be done – and it's up to Matthew to do it. Within six months of Eliza's death, her widower has entered into a new arrangement to restore a measure of order and felicity to the bereft, throughother and overcrowded house. In St Peter's Church in North Street, on 15 May 1876, he is married for the second time, this time round to a tough-minded widow and mother-of-three named Ellen Dowds (née Jordan). This step, indeed, doesn't ease the problem of household congestion; but in other respects, we may suppose, it engenders an improvement. The mystery is how Matthew Tipping persuaded Ellen Dowds to take on the hefty domestic burden he was offering her.

Her own children were then aged ten (Mary Ann), eight (Susan) and five (John), and when the newly-wed couple emerged from the chapel in North Street, instead of confetti they were showered with stones by Ellen's infuriated five-year-old in a bid to drive away the bearded old man who was stealing his mother. It wasn't an auspicious beginning – however, the newly configured family had no option but to settle down and make the best of things. Matthew, the champion 'begetter', promptly sets about founding an extra Tipping dynasty. Fortunately this time he stops at two. I think this final pair of girls may not have been entirely welcome in a house already bursting at the seams, but they quickly learned to stand up for themselves (and for each other). Their names were Ellen and Sarah, and they grew up mettlesome and attractive, with their leg-o'-mutton sleeves and tennis rackets and ability to gad about on bicycles in their spare time. Like all their half-siblings, they were put to work in a local factory at the earliest possible age (maybe the factory owned by their mother's relations), as veiners or stitchers or winders or smoothers. But a new century was dawning, and with it came an opening out of possibilities, hardly discernible at first but increasing as time went on. The last two Tipping daughters were among the brightest of the family – a family sufficiently extensive to form itself into cliques and groups, at one minute antagonistic, the next conciliatory. A saying of Matthew's, in this respect, has gone down to posterity. Ructions were going on upstairs in the tiny house, and Matthew was dispatched by his formidable wife to put a stop to the uproar. When he came back down, having quelled the noise, his wife Ellen demanded to be told what was going on. He shrugged. 'Ach, just the usual. Your childer and my childer fightin' wi' our childer.'

There must have been occasions when Matthew took his youngest daughters to visit the farm at Crossmacahilly where he grew up. I see these Lurgan girls, wearing black laced boots and pinafores, running through the fields, making daisy chains, searching for new-laid eggs, 'supping' buttermilk with oatcakes baked on the griddle. ... All right, a tinge of rose-coloured spectacles is entering into these images of alluring country pursuits, but for all that I don't believe they're unduly fanciful. What else would they have done? ... It's unlikely that Matthew's girls would have had any memory of their Uncle James (another James!), their father's older brother, since he died in 1884 when they were only five and three. But James's remaining offspring stayed on ... and on. The few that were left, that is: out of a family of eleven, it seems, only three survived beyond the age of twenty-five. One of these was a daughter, Bridget, who married a blacksmith from nearby Lylo. The other two turned gradually into a pair of those old bachelor brothers who feature strongly in the literature of the Irish countryside. 'Only Pad is married,' writes Polly Devlin in her enchanting memoir of County Tyrone, *All of Us There*; 'the other brothers, like so many of that generation, have continued to live where they were born.' And Benedict Kiely's story, 'Homes on the Mountain', has 'John and Thady ... still alive in the old house on Loughfresha. Like pigs in a sty ...'.

We needn't, I hope, attribute a comparable degree of slovenliness to Mattha (an archaic form of Matthew) and Barney Tipping, as their seniors and siblings one by one died or moved away from Crossmacahilly until only the two remained. The farm, by this stage, was known in the district as 'a ceilidhe house', where, as I've indicated, neighbours would gather on Saturday nights to hear Mattha read aloud the entire contents of the *Irish Weekly* (a weekend supplement of the nationalist paper the *Irish News and Belfast Morning News*) and debate the urgent events of the day. Mattha enjoyed a reputation as the leading Catholic intellectual of the neighbourhood, and his opinions carried a good deal of weight. When he died in 1922, his brother Barney took over his role. After all the years of overcrowding, the house has now come down to a single occupant. Barney lived on for a further twenty-two years, until 1944, after which time the farm fell into a state of dereliction. Returning to the clay, in William Trevor's potent phrase. Returning to the clay.

I don't think old men like Barney exist any more, living on in the houses in which they were born, eking out a diminished existence in deteriorating circumstances. They'd be whipped off to sheltered accommodation at the first sign of a memory lapse, or tea spilled down an ancient jacket unaccustomed to dry cleaning. But the past, in actuality and in fiction, is full of them. Michael McLaverty's short story, 'Stone', has one, Jamesey Heaney, 'sitting with his hands on his knees, his shoulders drooped forward, [waiting] for the fire to light. At his feet lay his black and white collie, her forepaws in the ashes, a wet nose on the flags. The closed door was slitted with light, and through the nests of cobwebs on the deep windows came a blue wintry brightness. It was cold.' It could be Barney Tipping he's describing.

The two unmarried Tipping brothers (my grandmother's cousins) had a good deal of local and national news, at various times, to air with their friends and neighbours. The fall of Parnell, the presentation and defeat of successive Home Rule Bills, the Boer War, the formation of the Ulster Volunteer Force and then the Irish Volunteers, gun-running at Larne, the signing of the Covenant, the outbreak of war with Germany, the 1916 uprising, Michael Collins visiting Armagh, Partition. ... And always and incessantly, trouble in the streets: the streets of Belfast, Lurgan, Armagh, Portadown. ... Trouble sparked off by deadly and ineradicable religious affiliations. As the novelist and satirist John Morrow has it, the problem with Ireland has always been sects (and you have to be very careful how you say it).

CHAPTER 5
ALL THE DEAD DEARS

Processionals of lives go by
On delicate, crisp treads;
Blurred fragrances, gently percussive,
Stir among leaves.
Top-hatted heads of firms and kitchen-maids
Visit the instincts of the eye.

Douglas Dunn, from 'The People Before'

Like everyone else in the world, I have four great-grandmothers. Unlike many people, though, I know their names: and there isn't an Irish name among them. Ellen Jordan, Catherine Harland, Emily Anne Thorpe, Mathilda Clara Maria Heller. The closest is Ellen Jordan's, though that name is likely of Anglo-Norman provenance; still, if your ancestors have been in the country since the twelfth century, I think you can call yourself Irish. She certainly did – and claimed an unbroken Catholic lineage to boot. She was my mother's feisty maternal grandmother. Nora's other grandmother, her father's mother, was Catherine Harland. At least, Harland was the name she went by. It was her mother's name. Young Catherine began life in post-Famine Lurgan under a serious social disadvantage. She was illegitimate. And unlike Helena Tipping, who was also born out of wedlock in the same decade, she didn't have parents who belatedly gave in to church and family pressures (if that was what Matthew and Eliza did). She didn't have parents, plural. As far as we know, her father's identity was never disclosed.

There's a story here, if only one could get to the bottom of it. Catherine was born in 1859 – and for succeeding generations, right down to the mid twentieth century and beyond, illegitimacy in the family betokened the ultimate loss of face. A sense of sin and degradation was tied up with failures of chastity, and it pervaded every religious group and every social class. A generation later, for example, we find even the worldly (and wealthy) Maud Gonne passing off her daughter Isolde as her niece. People were very prone to be sexually censorious, and if you knew of any irregularity in this respect among your immediate forebears, you'd simply have edited it out of the family narrative. I think it entirely possible that my mother never heard a word about her grandmother's dubious origin. I'm sure she believed Catherine Brady's family background to be as sound as anyone's. It was Catholic, that was the main thing. But was it? 'Harland' is not an Irish or a Catholic name. Harlands first set foot in Ulster in the mid seventeenth century, arriving as immigrants from County Durham. A lot of them then proceeded on to America and a prosperous life, but some stayed put, sinking roots into County Down and County Armagh. They belonged to the Society of Friends. They were very plentiful around Lurgan and Seagoe. They married wives with striking non-Irish names like Duck and Bullock. They called their daughters Elizabeth, Abigail, Rebecca and Catherine. And they remained committed to the Quaker faith – or most of them did. According to the 1911 census, Catherine Harland's mother Elizabeth Harland is the solitary Catholic of that name in the whole of County Armagh.

We can take it, then, that a switch of allegiance occurred at some point in some irresolute branch of the Harland family (which then died out); and as with the Tipping line, conversion to Catholicism goes hand-in-hand with a drop in social status. In 1861, when Catherine is two years old, a hotel called the Greyhound stands in Lurgan's High Street, and round the corner from it is a dodgy cobbled lane or court known as Greyhound Hotel Lane. In that lane lives a family called Harlan. (The Harlan and Harland spellings of the name are interchangeable.) Is this where Catherine grew up? Nothing is known about these obscure and lowly Harlans; but Catherine's mother Elizabeth worked as a servant for the well-to-do Johnston family of brewers at 19 High Street, close by, which suggests a connection in terms of propinquity, if nothing else. We don't know whether Elizabeth at the time was a live-in servant (and later cook) – but it wouldn't have been unusual to find her illegitimate child being brought up by its grandparents and fed an assuaging fiction: that its biological mother was just an older sister in the family.

The ascertainable facts (if they are facts) would have backed up this assertion, in Catherine's case. According to the 1911 census, again, Elizabeth Harland was twelve years old when she gave birth to her only child. (Not that she discloses anything of the sort to the census-takers: the spaces under 'children born' and 'children living' are blank.) We can work this out from her own stated date of birth, 1847. But is it a true date? I don't think so. Many people falsified their ages for the census returns, whether to prolong their working lives, because they'd simply got it wrong, being born before the era of record-keeping, or through forgivable vanity. And in the previous census (1901) Elizabeth had claimed to be fifty-nine years old, which pushes the year of her birth back to 1842. Whatever her true age, though, twelve or seventeen or something in between, Elizabeth was certainly young enough at the time of her daughter's birth to require looking after or shoring up. And maybe she got it at her place of employment. Maybe she kept the child with her in a back room of 19 High Street. Maybe the Church of Ireland Johnstons were sufficiently conscientious to try to do right by their 'wronged' Catholic maidservant – short of incorporating her into the family, of course. For what we have here – well, possibly – is a kind of *December Bride* situation.

In Sam Hanna Bell's novel, set on the Ards peninsula of County Down around the turn of the twentieth century, the eponymous bride Sarah Gomartin works as a servant of the Echlin family, Presbyterian farmers in a desolate spot, and in due course gives birth to a child whose father's identity she either doesn't know, or refuses to specify. Which of the younger Echlins is responsible for the girl's predicament, diminishing her standing in the eyes of the primitive, church-going, bible-clutching community? Either of the Echlin brothers would be glad to marry Sarah, but she holds out, biding her time, driven by an austere integrity, until circumstances bring about a change of heart. This occurs a long time after the initial transgression: hence the title. You read this novel for the pleasures of its Ulster rock-hardness, its spare but somehow picturesque Presbyterianism, the ancestral clock ticking away in the parlour, the scrubbed stone floor, the patchwork quilts. But I don't know if women like Sarah Gomartin ever existed, sufficiently grounded in their own self-reliance to go against community regulations. A nineteenth-century, pregnant, unmarried girl, you feel, wouldn't have hesitated to accept *any* offer of marriage, to get back her squandered reputation. Otherwise, it's all up with her: 'The neighbours will know of my black disgrace.' Propriety matters. 'The Girl's Lament', by William Allingham, gets at the essence of seduction and betrayal, Ulster-country style:

> In our wee garden the rose unfolds,
> With bachelors' buttons and marigolds;
> I'll tie no posies for dance or fair,
> A willow twig is for me to wear.

> For a maid again I can never be,
> Till the red rose blooms on the willow tree.
> Of such a trouble I've heard them tell,
> And now I know what it means full well.

The telling phrase, 'My apron-string now it's wearing short', encapsulates the sorry story, the whole grotesque (grotesque to our minds) atmosphere of shame and blame. It's important to stress how deep-rooted was the dread of community censure; no point in applying free-thinking attitudes of the present to past sexual misdemeanours (if that's what they were). I've uncovered quite a few lapses from strict pre-marital chastity among my forebears on both sides; but in most of these instances, *someone* intervened to put things right, before the social damage became irreversible. A hasty marriage was one thing; no marriage at all, another.

Certainly the most dramatic case is that of my great-great-grandmother, Elizabeth Harland. Picture an attractive young child-servant employed in a household containing three lusty boys, all around her own age: James (born 1839); William (born 1844); and Courtney (born 1846). It's not hard to envisage the kind of carry-on that might have taken place – or the inevitable outcome. I can't be certain about this, of course; I may be barking up the wrong family tree entirely. Everyone can point to missing forebears, broken lines of descent – and I've no reason to jam these brewing Johnstons into an ancestral gap of my own. Well, no reason except the obvious one. And suggestive silences and inactions. Where, for example, was the local priest with his holy water and domestic-regulatory impulse? If a young, available, Lurgan Catholic had fathered Elizabeth's child, you'd expect the pair of sinners to be dragged, protesting or not, before the altar. If the girl's condition had nothing to do with the Johnstons, you'd think they would wash their hands of their erring housemaid. But they didn't. We don't know what arrangements were entered into, but they kept her on. Time passed. In the natural course of things the Johnston parents died and the sons entered the professions (as managing director of the family business, tobacco manufacturer and practising solicitor respectively). Their Catholic housemaid Elizabeth Harland was promoted to cook. She never married, and neither did they. The three bachelor brothers and the spinster servant lived on and on in the same High Street house. One wonders what terms the unequal quartet were on: did Elizabeth turn into a stately elderly housekeeper, a known and respected figure in the neighbourhood, or did gossip and scandal plague her all her life? Did her juvenile disgrace stay with her, like a tin can tied to the tail of an inoffensive dog? Why did no one ever teach her to read and write? (The census return has her down as illiterate.) Was she brave or defeated? Did she acknowledge her daughter, or try to pretend she was some other relation? And where *was* baby Catherine during her early years?

Maybe her mother brought her up, as a single parent, and maybe Catherine knew who her father was, but was cautioned never to mention his name. 'If anyone asks – just say he's dead.' On second thoughts – this seems a bit too enlightened a course of action for close-knit, nineteenth-century, stuck-in-the-mud Lurgan. As for Catherine's father – he could have been a passing tramp, for all I actually know to the contrary, with Elizabeth too young or naive to understand what was happening to her when the child was conceived. Maybe the Johnstons were totally disinterested Christians. All one can be sure of is that Catherine was not abandoned, however her presence in the world was explained, and that mother and daughter were, and remained, on good terms. In later life, during the First World War, they lived together for a time in Glasgow. Elizabeth died in 1920, aged seventy-three (or perhaps a bit more). I don't know when the Johnston brothers died, or who inherited the brewing fortune. It was considerably depleted anyway, due to the large sums donated by James, the head of the family, to help fund the building of a Temperance Hall. Was this to atone for some form of intemperance in his past, one wonders? (Ah, irony.)

Family lore has Catherine, in her later years, inhabiting a house in Lurgan crammed with antiques – which suggests that some residue of the Johnston estate may, just may, have ended up with her. Alas, by this stage she'd taken to drink, and as the house was – conveniently – located next door to a pub, these valuable objects one by one found their way over the back wall dividing the two properties in exchange for bottles of gin. (Some of Catherine's grandchildren knew not to call in on her on their way to school if the curtains were drawn: this meant she'd had a rough night.) ... When she died in 1938, Catherine had sufficient resources to leave £5 (£185 in today's money) to each of her grandchildren, of whom there were many (my mother among them).

However and wherever she was reared, Catherine acquired sufficient sewing skills to get employment as a seamstress. It was the lower of the two standard occupations assigned to women in nineteenth-century fiction (the other was the governess, which I'll get to in a minute). Think of Little Dorrit, in the Dickens novel, going out daily from the Marshalsea Prison to sew for survival. Or Mrs Gaskell's heroine Mary Barton, who earns a meagre living as a needlewoman in congested, soot-stained Manchester of the 1840s; or the same author's Ruth, in the novel of that title published in 1853, who exemplifies the wronged-but-virtuous young dressmaker. Indeed, there's a whole 'seamstress' genre featuring long-suffering stitchers whose fate is either to rise in the world, via marriage, or to descend even further into prostitution and a lurid death. Bastard infants accompany them along the latter route. And even for those who will make something of their lives in the future, the present drudgery is unremitting.

> Work – work – work!
> From weary chime to chime,
> Work – work – work
> As prisoners work for crime!
> Band, and gusset, and seam,
> Seam, and gusset, and band,
> Till the heart is sick, and the brain benumbed,
> As well as the weary hand.

'Seamstress' indicates more than a job: it signifies an entire condition of female lowliness and ill-paid labour. I don't know to what extent the conditions evoked by Thomas Hood in his famous 'Song of the Shirt' were replicated in 1870s Lurgan, but certainly the town offered scope for hardship and exploitation, along with its sectarian delinquencies. Sore eyes and malnutrition. Perpetual exhaustion. Closer to home, too, and some way in the future, you have the poet 'Richard Rowley' (pen name of the businessman Richard Valentine Williams, who died in 1947) impersonating one of his own Belfast factory workers – 'The needles go leppin' along the hem,/And my eyes is dizzy wi' watchin' them' – in a tone akin to the resentment and fatalism of the Hood poem:

> Monday morning till Saturday,
> I sit an' stitch my life away ...
> An' what have I ever done or been,
> But just a hand at a sewing machine?

Catherine Harland, though, as the bastard child of an illiterate servant, might have counted herself lucky to gain a foothold in the sewing profession, whether she worked from home (wherever 'home' was), sewing shirts for a pittance, or, more likely, as a stitcher in a local handkerchief factory (maybe even the factory owned by the prospering Catholic Jordans). Later on, she describes herself as a dressmaker, which indicates a slight progression upwards. But she's married by then. Through her work, Catherine has met a young Lurgan tailor named Terence Brady, and the two of them get married in 1880 when they're both just twenty-one. (Unusually for my family, I don't think Catherine is pregnant at the time. But she'd have had the best incentive in the world to practise abstinence: her own situation, and her mother's.) To become a tailor, Terence would have had to serve an apprenticeship and gain necessary expertise, and as the wife of a respectable tradesman, Catherine could hold her head high and cast off the scandal of her origins. It was a triumph of a kind. Her mother's ill luck, or ill judgement, was not revisited on Catherine. (But Elizabeth, the Johnstons' servant, may have enjoyed a luxury unavailable to the vast majority of her contemporaries: a room of her own.)

Young Mr and Mrs Brady set up home at 37 Edward Street, where their first son William was born in 1881. He was my grandfather. He was followed swiftly by ten brothers and sisters, of whom only half survived into adulthood. Losses and gains. I'm happy that Catherine overcame her social handicap to fit into normal Lurgan Catholic plebeian life. But in some ways her mother Elizabeth had the better part – room to breathe and congenial surroundings. Yes, I know her work as a servant and cook was hard, but independence and security of a kind must have counted for something. And she'd have had time off, perhaps to lend a hand with her proliferating grandchildren, whether these were acknowledged as such, or not. Or perhaps I'm talking through my hat. What do I know about it? The details of Elizabeth's life, like those of innumerable other lives, are simply and utterly irretrievable. I've decided, though, that my great-great-grandmother was seventeen, not twelve, when her daughter was born. I'm basing this conclusion on the fact that many census respondents are overtaken by vagueness when it comes to the question of age. They make a wildly inaccurate estimate of the number of years they've been alive. The old rogue Matthew Tipping, for instance, claims a date of birth in 1841, which would make him ten years old when he first became a father. Sexually precocious he may have been, but we needn't cast him as a biological phenomenon.

Yes, Elizabeth was seventeen; and this makes the eldest Johnston son the most likely candidate for illegitimate fatherhood. But everything surrounding this time of drama – the shame and horror and remorse and agitation – is now lost for ever. The facts can never be recovered; and so, for the moment, I think, I've indulged in sufficient speculation about the matter. To stick with an unadorned sequence of events within a hundred-year span: Elizabeth gave birth to Catherine, who gave birth to William, who 'begat' Nora, who gave birth to me. While William lay in his cradle in a house in Edward Street, his future bride – already three months old when he came into the world – lay gurgling and kicking her heels in another cradle by the side of a hand-loom, in a house only a couple of streets away. She lay in her cradle, taking everything in, while her stern half-brother Henry Tipping prowled beside her with his hands clasped behind him, back and forth, back and forth, in the tiny room.

Henry is twenty-five, and may already have his eye on fifteen-year-old Mary Anne Dowds, his stepmother's daughter. But it will take another six years to get these two to the altar, though they've lived in the same house, along with all the rest of the mixed-up family, since 1876. When the Tipping/Dowds wedding takes place, it is – again – under duress.

Henry Tipping's greengrocer's shop in Edward Street, with Henry himself standing in the doorway

Mary Anne, twenty-one, is three months pregnant. No, says her grandson, my cousin Harry Tipping, it's not incest: though complications on the domestic front may suggest otherwise. Henry and Mary Anne are not related by blood; it's just that his father's wife is her mother (or as my grandmother and her full sister Ellen might have put it, testing their contemporaries with a conundrum, their mother's daughter married their father's son). ... And considering the conditions under which they all mucked in together, all the Tippings and Dowds and overlapping generations, it's surprising that more in the way of coital shenanigans didn't take place (as far as we know). ... At any rate, in September 1887, whether in a furtive or a festive spirit, Henry Tipping and Mary Anne Dowds (the gentle Mary Anne, she was known in the family) are pronounced man and wife and detach themselves from the whole jing-bang of John Street, from parents and siblings and half-siblings and step-siblings and all. Henry, showing a bit of enterprise, has already set himself up as a greengrocer, renting a small shop in Edward Street and the flat above it; twenty-odd years later, well into the new century, Henry transfers his business to rather better premises, still in Edward Street (76). Here his and Mary Anne's ten children grow up conscious of Orange hegemony and Catholic 'underdog' status, and in due course align themselves with the republican movement in the North, up to and beyond the signing of the Treaty. (I'll consider their activities at this time in the following chapter.)

Henry never came before a magistrate on a charge of riotous behaviour, and in this he failed to uphold the family reputation. They were great belligerents, all highly active on the nationalist side. I've already mentioned the young James Tipping (b. 1859) who was caught 'clodding' stones at poor John Hancock (who wasn't his enemy) and gaoled as a consequence (see p. 108–9). Henry's and James's brother Matthew,[1] born at Crossmacahilly in 1861 and likewise a dab hand with a cobblestone, was arrested in 1881 and charged with assault on the say-so of a Protestant youth named Thompson, who claimed he was innocently passing the Convent of Mercy in Edward Street when a stone flung by Matthew struck him in the face. It split his lip wide open, he complained, and broke a couple of his teeth. The incident took place in the early part of the summer, with the marching season imminent and sectarian passions running sky-high. Matthew's offence was beyond dispute, and the presiding magistrate, fed up with rowdyism and hotheads and endless faction fights disfiguring the streets, sentenced him to a month's imprisonment. (Matthew could have stayed at large if he'd had the resources to fork out twenty shillings and costs, but I doubt if this was an option for a poor factory hand.)

It wasn't the last of Matthew's court appearances. Four years later he's up again before the same JP, Colonel Waring, after supposedly running with a crowd in North Street pelting the police with stones and bottles, shouting and rampaging and barging their way through to a Protestant quarter. A St Patrick's Day parade was the occasion for this particular fracas. The nationalist faction was asserting its right to march along a stretch of ground at Church Place – between North Street and Edward Street – which the Protestants held to be Orange territory. It was the usual recipe for a flare-up of violence, with the usual police injuries suffered as a consequence – for which, in this instance, Matthew Tipping was held responsible. He denied the charge but several witnesses put him at the scene, making a guilty verdict inevitable. This time, it was a forty-shilling fine or two months' imprisonment. I don't know which of the two Matthew opted for. But by proclaiming his innocence, he added fuel to the nationalists' burning conviction of being unfairly targeted, penalised and kept down, in a hostile state. It was always and ever, 'us and them'. 'There was then,' William Carleton had asserted earlier in the century, 'no law *against* an Orangeman, and no law *for* a Papist.' The nineteenth-century Tippings would have gone along with that, and no doubt could have cited experiences of their own to back it up. But it was only from the 1880s on, in the bitter, grimy, insubordinate streets of Lurgan, that their Papist orientation blossomed into a full-blown commitment to all things Irish. Playing Gaelic football, joining *Cumann na nGaedhal*, attending every local ceilidhe and Irish concert, marching with *Na Fianna Éireann* and *Óghlaigh na hÉireann* ... these activities brought a charge of glamour and purposefulness to workaday Catholic existences, and Tippings were there in the thick of them, along with other prominent local families, Thornberrys and Bradys and O'Hagans and Haugheys and others. (I'll go into this more fully in Chapter Six.)

Another of that unruly generation, the first Matthew's oldest son and Henry Tipping's brother John, fulfilled family expectations by getting himself arrested in his turn for disrupting the peace. Twenty-eight years old, John faced a charge of being drunk and disorderly and assaulting a sheriff's officer in the street. The date of this particular shindy was September 1882, and the magistrate, wearied, no doubt, by all the unrepentant Tipping faces popping up before him, one after the other in a grim succession, delivered a typical verdict: ten shillings or fourteen days. I'm sure Colonel Waring hoped he'd seen the last of them. But then, only a month later, up comes yet another of the hooligan crew. Bernard Tipping, born in 1862, the youngest of Henry's brothers. This time, though, proceedings are the other way round. Bernard is the plaintiff here, charging a youth named James Mulholland with having stabbed him in the left side during an encounter in Market Street on the night of 9 October. 'Some blows were struck between him and me before I was stabbed,' Bernard declared; and, in a burst of candour, 'I believe I struck the first blow when we "squared" out to fight.' Mulholland, an employee of Bullick, Hamilton & Co.'s linen factory and a Protestant, said he happened to be carrying an opened knife when Tipping hit him in the eye, implying that the subsequent stabbing occurred more or less by accident. Confronted with exhibit A – Bernard's bloody shirt – Mulholland insisted he was so frightened and damaged that he couldn't help striking out with the knife. Matthew, Bernard's father, then weighed in with a statement to the effect that a Dr Gribben, summoned by him to patch up his bleeding son, had pronounced Bernard 'dangerously ill'. This drew from the exasperated Colonel Waring a surprising retort. 'I would not take Dr Gribben's evidence as to the health of a cat,' he snapped. The case was adjourned – and as the press failed to follow it up, the outcome remains unknown. I suspect that Bernard won a small amount of compensation, but I can't be sure about this.

One does not envy Colonel Waring his job as presiding magistrate at Lurgan Petty Sessions Court in the 1880s, inundated as he was with batch after batch of cases involving sectarian delinquency. The old courthouse on the corner of William Street and Charles Street might have been purpose built to discourage Protestant-versus-Catholic street-ferocity. Not that *any* deterrent was sufficient to restrain ancestral, or quasi-ancestral, convictions, during encounters between immemorial opponents. But local JPs did their best. And irony, albeit unrecognised irony, was not excluded from the courthouse precincts. I'm thinking not only of the Tipping/Blacker connection, with its implications for neutralisation, but of slighter anomalies which inevitably crept in. For example, in the case of Tipping versus Mulholland, a member of the bench was John Johnston, Esq., JP – original employer of the child Elizabeth Harland and father of her three contemporaries, James, William and Courtney. If my suppositions regarding the Johnston family have any substance, the JP is involved at this moment in passing judgement on his infant great-grandson's future wife's half-brother. Ah, Lurgan interdenominational, cross-community complexities.

This was the world into which my grandmother arrived at the tail-end of a boisterous family, in a house filled with firebrand half-brothers and flouncing half-sisters, a world of grievances, street brawls, arrests, consternation and uncertain tempers in the home. Born on 10 July, she'd have woken, at two days old, to the sound of Orange menace, drum-beaters and Taig-baiters marching in a show of domination and pageantry. It was a day for Papists to stay behind firmly closed doors (though many didn't). My grandmother is getting a foretaste of the life of contention in front of her, with which certain well-honed survival skills, including self-reliance, humour and assertion, will enable her to cope. I don't see her as suffering from the character defect she later attributed to me, when she'd inform all and sundry that I was 'very backward in coming forward'. She meant it kindly, but it bewildered her. Shyness was not an option in the household to which fate had consigned her. The quality she most admired was gumption, and in this, at the time, I was sadly deficient.

When Sarah is just eight years old, her father Matthew has his turn before the magistrates – not in the guise of an elderly brawler backing up his street-fighting sons, as you might think, but standing accused of selling ale from his front-parlour shop without a licence to deal in liquor. Some 'begrudger' has tipped off the police, who raid the John Street premises and confiscate a half-barrel of ale. Matthew claims the ale was brought in for his own use, to appease a weak digestive system which baulks at milk and tea. (Was there laughter in court? And did the aforementioned Dr Gribben testify on Matthew's behalf? One wonders.) He pulls it off. The case is dismissed. Counsel for the defence, a Mr Menary, is eloquent about the state of affairs that leaves 'a rich man's cellar' free from intrusion, while a poor man's solitary half-keg of ale makes an occasion for a criminal prosecution. His remarks raise a cheer in the courtroom, where it is felt that some kind of democratic principle has been asserted. Matthew's ale is returned to him. His wife Ellen Jordan, herself a tremendous 'argufier' by all accounts, would have relished the verdict but found it mortifying to be so publicly designated 'poor'. Ellen has many obstacles to surmount in her bid for respectability, with the antics of her immediate family high among them.

It's 1889, and Lurgan resounds to the blare of factory hooters, the din of rappers-up rousing people out of their beds to hasten to their work, the clip-clop of horses' hooves, the raucous voices of bulky Belfast women, just off the train and trundling handcarts towards the Thursday market. Dealers in second-hand clothes and poor people's delph. The raggedy, heavy, crow-black clothes of these market women would have rendered them slightly sinister in the eyes of local children, including eight-year-old Sarah Tipping on her way to and from her girls' elementary school in an outbuilding attached to the convent in Edward Street. Baba Yaga. The Hansel-and-Gretel woman. Not that Sarah isn't venturesome and alert, for ever on the go, dodging in and out of the crowds, maybe licking a toffee apple or buying a penny bun from a countrywoman come to town with her huge wicker basket full of wares. Is the eight-year-old dressed in a pinafore over a woollen dress and black laced boots? (I don't want to superimpose an E. Nesbit garnish over nineteenth-century Lurgan realities, but some images stick in your head and won't be eradicated.) Is her sister Ellen larking about with her, or her best friend Minnie Cochrane? If they step incautiously into alien territory, are their ears assaulted with sectarian taunts (while they give as good as they get: 'Fenian scum'; 'Proddy pigs' – accompanied by giggles and scurrying down the nearest alleyway)? ... Well, I know you can't conjure up a truthful picture of ancient unrecorded activities; but perhaps if you make an effort you may just catch sight of some ghostly ancestral figure vanishing round a corner – the corner of Wellington Street and Black's Court, say – with a swish or a flash of an antique garment, corduroys or britches or a ground-length woollen skirt, intent on some pursuit of the far distant past.

Grandmothers, great-grandmothers. In my particular line of descent, the counterpart to Catholic Lurgan is Protestant Wexford. However, the great-grandmother I know least about is the Wexford one, Emily Anne Thorpe. My paternal grandmother's mother. Born in Enniscorthy (I think), c.1849. She was farmer William Lett's second wife, and that date of birth would put her at forty when her only child, my father's mother, was born. (As with the Lurgan Tippings, there were Lett half-siblings about the place.) Am I right in attributing to Emily Anne a background filled with Enniscorthy shopkeepers? Perhaps. Some 'modest gentlemen's houses' in the neighbourhood were inhabited by people with the name of Thorpe – Castle View, New Ross, for example, Knockroe House, New Ross, and Shanballyroe House, also in New Ross – but again, I can't pin down a connection to any of them. I wish I could, for these are elegant, evocative, stone-built, eighteenth- or early nineteenth-century houses, not unlike the house in Antrim in which I've lived for the past decade or more. ... As a passionate conservationist and architectural aficionado, I offer thanks to God, or whatever means the good (and to the Irish Georgian Society), that so many ancient Wexford houses have survived into the twenty-first century. I don't care if these houses carry associations with yeomen or Orange magistrates or Protestant supremacy or any other historical embodiment of devilishness. Even those disfigured by oppression or bloodshed have long transcended the darkness imposed on them. Their aesthetic impact today is the thing that counts. They are vivid conduits to an earlier life. They are part of the Irish heritage common to all of us, high or low or at whatever point in between.

Having a Wexford grandmother and further-back relations from the tail-end of the country, was for me a way of boosting my Irishness in the eyes of my contemporaries – as long as I didn't mention the awkward Protestant bit. Wexford, Loch Garman, was all to do with heroic pikemen, 1798, 'The Croppy Boy', the thatched houses of the Irish poor, extreme devotion to the Catholic church. It's hard to fit Letts and Thorpes and Hornicks into that cultural dynamic, but I was happy if the implied indigenousness passed unchallenged. I suppose I was hoping to transmit an impression of my grandmother as a barefoot *cailín* in a red cloak on a wild mountainside surrounded by gorse and heather and the fumes of turf.

The turf may be authentic, but the rest was not. It derives from a picture postcard, *c*.1910. (I shouldn't forget the Connemara donkey-and-cart along with the rest of the 'autochthonous' baggage.) My grandmother's father belonged to the 'strong farmer' class; he kept indoor and outdoor servants and slept in a four-poster bed. He attended the local Church of Ireland church. He had four daughters and a son – the son he disinherited in a fit of pique in 1928. Everything he owned was willed to his second (unmarried) daughter, Annie Tennant Lett. Well, aside from two bequests of fifty pounds each, one to his daughter Emily Craig. Father and daughter must have been reconciled by this stage – if reconciliation was required. I'm guessing again, but there is evidence to suggest they fell out earlier, and it's possible that Emily came very close to being disowned altogether: she was a wayward girl! (I see the hand of Aunt Annie as a peacemaker in any subsequent mending of relations.)

I was thirty or thereabouts when my grandmother Emily died, but I never got to know her well, or felt that she and I had a great deal in common. True, until I was twelve or so, I was taken at least every other Sunday to visit her Dunmurry home, travelling with my parents from Belfast on the Hillhall bus; and after that time I'd still see her at regular intervals. But I never spent time alone with her. The gate lodge was always coming down with grown-up relations and other visitors, and I'd escape into an outhouse to leaf through mildewed copies of *Woman's Home Journal*, or a pile of my Auntie Hazel's old *Girls' Crystals*. Or I'd borrow an old rusty bike and keep on wobbling round and round the house until I'd actually succeeded in staying on the rickety thing, sailing past the kitchen window before the amazed eyes of assembled grown-ups. (Perhaps.) That was how I learned to ride a bicycle, in my tenth year. Some relations I was pleased to see (and the spaniel Sha), but my grandmother's presence I just took for granted. She was part of a world filled with fixed points of reference and changeless circumstances, changeless as the whitewashed gateposts and Belleek china tea set laid out on the damask tablecloth. Besides, old people really were old in those days – nowadays they're Claire Tomalin or Joanna Lumley. My grandmother would only have been sixty-something when I knew her best, but she seemed ancient to me, slippered, toothless, shapeless, clad in a patterned overall, a hairnet enfolding her thin grey hair.

So it came as quite a surprise when I first saw a photo of the young Emily Lett – or Emily Craig as she'd have been at the time (you can see her wedding ring). It's a formal photograph of a well-dressed couple seated side by side on elaborately carved chairs in some photographer's studio, my grandparents in their glossy youth. They gaze impassively at the camera, seated bolt upright, he with folded arms across a well-cut jacket and waistcoat, she in a pale cotton, high-necked blouse, thick dark hair arranged on top of her head in accordance with the style of the day. The very image of a handsome, well-omened Protestant Irish pair. They seem to be asserting their presence in the world, and their commitment to one another. There's an innocence about her, however, a guilelessness, while he wears a challenging look. And what you don't see in the picture is the drama and agitation surrounding their wedding, the tears and recriminations and delays. Neither do you see their infant son Stanley, born in October 1910. The Craig/Lett marriage was solemnised just a month earlier, on 7 September. A significant date: it was also my grandmother's twenty-first birthday, the day she came of age. You'd have to infer from this that Emily's engagement to William Craig did not go down well with the Clonleigh household. I don't know if Emily's mother was still alive (she wasn't a year later, I learn from the 1911 census). She is missing from the domestic fracas. But the girl's father was there, a man of strong opinions, and something impelled him to keep his fecund daughter from 'regularising' her situation until the last possible moment. Had he had other plans for her? It made no odds. The instant she was free to do so – and just in the nick of time – Emily Lett married William Craig. Had she already run away from home and moved in with the villain of the piece at his New Ross lodgings? Or did she remain at Clonleigh and brazen it out before the neighbours, all the while enduring paternal anger and disapproval? It can't have been an easy time – and I'd never have thought of my grandmother as bold or strong-willed or enterprising; a pliable girlhood, I'd have attributed to

Patricia Craig's grandparents, *c*.1911

her, a docile, amiable disposition. Perhaps I was wrong. Or perhaps none
of the above scenarios existed. But you can't get away from the facts, the
dates of the marriage and of Stanley's birth.

Stanley – or Robert Stanley, as he was christened – was born in Ayr,
far from Clonleigh and its contretemps. The previous month, as we've
seen, his parents were married in the parish church of Templeudigan,
County Wexford (St Peter's), where the officiating vicar no doubt
averted his gaze from the bride's protuberance. The witnesses were an
Annesley Kavanagh and an Annie McClintock (about whom I know
nothing whatever). The bridegroom's place of residence is down as 'New
Ross'. His occupation is 'coachman'. The fathers of bride and groom
are both described as farmers. (Why do I think my great-grandfather
Craig was at one point in his career a policeman on the Lisburn Road
in Belfast? Either it's a genealogical fallacy – and a few of those will
creep in from time to time – or there's an explanation for the change
of occupation which I may find later.) Once married, the errant couple
hasten to Scotland, where as far as anyone knows they've been man and
wife for years. In a short time Robert Stanley comes into the world (was
the 'Robert' in honour of Burns? Again, I have no way of knowing). Did
my grandfather obtain employment as a coachman? It would have been
something to do with horses anyway, he worked with horses all his life.

With a name like Craig, you would think the small family would fit like Cinderella's foot in the slipper into lowland Scottish life. But less than four years later we find them domiciled in Dublin where a second child is born. The abundantly named Emily Charlotte Annie Marie Heller Craig – fortunately soon abbreviated to plain Marie – is the first of four daughters. The original delinquent pair are now well settled and forging ahead as unimpeachable procreators. And if it wasn't for nosy descendants prying into their private history, the initial sexual transgression would never have surfaced to slightly undermine their church-going respectability. As with my mother and Catherine Harland, I don't believe any of their children knew a thing about it.

But who exactly was this William Craig whom farmer Lett declined to take to his bosom? (As far as I know.) A wild boy who'd run away from home in 1898 at the age of fourteen and got himself taken on as a stable hand at Finnebrogue, near Downpatrick – in defiance of his parents' project to secure for him a start in life as a railway clerk. They thought it would make a good career for him, but he wasn't having any of it. He knew what he wanted, and it didn't include dispensing tickets to the travelling public, or sitting on a high stool poring over a ledger. So he fled to Finnebrogue. How he subsequently arrived in County Wexford, or when he first encountered the comely but vulnerable Miss Lett, I have no idea. He seemed to get around, my grandfather, before he brought his family to settle in Dunmurry where he took up a post as head groom to the Charley family, sinking roots into the district and adapting to its ways. Here, at the end of 1917, a third child, christened William Albert Thomas – my father – was born. As for my grandfather's father, the coachman/farmer/policeman who may or may not have been born in Dublin, but who definitely had connections with Leitrim, Donegal, the Ards peninsula and Belfast ... I know only a little about him. I know his political persuasion was as Orange as William Johnston's of Ballykillbeg. And I have his death notice from the *Belfast Telegraph* of 28 April 1925. '... Suddenly, at his residence, Drumawhey, Newtownards, County Down ... late of Kinlough, Bundoran.' Seventy-five years old, so he'd have been born in 1850. His grave is in Belfast's City Cemetery – ten minutes' walk from my birthplace. Between himself and his peripatetic second son, my grandfather, a good deal of Irish ground gets traversed. If they'd had a more distinctive name than Craig – Tipping, Topping, Twyble, Trimble, Turkington – their antecedents might be discoverable. As it is, researchers

135

are stymied by the nearly generic patronymic. (When I was eighteen and determined to be as Gaelic as possible, I was known as Pádraigín de Creag: of the rock.)

Well, I could claim the family originated in Ayrshire, Aberdeen or Orkney, and that one of them – the Reverend John Craig – was a colleague of John Knox, and therefore implicated in the start of the Covenanting movement and the whole exodus to Ulster. But hypothesis and probability can only take us so far. My Craig great-grandfather remains essentially unknown, along with all his forebears. With his wife, however – his first wife, my great-grandmother – it's a different matter. And here my religious ancestry takes an unforeseen turn. To the whole admixture of Catholicism, Protestantism, Quakerism and probably Scottish Presbyterianism, I have to add a German Lutheran dash. In 1881, the three-generations-back William Craig, definitely a coachman at this stage, had married a young German governess named Mathilda Clara Maria Heller (she was known as Marie).

Both of them were employed by the May family, one-time sovereigns of Belfast. We've now gone back to the 1870s and the Dublin residence of the Rt Hon. George Augustus Chichester May, Lord Chief Justice of Ireland between 1877 and 1887.[2] George Augustus and his wife Olivia (née Barrington) had a lot of children, including Charlotte Olivia, Edward, George, Stella and Josephine (who died in 1873, aged four) – ten in all. During the months of winter and spring, the May family lived at 13 Fitzwilliam Square, in the lofty and punctilious manner appropriate to their standing, and to the era. The handsome square with its enclosed central garden was home to a lot of doctors and lawyers, soldiers and academics, and many of the families occupying its elegant, five-storey Georgian houses were related to one another. For instance, the younger Mays had hordes of cousins – Barrington, Jellett and le Fanu cousins – living close by, creating a juvenile network of gaiety and seasonal pursuits. A treat for the children might consist of a walk to College Green, in the charge of a nursemaid, to view the illuminations celebrating the Prince of Wales's marriage; or a visit to the pantomime at the Theatre Royal, going through dark winter streets festooned with stalls attended by women selling apples and oranges by the light of lanterns made out of paper bags. On Sundays, they were all marched to church at St Stephen's, Mount Street, with their parents walking arm-in-arm behind them, 'after the fashion of the day'.

PC's great-grandmother Marie Heller, *c.*1878

A pattern for the children's upbringing went something like this. A nurse or nursemaid for the infants, followed by a governess once the age of reason was attained. Then, at ten or so, the boys would be enrolled at a Dublin day school, before going on to Rugby in Warwickshire (or some similar establishment). By this stage they'd have had manliness instilled into them by being encouraged to kill every bird, fish or non-domestic animal that came within their orbit. It was called sport. It was a preparation for killing Boers, Asiatic wild animals and Irish insurgents, when 1916 came around.

I learn all this, and more, from a very stilted book of reminiscences by an old soldier, Major-General Sir Edward Sinclair May.[3] When Major-General Sir Edward S. May was a boy in Fitzwilliam Square, he listened to a lot of servants' gossip about the Fenian Brotherhood and its hopes for Ireland, and among the things that stayed in his mind was a recollection of daily walks with his governess past Mountjoy Prison, while Fenian trials were taking place inside it. He doesn't say what his attitude to the Fenian uprising was, but I think we can take it that it wasn't approving. The governess in question can't have been my great-grandmother as she was only thirteen at this time, and still living with her family in Bremen. (Edward May was two years younger.) But she may have come next in the succession of May family governesses. She was with the family in Howth on her twentieth birthday in July 1874, and the cards she received on that date from her employers – and kept for ever after in her personal photograph album – suggest she was held in high regard by the lot of them.

This wasn't the usual situation of the nineteenth-century governess. Numerous novels, journals and autobiographies tell a different story, one of taunts, privations and humiliations. Between *Jane Eyre* and *The Turn of the Screw* – between the force of destruction emanating from the attic, and exposure to extreme psychological or psychic peril – the young woman teacher sent out to make her way in the world requires constant vigilance to keep her from harm.

She also needs to be endowed with fortitude. At a time when most women never moved far from the place where they started, the idea of uprooting oneself and living among strangers must have loomed like a nightmare before the faint-hearted. But my great-grandmother, not a whit daunted, left her home in Bremen with her Saratoga trunk, waved goodbye to her parents and siblings, and crossed the North Sea and then the Irish Sea to reach her destination in Dublin. It was a great adventure. The Mays, for their part, would have got what they paid for: a young woman well equipped to instruct and win over their daughters and younger sons, and keep order in the schoolroom. They were well enough placed to pick and choose among the applicants for the post of governess, and something about Marie Heller must have commended itself strongly.

A lot has been written about the socially ambiguous status of the governess in a grand family. Is she a servant or isn't she? What degree of hobnobbing is permitted between her and her employers? How does she deal with resentment in underservants obliged to wait on her? Each case was different, of course, and I get a sense that Marie Heller was something of a pet with the Mays and their social circle, perhaps because of the novelty of her origins. (She was also a good deal better educated than most of them: I know of her immersion in the world of literature, and I'd like to attribute to her a certain moral and intellectual refinement as well.)

She was born in Berlin, a city of tall houses, balconies and linden trees, in 1854. The previous year, her father, Friedrich Wilhelm Heller – how German that is! – had received an honourable discharge from the Prussian army, and was free to resume his original, ancestral occupation. He was a potter, the third son of a master potter, born in a place called Zellin, in 1814 – Zellin being located in Prussia then, though I think it was ceded to Poland after the Second World War. At any rate, it was somewhere close to what is now the border between Germany and Poland. His wife, Maria Bertha Dorothea Vogel (b. 1820), had a different upbringing as a Berliner and the daughter of a piper in the king of Prussia's army. The names of Maria Bertha Dorothea's parents were Johann Gottlieb Vogel and Julianne Stolzenbach – and that's as far back as I'm going along the German line. These are only names to me, and foreign names at that. I can hardly comprehend that people called Vogel, Heller and Stolzenbach are among my direct ancestors: but there they are. Their northern European faces – those born in the age of photography, that is – gaze out inscrutably from the pages of Marie Heller's family album. There they stand, in their studied poses, frock coats and nineteenth-century silhouettes, transfixed in a faraway realm of the past and utterly unapproachable. An image has survived of my Berlin great-great-grandmother Bertha Vogel, but it's as enigmatic as the apparition of Miss Jessell in the Henry James story, and as wispy as woodsmoke. Indeed, I have very little grip on my German forebears; though – when I think of historic European cities with mediaeval courts and cobbled streets and four- or five-storey, half-timbered houses, I could wish it was otherwise. '*Je regrette l'Europe aux anciens parapets.*'[4]

When Marie was five, the family upped sticks for the Free Hanseatic city of Bremen (with a population of about sixty thousand, as opposed to Berlin's nearly half a million). To move home at the time was quite a business, requiring all kinds of certificates including one which stated that the Hellers 'had given no cause for complaint' while they lived in

Berlin. An unimpeachable family then, to which were added several offspring during the 1860s (though Bertha was well into her forties by this date). Marie, the fourth daughter, would have been a bright little girl who shone in the schoolroom (just like her future granddaughter-in-law, my Lurgan mother), with a good grasp of languages and a love of German literature. Heinrich Heine, Ludwig Uhland, Joseph von Eichendorff and Karl Simrock were among the poets whose works she wrote out meticulously – page after page – in a special poetry notebook: a resource for difficult times, a talisman she kept by her for the rest of her life. Marie's future as some kind of teacher was already marked out, perhaps, at an early stage; though no one could have envisaged her eventual resting place in a desolate Leitrim graveyard with incessant Irish rain coming down in sheets against the headstones, and the wind soughing among the yew trees.

Interspersed with the German family photos in Marie's album are sepia pictures of the beau monde Mays and their acquaintances, and of the young governess's Dublin friends. Among the latter is Miss Maria Merrin who seems also to be a resident of 13 Fitzwilliam Square – was she perhaps another May employee? Marie has inscribed a photograph of herself, a present for this Miss Merrin, with the words: 'Remember in later years always your old friend in pleasure and pain, Marie Heller. 19 November 1876.' The photographic studio is that of Geo. Mansfield, 90 Grafton Street, Dublin. You also find a Cissy Dempsey in the album, and Louise Helms who writes to Marie, 'Forget me not', in the standard sentimental fashion. One of the governess's twentieth birthday greetings comes from her employer Mrs Olivia May, 'with affectionate love'. It is dated Locksley, 16 July 1874. There was a country house called Locksley, of recent construction (1860s), one of a pair, the other being Rosedale, built at Howth for the Guinness family – is it the same Locksley? Possibly the Mays had rented the house for the summer. Other summers saw them ensconced at Violet Hill, near the seaside resort of Bray, at Killarney Wood or Bray Head House (the property of the Putland family). No doubt there were picnics, with hide-and-seek and the younger contingent dodging in and out of the trees, croquet on the lawn and excursions by carriage to local beauty spots.

And there in the midst of all these decorous goings-on is my youthful ancestress, revelling in her popularity, speaking German or French to her charges, contributing to the gaiety of every innocuous occasion. I like to think that Marie Heller crammed a lot of enjoyment into the thirty-six years vouchsafed to her. I see her as a small girl with a watering-can attending to geraniums, nasturtiums or climbing roses on a balcony in Berlin; or – wrapped in rugs – being drawn on a sleigh through the snow-laden streets. Christmas, the great festival of the German year, was a time of magic and wonder to her. 'O Christmas, Christmas! Highest feast!/We cannot comprehend its joy ...'. These lines, in German, by the poet Nikolaus Lenau, have a place in Marie's hand-written anthology. Her relish for the Christmas season may have been transmitted to me, genetically – I can't otherwise explain my delight in the changed atmosphere obtained by the glittering fir tree and other trappings of the time of year. I'm not and never was a crackers-and-paper-hat person; but each December, and more so as I get older and older, I insist on bringing into the house a Christmas tree to be festooned with antique baubles. This frivolity certainly isn't an inheritance from the other side of my family, for reasons I'll touch on later. Even my mother, who made something utterly enchanting of *my* childhood Christmases, was apt, on her own account, to disparage the whole annual fuss-about-nothing and tinselly tomfoolery (as she saw it). There was a defensive element to this, supposedly common-sense rejection of festive indulgence, as we shall see.

I don't know if Marie Heller ever made the return journey to Germany once she'd left home to be a governess, but I am sure the pull of the homeland remained. ... However, her position with the Mays is consolidated; and, in the great houses of her employers, she is sheltered from the fraught events of the day – Land Wars, evictions, boycotts, assassinations. The legacy of the Fenian movement. Time passes – 1876, (bringing the death of Mrs Olivia May, with what repercussions on the governess's position, I don't know) ... 1877, '78 – and, on the home front, trouble occurs. Does the twenty-two-year-old son of the family cast a seigneurial eye on the twenty-four-year-old governess, or is it someone else who has designs on her? The truth can never be known now, but an established fact is that, in the early summer of 1880, the young German woman finds herself in an age-old predicament. Like Eliza O'Hara, like Elizabeth Harland, like her future daughter-in-law Emily Lett, she is pregnant out of wedlock. I am sorry to harp on all this amatory irregularity raging through my background like wildfire on a heath – and perhaps the source of the 'bad blood' attributed to me by the nuns of St Dominic's High School in Belfast – but I can't seem to get away from it.

Bad enough for this to happen within a familiar, more or less supportive community, like Catholic, rural Crossmacahilly, or a family primed to take the matter in hand and act for the best; but for a lone German girl away from home, a 'respectable', God-fearing, Lutheran German girl committed to rectitude in holy Victorian Ireland, the shame and stress must have been excruciating. Talk there would have been, salacious gossip and avid speculation (such as I'm about to go in for). Was Marie shunned by her erstwhile friends Maria Merrin and the Helms sisters? Did Cissy Dempsey turn up her nose, once she'd enjoyed being properly shocked and enthralled? Above all, what was Marie's view of her situation? Was she defiant or demoralised? Even if she lacked the adamantine integrity of Jane Eyre, she'd never have cast herself as a Hetty Sorrel figure. How deluded was she, and by whom? Were her employers sympathetic, or not? Was the future Major-General Sir Edward Sinclair May, who married at forty and sired five daughters and a son – was this individual, at this dramatic juncture, in a study or billiard room shaking in his shoes; or holding himself aloof and a bit contemptuous from a family emergency that really and truly had nothing to do with him?

The unanswerability of these questions doesn't make them any less pertinent. The elder Mays, at the very least, bore some responsibility for Marie's welfare, being in a sense *in loco parentis*. They'd hardly have put her out on the street, but what did they do? Was she sent away to some distant place of refuge or private nursing home? Was the whole thing just a botheration and annoyance to them, or did they know themselves to be more deeply implicated in Marie's disgrace? How were the young May daughters shielded from the evidence of immorality? What urgent negotiations were carried on? All impossible to determine. Documentary evidence gives a little, just a little, to go on; and it discloses Marie, still single, in February 1881, with a baby in one hand – and no doubt her book of poems in the other.

Enter the demon-king coachman William Craig. (I'm joking; it's just that his copious moustaches, in the one photograph I have of him, make him the perfect model of a pantomime villain.) On the other hand, perhaps this person has been in the picture all along, a known seducer with an aversion to matrimony – at least, when the prospective wife is not an Irish girl (he married again, after Marie's death). Perhaps he really

The 'demon-king coachman': PC's great-grandfather William Craig

is the father of the child, the baby Bertha, called after Marie's mother back in Bremen. Certainly I never received the smallest intimation that all was not as it should be with the parentage of 'Aunt Bertha', as the 1880s baby became known to my father and his siblings. Of course I didn't; it was the 1950s, when respectability reigned and no one in their right mind would have brought up an ancient scandal in the family. No one would have given any credence to it, either. All right, you can't get round the date on the marriage certificate, April 1881, proclaiming extraordinary tardiness on the part of bride and groom – but no need to go further and make it a marriage of convenience into the bargain.

I can't quite accept this version of events. The marriage was certainly a come-down for Marie Heller. Coachmen were very numerous in the carriage-owning era, and for all their sumptuous livery they were classed as servants; whereas she was on the next thing to an equal footing with the employing family. I can't believe that this accomplished young woman, speaking several languages fluently, and possessed of a certain European urbanity, would choose to throw in her lot with a rough Irish coachman, had any reasonable alternative been available to her. The alternative she faced was, of course, social ostracism and probably penury, as an unmarried mother at an especially censorious time.

The scenario I envisage is this. Some unknown person beguiled and bamboozled Marie, conscripting her for the sorrier role in the standard, not to say trite, seduction-and-humiliation plot. The Mays,[5] whether interested or disinterested parties, were then faced with the task of finding a husband for matrimonially downgraded Marie, and the best they could do in the circumstances was the coachman. And that only after protracted to-ing and fro-ing. Perhaps a financial inducement was proffered, or an undertaking given, *de haut en bas*, that a well-disposed eye would be trained on any future children born to Marie and William Craig. (And so it proved. At any rate, my grandfather William Henry experienced no trouble in finding employment as a coachman, a stable hand or groom with local grandees at Finnebrogue, in Wexford, in Scotland or, eventually, in the Lagan Valley.)

Marie's life was in shreds, however, and she opted out of it, ten years and five children later, by turning her face to the wall. I doubt if she'd ever have become acclimatised to the moods of the Irish countryside, or a day-to-day existence decidedly at odds with the future she might have mapped out for herself. Perhaps sex was a consolation – or a punishment accepted in a penitent spirit for the mess she'd made of things, her social wrongdoing and foolish gullibility. At any rate, the children of the marriage came quickly, following on from John in 1882 (my grandfather was next, in 1884), and from the first son on were indubitably Craigs. But over Bertha, I think, a question mark remains.

All this may be wrong. But there *is* that fact of the back-to-front sequence of birth and marriage. Another fact is that her Germanness and his Leinster identity (if that's what it was) combined to breed a family of Ulster unionists and Orangemen. They signed the Covenant in 1912, at the height of the stupendous outcry against Home Rule. They paraded on the Twelfth with their sashes and banners. In her well-tended, hedged-in garden at Dunmurry – her special domain – my grandma Craig grew clumps of Orange lilies.

George Augustus May outlived his children's German governess by a year. He died, for some reason at a house called Lisnavagh in County Carlow, in 1892, aged eighty-seven. He died as he had lived, a toff, unknown to the ceilidhe house, the agitators' meeting place or the soup kitchen. The household over which he presided during his heyday would have been a conservative one, committed to 'ascendancy' values. The glamour of the Fenian movement, 'cultural' Irishness or an affinity with the aspirations of Charles Stuart Parnell would have passed it by. Irish disaffection would have been anathema to it. Particularly, at one end of the century, George Augustus might have remarked the fate of a predecessor in the role of Lord Chief Justice, Lord Kilwarden, murdered by a mob in Dublin during the uncoordinated rebellion of Robert Emmet; and at the other end, in 1882, he had the Phoenix Park assassinations of Lord Frederick Cavendish and T.H. Burke by a reprehensible offshoot of the Irish Republican Brotherhood called the Invincibles, to underscore in his eyes the fiendish nature of Fenianism.

None of this would have meant a thing to the girl from Bremen. But, worldly or workaday, it was Protestant Ireland, not Catholic Ireland, that reeled her in. Her Lutheran sensibility chimed with a Church of Ireland decorum (leaving aside the lapse of chastity rebarbative to both). She wasn't to know that, a long way in the future, a renegade grandson would throw in his lot with the other camp and help to build barricades in Belfast against a 'Protestant' onslaught, during the troubles of the early 1970s. (At the time I'm writing, that grandson, my father, is a healthful and cheerful ninety-three-year-old, loosely attached to the Catholic church at Kilclief, near Strangford, County Down, and strongly attached to his local Catholic community.)

Take a year at random in the nineteenth century – say, 1859. In the north of Ireland the great religious revival is gathering a head of steam, as Presbyterian staidness flies out of the window and unbridled hysteria enters in. Susceptible people all over the place are 'saved' or 'converted' with maximum melodrama. A situation prevails in previously inexcitable Ulster communities which is curiously akin to Lewis Carroll's 'reeling and writhing and fainting in coils'. The social commentator James Winder Good, writing in 1918, describes what happened:

> From the North of Antrim, where the first manifestations were displayed, the fire spread rapidly south, until ... practically the whole of Presbyterian Ulster was ablaze. The enthusiasm was even more vehement in towns than in the rural districts ... [with] 'screams of the most unearthly description proceeding from places of professedly Christian worship at all hours

of the day and night, girls with dishevelled hair and pallid faces ... supported in the arms of young men and young women, to their homes from the churches where they had been struck ...'.

(The quotation comes from an embarrassed observer of these unprecedented antics, the Reverend William McIlwaine.) Trances, seizures, visions and 'miracles' are the order of the day – and one can envisage the bemusement of Catholic onlookers as *their* church's reputation for 'superstition' and emotionalism is suddenly and exorbitantly overtaken.

Among the latter, possibly, are Matthew Tipping and his wife Eliza, a young couple still occupying part of the Crossmacahilly farmhouse with its linen-weaving accoutrements and its apple orchard in full fruition, and with a new arrival – their son James, the future Lurgan stone-thrower – added to the rest of the inhabitants jostling for a bit of space. ... In another part of County Armagh, eighteen-year-old Ellen Jordan (Matthew's next wife) may also be witnessing unexpected religious excitements among the overwrought of the area, and thanking her lucky stars for her own ancestral, sensible and dignified, Catholic creed. She may also, in the usual way of spirited adolescents, be exhibiting impatience with her parents' harping on the awful old Famine (safely in the past), and on the failed, and farcical, uprising of 1848 – though she is probably herself a supporter of the embryo Fenian movement. There is plentiful news of evictions and other evils in the Irish countryside to keep Ellen's nationalist instincts working at full throttle.

In the town of Lurgan itself the young domestic servant Elizabeth Harland is giving birth to her daughter Catherine, an occasion not calling for rejoicing on anyone's part – though, as we've seen, Catherine does not allow herself to be disabled by her origins. Catherine's route to respectability, her future husband Terence Brady, is at this moment taking into his infant lungs the purer air of County Cavan – 'lakeside orchards in first bloom' – though before long he too will be transplanted with his family to dusty, sect-ridden, throughother Lurgan.

I haven't the smallest peg on which to hang speculations about the setting or the circumstances of my great-grandfather William Craig's upbringing (he who ended up buried in the City Cemetery in Belfast). Nine years old in 1859, and Protestant to the core (that much at least

I can infer), the future coachman may already be working with horses, somewhere in the south of the country – though not as far south as County Wexford, where another forebear, young William Lett, is getting the hang of the farming business in the face of a severe agricultural depression afflicting the country (and becoming entrenched in his Church of Ireland identity). In the nearby town of Enniscorthy, ten-year-old Emily Anne Thorpe. ... But here I really do come up against a brick wall of total ignorance. Whatever she's doing, I have to leave her to get on with it.

It's easier to conjure up a picture of Mathilda Clara Maria Heller, a solemn little girl of five, saying goodbye to Berlin and the balconies and cobbles and flower shops, the Kranzler-Ecke, the fish market, the smell of coffee and confectionery, the carts laden with branches of young birch trees in the spring and streets thronged with officers in military uniform. Utterly unaware of remote, bleak Ireland and everything to do with it, she is on the way to Bremen, where her father will set up his pottery business. I hope there is space among the family's possessions for her cherished children's books and books of poems (I'm sure she owned some of these). All right, I know I'm attributing some of my own proclivities to this unknown great-grandmother, but it's not entirely without foundation.

John Hewitt has recorded in verse his mild antipathy towards his Methodist grandmother, describing her as 'stiff and hard'. But, he adds, she had a mitigating feature: she carried a cache of poems clipped from newspapers in a pouch on her garter. Tennyson, Whittier, Longfellow, George MacDonald. And, 'remembering that satin pouch of poems / I clasp her bony hand'. Yes, keeping poems by you seems to be a measure of integrity – one I'd go along with anyway. And to bolster that conviction in my mind I have those skilled amateur anthologists, my mother and my father's grandmother, bequeathing to me an intense susceptibility to the power of poetry. And it was probably that dual genetic inheritance that predisposed me to become an anthologist – if not entirely a poetry anthologist – myself.

At school in Belfast in the 1950s I never won prizes for anything – with one exception. When we were twelve or thirteen, and in Form 2A at St Dominic's, our English teacher, Miss McVerry, announced one morning a competition for the class. 'Now, children, I want each of you to take an unused exercise book. And in it, in your best handwriting, between now and the end of term, I want you to copy out any poems or pieces of prose that you particularly admire. It must be your own choice, remember, and it can be absolutely anything you like, from a nursery rhyme to a passage from Shakespeare. If any of you have a clean exercise book in your desk, you can start now by writing "My Anthology" on the first page. [She then proceeded to chalk up these words in large letters on the blackboard.] And at the end of term, there will be a prize of a book-token for whichever of your efforts I judge to be the best. Now – any questions, or does anyone have any idea about the sort of thing you might start with? Yes, Mary?'

It was the first time I'd heard the word 'anthology', but I knew at once that this project was right up my street. I couldn't wait to get it under way. In fact I produced two 'anthologies' (the first exercise book was filled pretty quickly), spending most of my evenings over the next couple of months seated at the kitchen table surrounded by papers, books, paint-boxes and jars of dirty water. I went one better than everyone else by illustrating my choices, mostly with pictures copied from books I owned ('Where is Persephone, you naughty sea children?'; 'He tied Lucy and Henry to the kitchen table'). I was nothing if not an eclectic compiler. I had Chaucer (surprisingly, in the Middle English versions) and Spenser alongside Louisa May Alcott and 'Roddy the Rover'. Kipling's poem about not 'giving your heart to a dog to tear' (I was very fond of dogs) is followed by 'Charlotte Bronte's Creed'. Poetry and prose are intermingled throughout. Thus was the pattern set – minus the illustrations – for my Blackstaff *Belfast* and *Ulster* anthologies, and *Oxford Book of Ireland*.

I won the prize. It was a book-token for seven shillings and sixpence. I'd like to say I bore it off to Mullan's or Erskine Mayne's and exchanged it for something like *The Faber Book of Contemporary Poetry* or Sean O'Faolain's translations from the Irish, *The Silver Branch*. But I know it was expended joyfully on the *School Friend Annual for 1956*, or *The Secret of Grey Walls* by Malcolm Saville. I needed poetry to amplify my life, but I also needed – and still need – a large element of frivolity in my bedtime reading. (Nowadays it's supplied by wonderful contemporary thriller writers like Andrew Taylor, Sue Grafton, Michael Connolly, Alafair Burke and the incomparable Reginald Hill.) I was – and still am, as a collector – a children's books addict.

As for the poetry business – some of my ancestors on both sides,

I am sure, never gained pleasure from a line of verse in their lives. But it's not fair of me to single out the two who did, and elevate them, for that reason alone, above all the rest. And, if you make assumptions about people's relations to literature, you may be setting yourself up for a salutary comeuppance. My utterly unpoetic and ill-educated father could, for example, in his prime, recite from start to finish not only 'The Shooting of Dan McGrew', but Portia's central speech from *The Merchant of Venice*. And my two-times-over half-great-uncle Henry Tipping – but hang on a minute, I'm getting entangled here in the skein of my own ancestral complications. Two-times-nothing; that only applies to his and Mary Anne Dowds's children. His mother Eliza O'Hara was not related to me. My half-great-uncle Henry Tipping, then, an uncouth and grumpy old sod by all accounts, nevertheless revered Thomas Davis's 'Fontenoy, 1745' – to the point of not restraining his rendering of it in the presence of his terrified infant half-sister Sarah.

> ...The treasured wrongs of fifty years are in their hearts today –
> The Treaty broken 'ere the ink wherewith 'twas writ could
>   dry,
> Their plundered homes, their ruined shrines, their women's
>   parting cry,
> Their priesthood hunted down like wolves, their altars
>   overthrown –
> Each looks as if revenge for all were staked on him alone.
> On Fontenoy, on Fontenoy, nor ever yet elsewhere
> Rushed on to fight a nobler band than these proud exiles were.

Fontenoy was the site of the battle in which the Irish troops of King Louis XV inflicted an overwhelming defeat on the English forces under the command of the Duke of Cumberland – 'the Bloody Duke of Cumberland'; and, of course, you could say it's not so much poetry as patriotism that animates great-uncle Henry as he roars out the list of 'treasured' enormities. The wrongs done to the Irish were entwined in his heart and head – and never mind if the blood of those on the side of Thomas Davis's plunderers and desecrators has sneaked to an extent into his own bulging nationalist veins. There's no one to say, 'But hold on a minute,' to disturb his conviction of possessing an unblemished Irish ancestry.

CHAPTER 6

CULTURAL CONFUSIONS

The roll call in the side chapel of the Royal Irish Fusiliers
might have taught us something: O's and Macs mingled in
death with good Proddy names, Hamilton, Hewitt, Taylor,
Acheson.

John Montague, from 'History Walk'

Throughout the nineteenth century, savage street-fighting occurred
periodically in key towns in the North, including Belfast, Derry,
Portadown and Lurgan. Belfast's bad reputation in this respect goes all
the way back to 1813, when two men were shot dead in North Street –
victims, as George Benn has it, of 'party collision'.[1] The affably sardonic F.
Frankfort Moore, in *The Truth about Ulster* (1914), records an experience
of his early life, when a careless nursemaid led him into a turbulent
quarter of the town while a riot was in progress. Too young to understand
what was going on, but quite old enough to relish the excitement of the
occasion, he stood with his nose pressed against an upstairs window of
a local house into which his nurse had hastily bundled him, watching
Belfast go about its usual stormy business. 'I saw a flying crowd of men
and women, boys and girls of the mill-working order, and behind them
were riding at the trot three dragoons with their sabres drawn and at
the "carry".' It was 1857, Twelfth-of-July parades had just taken place,

and rumours of 'Papist' threats to cherished Orange clergymen such as Dr Cooke and Dr Drew had inflamed the situation. Protestants and Catholics were once again at one another's throats.

Paving stones, porter bottles and iron nuts all came into play and inflicted considerable damage on sectionally undifferentiated heads and limbs. The most vicious and violent years of the century were 1857, '64, '72 and '86, the last tied up with the Liberal government's first Home Rule bill (and Protestant jubilation over its defeat). Major sectarian outbreaks were a feature of Belfast, where street-fighting had swiftly assumed a strategic character, but provincial towns like Lurgan weren't behindhand in taking up the cudgels in support of one side or the other. Most of the combatants fuelled by factional fury would have had nothing in their heads but enlarged folk-memories of atrocities perpetrated against their co-religionists – or perhaps not even that. For some it was just a matter of a distorted birthright: if you're born a Protestant the onus is on you to fight the Taigs, and vice versa. You don't need to know what it's all about.

Hence the missiles propelled into Protestant faces by Tipping hard men of the 1880s. The first Lurgan generation – sons of weaver/shopkeeper Matthew – had nothing to lose, and something to gain in the way of community prestige, by standing up for their Catholic entitlements. I don't think their actions at street level – assault and rampage – were motivated by any idea of political reform. It was more instinctive than that. It was bred in the bone and expressed with the fists. As for their Protestant counterparts – well, from the year of Emancipation on, 'the theory of insatiable Catholics extorting privilege after privilege at the expense of harassed Protestants colours all Orange thought', wrote the social commentator and historian James Winder Good in his study of 1919, *Ulster and Ireland*. True – but again at street level, thought didn't come into it. Nothing more elaborate than blows struck at foes was the rationale.

But things are about to change. The succeeding Tipping generation is rather more perspicacious and better informed, and its militant instincts become attached to an ideology. This is true at least of the family it suits my purpose to concentrate on – for you needn't worry that I'm about to delve into the procreative histories of all the Tipping offspring of Matthew and his wives. For the moment at least, I'm sticking to the progeny of one son, Henry and *his* wife Mary Anne Dowds – quite enough to be going on with. Four daughters and six sons were born to this pair between 1888 and 1906. All of them grew up devoted to Ireland and their mother, but at odds with their father – except perhaps the youngest, Bertie, the sole beneficiary, in 1938, of Henry's will. Henry was not likeable. Even if he failed to manifest the backstreet truculence attributable to his brothers, Henry possessed a nasty feral streak of his own (according to his grandson Harry Tipping), and would sometimes incite his sons to bash one another in the face, this being his idea of fun. The sons were great pals, as it happened, and if they went along with this, it really was only a game as far as they were concerned. Family solidarity was strongly developed in this branch of the Tippings – with father in his brown grocer's overall, maybe, excluded from its benefits. (Though Henry did stick up for his sons when they got into trouble, as we shall see.) The girls in particular had no cause to love their father, whose position on women's rights was not advanced. Despite this, I think, Mary Anne Dowds kept her husband more or less in order, and exerted as much of a civilising influence in the home as she could manage.

Outside the home, other, enlightening, nationalist and cultural influences were mustering. In 1892, in a lecture delivered to the Irish Literary Society in Dublin, you had the Protestant *Gaelegoir* Douglas Hyde calling for the total 'de-anglicisation' of Ireland, and, in furtherance of this object, going on to found the Gaelic League (with a little help from Glenarm man Eoin MacNeill, and others). It was a crucial moment in the history of Ireland: 'I have said again and again,' wrote Padraig Pearse, 'that when the Gaelic League was founded the Irish revolution began.' The existing Henry Tippings were only babies at the time, too young to sit up and take note of what was happening in the sphere of nationalist politics; but for reasons of birthright, location and so on, they were predestined to be responsive to all the exhilarating forces coming at them from various directions.

The first of the family, Anne Theresa, was born in 1888. Once she'd come of age, the eldest Tipping daughter washed her hands of Lurgan and its turmoil by emigrating to Rhodesia and passing out of this story. (She kept in touch with her family, though.) A batch of brothers followed the birth of Anne Theresa, starting with Matt in 1890 and interspersed with Lily, May and Monica (Monny). By the time the oldest were into their teens and twenties, an Irish cultural revival was dominating the social climate of the day. Just after the turn of the century, people like the young Quaker nationalist Bulmer Hobson were flocking to join the junior branch of the burgeoning Gaelic League which met in a hall in Albert Street in Belfast, poring over Irish-language primers to the detriment of their nerves and eyesight, and flinging themselves with abandon into violent games of hurling at the back of the old Falls Park. The *caman* – hurling stick – became a symbol of a new and exuberant nationalist *aithbheodhchaint*.[2]

Some time during 1902, and in collaboration with Constance Markievicz, Bulmer Hobson conceived a brainchild, Na Fianna Éireann – an organisation geared to train up boys, North and South, in the ways of patriotic thought and activism. (It only got going in the North after 1910.) The young Lurgan Tippings got themselves enrolled in the local Fianna branch as soon as they were of an age to do so, and joined with a will in its marches, merrymaking, and Gaelic games. I don't know if any of them ever became adept Irish-speakers, but they were great at Gaelic football. They were energetic goalkeepers, players and administrators of the team known as the Lurgan Davitts. All were deeply attuned to the Fianna's *raison d'être*, which – here comes an irony – was devised by a Protestant Irishman as a strenuous riposte to the Catholic Boys' Brigades which functioned at the time as a kind of recruiting centre for the British Army.[43]

Hobson's biographer, Marnie Hay, tells a story about the young Quaker taking over a class of boys in a building attached to St Paul's Church on the Falls Road in Belfast, and proceeding to dun into their more or less attentive heads the Lord's Prayer in Irish. He had them chanting away in unison, '*Ar nAthair ata i Neamh ...*', while people passing by in Cavendish Street outside wearing shawls and caps might have wondered what the hell was going on. Marnie Hay records the surprise of the St Paul's curate on entering the classroom and finding a *Protestant* engaged in this activity.

He needn't have been surprised, really. It was Protestants who saved the language when native Catholic Irish-speakers were desperate to gain a bit of fluency in English and rise in the world. It was Protestants, by and large, who had the leisure and resources to go about the work of collecting and preservation. They were rectors' sons like Douglas Hyde, businessmen like Robert MacAdam, or ex-Trinity students like Samuel Ferguson, whose commitment to Gaelic culture *and* unionist politics has often been remarked. Ferguson acknowledged absolutely no incompatibility between the two. The term that quickly came into being was 'cultural nationalism', with the unspoken exclusion from it of any political follow-up.

If you'd been around, say, in the fifty years between 1870 and 1920, you might have found it a bit of a strain to grapple with all the overlapping, contradictory, competing, evolving and ingrained versions of Irishness floating around in the public sphere. First of all you had the fundamental divisions, Protestant and Catholic. ('Not men and women in an Irish street,' William Allingham lamented, 'but Protestants and Catholics you meet.') But being Protestant, in many people's eyes, needn't debar you from proclaiming an Irish identity, being a Gaelic-speaking aficionado or embracing separatism (to whatever degree). There were liberal Protestants and diehard Protestants (I'll get to the latter shortly). Among Catholic nationalists were many who welcomed the enlistment of non-Catholics to the national cause, holding fast to Wolfe Tone's idea of an inclusive nation. They thought it didn't matter what faith, or non-faith, you subscribed or didn't subscribe to, as long as you had the good of the country at heart. But then there were others for whom the concept of being Irish was absolutely entwined with Catholicism, who believed you couldn't be one without professing the other. And it mattered that you were a 'cradle Catholic' of impeccable lineage like my great-grandmother Ellen Jordan, rather than simply adopting the faith like the renegade Leslie of Castle Leslie in County Monaghan (say) who changed his name from John to Shane and went about clad in a saffron kilt.

The Church had for some time been increasing its hold over its adherents, and by the turn of the century it had many of them in its vulturine grip. In 1902, an actual 'Catholic Association' came into being to oppose Protestant influences and impose a priestly formulation on cultural activities (let alone daily activities). Clear the way for D.P. Moran and his 'Irish-Ireland' movement. 'The Irish nation is de facto a Catholic nation,' the author of *The Philosophy of Irish-Ireland* unequivocally declared. Short shrift was given in this philosophy to Yeats's and Lady Gregory's campaign to add dignity to Ireland in the face of ongoing 'Paddy-and-shillelagh' slurs. A different brand of dignity, decidedly church-based if not positively awash in holy water, was postulated by Moran's Irish-Irelanders. It might be embodied in pious peasants or dressed-up ecclesiarchs. But it didn't reside in emblems extracted from sagas and folk-tales – perish the pagan thought – or in a cornucopia of crepuscular allurements. The literary achievement of the Revivalists was beside the point when the spirit of the nation eluded their best efforts. The Catholic spirit of the nation.

It isn't too hard to understand the resistance of Orange Ulster to all this, or even to accord a little, just a little, credence to the slogan of the day: Home Rule is Rome Rule. But alas, the Orange version of ethnic identity carried an obduracy and intolerance all its own. Clear the way, again, for Sir Edward Carson and his Ulster Volunteers recruited from Orange Lodges and geared to the fullest extent to withstand any impulse in Ireland towards democracy. You can see the shade of the 'No Surrender' bard William Blacker presiding over Protestant preparations for defiance, when it seemed the spectre of Home Rule was about to become a reality.

What form did these preparations take? First you had 'Ulster Day', 1912, when a 'Solemn League and Covenant' against Home Rule was signed by nearly half a million Ulster men and women, all afire with loyalist indignation. Ulster Volunteers take over local fields, set up rifle ranges in them, and practise shooting in anticipation of a civil war. They wear badges proclaiming 'No Surrender'. The future poet George Buchanan, eight years old at the time, observes these activities going on in the vicinity of Larne where his father is a Protestant rector. 'Ping-ping! The shots strike the targets. The Volunteers are learning how to kill.'[4] A short time later comes the famous gun-running episode of April 1914, when arms and ammunition from Germany are brought ashore at various seaports along the northern coast. George Buchanan continues his lively account:

> ... all through the night, on the road beside the rectory, we can hear the cars and we can see the trees constantly illumined by their headlamps. In the morning it is understood that an extraordinary event has occurred. A ship from Germany landed a cargo of arms at Larne Harbour. The police barracks were surrounded and the telephone wires cut. Already the arms have been distributed to points through the province, some being concealed under chancel floors in Protestant churches.

But the wind is taken out of anti-Home Rule sails by overwhelming events occurring elsewhere. It's 1914, and an entire world war is about to engulf the nations. The Protestant sons of Ulster, jettisoning their Orange outrage for the moment, rush to enlist in the British Army – which only a month or so earlier they'd planned to engage in battle – and distinguish themselves at the Somme and other major theatres of conflict. So do thousands of Irish Catholics, among them my grandfather Brady – though in deference to a nationalist imperative he enlists with the Dublin Fusiliers rather than any of the Ulster regiments. He does so in the company of Lurgan friends and connections-by-marriage, including his wife's half-nephew two times over, Henry and Mary Anne's son Frank Tipping. I believe these innocent recruits would all have regarded the prospect of training and fighting as something of a lark, before hell set in around them. I think of the Heaney poem about Francis Ledwidge, the 'Tommy's uniform', the 'haunted Catholic face, pallid and brave'. Some of the Lurgan army boys with their Catholic faces came home to tell the ghastly story, and some, like my grandfather, didn't.

A few months earlier, in the autumn of 1913, the Irish Volunteers had come into being as a counterblast to Carson's Ulster Volunteers. While the latter were motivated by the most implacable determination 'to resist Home Rule to the very death, [and] keep "the Covenant of God"',[5] the former held fast to the primary purpose of fighting for Ireland. Some among the Irish Volunteers achieved this purpose, when 1916 came around; while others, like their Ulster Protestant counterparts, though from an entirely different standpoint, were undergoing bombardment elsewhere. I don't want to go into the reasons why, after 1914, some Irish Volunteers joined the British Army without relinquishing their nationalist principles, while others stuck to their republican guns. Most of us know the reasons, and the outcome, the uneasy resolution imposed on the country by the Government of Ireland Act of 1920. As many historians have pointed out – with more or less glee – what unionists acquired after 1922 was a version of the Home Rule against which, with so much hullabaloo, they had previously set their faces.

On the scale of ironies, though, that's only about halfway up. It was the *nationalist* version they'd resisted, and that had been warded off, even if the terms of the eventual compromise were thoroughly satisfactory to no one. On the subject of ironies – here's another which I can't resist noting, having come across it while reading Jonathan Bardon's *History of Ulster*.

It concerns Sir Edward Carson and *his* muddled family. It was a cousin of Carson's, I learn, called Maire Butler, a member of the Gaelic League, who coined the imperishable term 'Sinn Féin'. And, '...we in Ulster will tolerate no Sinn Féin,' thunders Carson in 1920, addressing an assembly of twenty-five thousand Orangemen, 'no Sinn Féin organisation, no Sinn Féin methods ...'. The comforting solidarity of 'Ourselves', it seems, can accommodate or repudiate whomever it pleases. ... But we needn't be surprised by anomalies of consanguinity, which pop up to intrigue us all over the place, once we start to look for them. Take another pair of unlikely cousins, Charles Stewart Parnell and Sir Basil Brooke[6] – and then imagine yourself located somewhere above the whole cat's cradle of Irish affairs, looking down in bemusement.

As for the subject of my immediate interest, my own family connections: half of them were signing the Covenant at the appropriate moment, while the other half were shaping up to be republican activists. (All right, I'm simplifying things to underscore the point.) My Craig grandfather certainly celebrated 'Ulster Day', at least in spirit,[7] along with his father and brothers. But the outbreak of war with Germany placed him in a double bind. He didn't volunteer to join the British Army – well, how could he? He was half-German himself and disinclined, I am sure, to take up arms against his close relations. I don't even know if he was eligible for army service, given his background. But I do know that no hint of 'Hun' affiliations would have passed his lips, or those of his children.

One of the most cogent and entertaining discussions of confusion and complexity in Ulster politics was published in 1919, and has long been out of print. It is James Winder Good's *Ulster and Ireland*. I've already alluded to this study here and there, and I applaud it again for its adept engagement with contemporary – and perennial – issues, and for its liberal stance. It employs the kind of logic that undermines ideological idiocies. I recommend it to any student of Ulster inconsistencies. The mode in which it is written is that of satirical common sense. For example, when Good points out that 'during the progress of the Home Rule controversy the unionist case has been twisted right round', you want to stand up and cheer. First, in his speeches, Sir Edward Carson expressed vehement sentiments culled from Fitzgibbon and Castlereagh, but before the thing was over, Good says, 'his denial of the right of British statesmen to intervene in Ulster was uncompromising and passionate enough to have satisfied Wolfe Tone himself'. Sinn Féin Abu.

And here is my own fundamental contention in a nutshell. Compiling a list of speakers on a Protestant platform, all of them immersed to the hilt in the business of preserving Ulster's Orange integrity, Good is surprised – or perhaps not surprised – to find names like Maguire, Murphy, Quinn, Moriarty, MacNeill, O'Neill and O'Donnell occurring over and over among the denouncers of 'Romanism' and Fenianism. The names themselves, he says, 'are the best refutation of the doctrines their bearers preached'. Quite so.[8] And just occasionally, against the grain of Ulster fixity, you find the bearer of such a name endowed with sufficient aplomb to revel in the contradictions thereby adumbrated. I'm thinking of someone like the nineteenth-century anti-Papist firebrand cleric Dr Kane, Grand Master of an Orange lodge and pioneering member of the Gaelic League. 'My Orangeism,' Kane said (quoted by Good), 'does not make me any less proud to be an O'Cahan.' And an even more thoroughgoing proponent of the eccentricities-of-allegiance school of behaviour was the lawyer John Rea (c.1822–1881), whose Belfast house sported Orange and Green flags flying side by side, no doubt to the bewilderment of his neighbours. At one moment, Rea appears at the head of a procession of Orangemen asserting their right to public assembly and free speech, and at the next moment, mounted on a horse and waving a green flag, he's leading nationalists engaged in a similar demonstration. John Rea's label for himself, 'her Orthodox Presbyterian Britannic Majesty's Orange-Fenian Attorney-General for Ulster', might put us in mind of Walt Whitman's 'Do I contradict myself? Very well then, I contradict myself, / I am large, I contain multitudes'.[9] Alas, the general run of Ulster's larger-than-life figures were all on the side of their own preferred faction.

The exceptions like John Rea are heartening, but they're only exceptions. They do, however, recur from time to time to bolster the sense of limitless possibilities in Ulster affairs. Alongside the sticklers for sects are those who refuse to be constrained by factional requirements of any kind. Like Dr Kane before him, Frank McCollum of County Antrim was Grand Master of an Orange Lodge in the 1960s, and at the same time chairman of the Irish Musicians' Association, Comhaltas Ceoltóiri Éireann, when a branch of the latter was established in his home town of Ballycastle. Well, traditional music, as the fiddle-player Alex Kerr was fond of pointing out, 'knows no border, nor no creed'.[10] This is true, or ought to be true, but immediately a contradiction arises when you consider the effect of certain 'traditional' party tunes on the tempers and dispositions of clashing partisans. Anything, *anything* native to Ulster can be turned to an integrating or a disintegrating purpose.

As the stuff of fiction, the Home Rule crisis of the early twentieth century engendered one outstanding work, a narrative equivalent of an aspect of *Ulster and Ireland*. It is George A. Birmingham's *The Red Hand of Ulster*, published in 1912. Birmingham's central character is an astute and genial Irish peer of the realm who observes with a certain playful detachment the complete volte-face overtaking rival camps whose standpoints vis-à-vis Great Britain have somehow got interchanged. For example, a character in the novel is an ardent Sinn Féiner who, having sought out the most potent source of rebellion against Britain and locating it amongst the unionists of the North, cheerfully accepts the editorship of a 'loyalist' newspaper. And all around him, loyalists are tying themselves in knots in the effort to assert their loyalty to Britain at the same time as disembarrassing themselves of it. And, once the refusal of Home Rule is backed by a demand for a complete British withdrawal from Ireland, a state of semantic deadlock is brought about, and the author has tremendous fun with this and all the other egregious anomalies which make up his theme.

It's not the first time the sectarian instinct in Northern Ireland has had salutary fun poked at it. You will find, for example, a wonderful set-piece in William Carleton's novel of 1843, *Valentine McClutchy*. It exploits to the full the farcical element in sectarian inflexibility. What Carleton presents to his readers is a pair of complementary converts, an ex-Catholic Protestant and his ex-Protestant counterpart. Both men are bursting with new-found zeal and quickly square up to one another as the author brings them face-to-face. However, in the course of the ensuing argument, each man involuntarily reverts to his original theological position. The one-time Orangeman atavistically curses the pope, while the supposed ex-Catholic comes out as a Papist partisan. By this stage a crowd of supporters has gathered, an equal number of Prods and Taigs, and, Carleton tells us, 'the Catholics, ignorant of the turn which the controversy had taken, supported Bob and Protestantism; while the Protestants, owing to a similar mistake, fought like devils for

Darby and the Pope.' It is hard to think of a more telling indictment of the whole incorrigible business, or one more drily expressed.

But these are works of fiction, you may say, whose impact would not amount to much among hardliners in the streets of Lurgan or Belfast. Well, yes, but such things work, or should work, both in cumulative and subliminal ways, and at the very least suggest a structure for thoughtful, rather than instinctive, action. There are truths to be found in books which may filter down even to the non-reading public – even to the illiterate.

It's likely that my grandmother's parents, and her older half-siblings, could read but not write (unlike her father's country cousins, who were adept at both); but she herself was fully literate, as I can testify: a skill she owed to a short and piecemeal education with the Mercy nuns of Edward Street.[11] According to the census of 1901, the previously jam-packed house in John Street had dwindled by that date to three occupants: Matthew and Ellen Tipping, and their daughter Sarah. Sarah's age is given as nineteen, and her occupation as 'veiner' (that is, a person sewing veins in flowers decorating pieces of muslin, probably a factory job). ... Move around the corner to 37 Edward Street, and here you find a whole family of reading-and-writing Bradys, plus three old aunts named McManus who seem to have lived with them. I assume these were Terence Brady's maiden aunts on his mother's side,[12] since his wife Catherine's relations, as we've seen, were not conspicuous about the place, or at least not acknowledged as such. ... Here is the oldest Brady son William, also aged nineteen and a plasterer by trade. (His nearest brother James – Jim – is a draper's assistant, though at some point, I think, 'Uncle Jim' gains experience as a soldier with the British Army.)

Like the Tippings, the Bradys are ardently Catholic, and this means the courtship of William and Sarah is conducted at church-hall dances and ceilidhes, fund-raising concerts, outings organised by St Peter's Church and in the company of co-religionists. Do they ever duck out of priestly and family supervision and get away by themselves? Probably, for I don't doubt the pair of them were properly spirited young people, despite the pinched and seedy circumstances surrounding them. My grandmother was always one for a good laugh. And she's already been complicit in the elopement of her friend Minnie Cochrane (with a boy called Thornberry), whose luggage she helped deposit on the Belfast train.

Other escapades I have no knowledge of, but I'm sure they took place. My grandmother was voluble and filled with strong opinions. When I was fifteen or sixteen, she advised me to go about only with good-looking friends, lest those of unattractive appearance should drive boys away. (Or maybe she meant I needed a counterbalance to my unglamorous looks.) She wasn't a gadabout, I think, being always conscious of life's serious aspects. But she enjoyed gossip, as well as taking an interest in events of the wider world (and reading detective novels). She followed the Suez crisis and understood the implications of the death of Stalin. She wore smart coats and hats with veils.

Young Sarah Tipping and William Brady have the whole of Lurgan Park to go wrong in – not that I think they did – not to mention the shores of Lough Neagh, or the fields and country byways surrounding their grim home town. I can't say what drew them together, never having known my grandfather, but he'd have needed a certain robust self-assurance to go after the redoubtable Miss Tipping (she was still redoubtable in my day, though life had knocked a good deal of the undauntedness out of her). They were married in April 1902. She remembered washing her hair on the morning of her wedding day, and drying it in front of the kitchen fire. If she wasn't pregnant at the time – and I don't think she was – she quickly became so. The newly-weds had moved in with her parents at John Street, and there their first daughter Elizabeth – Lily – was born in January 1903 (nine months almost to the day).

She was followed by Ellen, or Elly – later Eileen – ('It was a cynical babe'[13]) two years later; then came Mary Joseph (Molly, or 'Ructions'), sweet-natured Catherine (Kathleen), and finally my mother Nora Theresa in June 1913. At some point – probably after 1910 when Sarah's father Matthew Tipping dropped dead in the street, causing consternation ('Dear God this holy day and hour') – the younger Bradys had installed themselves in a house in Edward Street: a better house, still opening on to the pavement, but with stairs leading up to an attic (as my mother recalled it). A few doors away lived Sarah's sister Ellen, also called Brady, and *her* expanding family (nine in all). To the David Brady household was added the widowed Ellen Tipping, who lived on until 1927. So: in Lurgan's Edward Street were domiciled two cousins – David Brady and William Brady – married to two sisters – Ellen Tipping and Sarah Tipping; also resident in the same significant street was a whole different bunch of double-kin: the Henry Tipping tribe (I hope you have all this clear in your head). All were in the grip of ideological grievances, coupled with a bit of blissful ignorance. As we've seen, all of them exemplified some undisclosed dilution of the Catholic, 'true-Gaelic' line.

Times were hard. There was no way round incessant scrimping and saving. A plasterer's wage wasn't adequate to keep body and soul together, not in a household consisting of seven anyway. And work for the breadwinner was not always available. So the call for British Army volunteers, when it came, fell on receptive ears. It was suddenly permissible for Irish nationalists to align themselves with Britain in the worldwide 'fight for freedom'. The expectation was that Home Rule would come out of it ('For England may keep faith ...'[14]). And never mind that a contradictory expectation sustained huge numbers of Ulster unionist volunteers.

Frank Tipping[15] was eighteen years old when he joined the 6th Dublin Fusiliers along with his Aunt Sarah's husband William Brady. Frank's son Brian Tipping later recalled his father's support for John Redmond, and his belief in the rightness of the Irish Parliamentary Party's pledge to join in the conflict on the side of England. The Redmondite 'National Volunteers', twenty-seven thousand of them, had come round to the new way of thinking. But the change of heart was not universal. Irish Volunteers held fast to the old, anti-British, separatist ideal. Their flag was hoisted under the slogan, 'England's difficulty is Ireland's opportunity'. Their path was set towards 1916 and the Easter Rising.

When it came to the bit, a fair number of Irish recruits may have been uncertain about what exactly it was they were fighting for, and how it chimed with nationalist aspirations. What had Salonika and the Dardanelles to do with Ireland and conditions at home ...? For this heat-scorched, utterly alien territory was the place the 6th Dublin Fusiliers found themselves in 1915, and where Frank Tipping sustained a leg wound in the fighting around Suvla Bay.

I don't know if my grandfather ever had a chance to go at an actual enemy, after all the months of training. He may have evaded involvement in combat activity by dying too soon. It wasn't only on the battlefields that casualties by the hundreds and thousands occurred. *The War Diary of an Irish Soldier*,[16] by Captain David Campbell, tells a shocking story of non-existent hygiene among the troops in the Dardanelles, plagues of insects, ants and flies unavoidably swallowed in droves along with bread and bully beef. Dysentery, Captain Campbell says, played havoc with the Irish battalions, and William Brady – perhaps lacking a strong constitution to begin with – fell a victim to it. There's a grave bearing his name and the date, 14 September 1915, in the Military and War Memorial Cemetery in Alexandria, though among some of his descendants a belief exists that he died and was buried at sea. I have his wedding ring on my finger. It was returned to his widow, who gave it to her youngest daughter; and when she died, it came to me.

Nineteen fifteen has been described as the year of the telegrams, as postmen burdened with appalling news knocked at door after door. To Edward Street in Lurgan in due course comes one of these ominous messengers, and life thereafter for the William Brady family assumes a stricken and savourless character. But my grandmother Sarah Tipping – like *her* great-grandmother Sarah Magee – has reserves of stoicism which she summons up to help her adjust to her new and unwelcome identity: war widow. Instead of a husband, a partner and helpmeet in the upbringing of five young daughters aged between twelve and two, she has a solid bronze medal, four and three-quarter inches in diameter, inscribed with her husband's name and the legend, 'He Died for Freedom and Honour'. Freedom and honour, *mar 'eadh*. 'Dead Men's Pennies' was the name the irreverent gave these medals. And in Catholic Lurgan, the thing was an ambiguous token.

My Catholic, Irish-nationalist grandfather gave his life for England. That much is indisputable – but no uplifting rhetoric of the 'Tell England' variety was available to mitigate the bereavement of his and all the other Irish war widows. 'Know that we fools, now with the foolish dead,' Tom Kettle wrote,

> Died not for flag, nor crown, nor emperor,
> But for a dream, born in a herdsman's shed,
> And for the secret scripture of the poor.

Dying for England was one thing, and an equivocal thing, dying for Ireland another. Easter 1916 came with all its confusion, upheaval and glory, and when the Rising was quelled and its leaders executed, there were those in the Irish battalions fighting in the First World War who wondered if they'd made the right decision. Popular songs like 'The Foggy Dew' took up the theme of bravely but mistakenly transferred loyalties:

'Twas England bade our Wild Geese go,
That small nations might be free;
But their lonely graves are by Suvla's waves,
Or the fringe of the great North Sea.
Oh, had they died by Pearse's side,
Or fought with Cathal Brugha,
Their names we'd keep, where the Fenians sleep,
'Neath the hills in the foggy dew.

When I was fifteen or thereabouts I had an old 78 record of this and other rebel songs which I played over and over on a second-hand record-player in the front room of our red-brick, semi-detached house at 551 Donegall Road, Belfast. These songs made my hair stand on end. 'All Around my Hat I Wear the Tri-Coloured Ribbon-O' – I did indeed, at least in a metaphorical sense. Like John Hewitt's grandmother with her cache of poems, I had images, clipped from newspapers, of Padraig Pearse and other 1916 leaders which I carried around in my purse, until they eventually fell to pieces.

My single-minded admiration for every proponent of an Ireland free and Gaelic and unique and righteous eventually fell to pieces too, but not before it had bitten pretty deep into my psyche. Revisionism made sense when I became aware of it in later life, but during the romantic-Irish years I vastly preferred the crepuscular view, the clandestine affiliation, the unimpeachable cause. I remember a ferocious argument with some would-be cynical schoolboys over the integrity or otherwise of the hanged republican Kevin Barry. 'He was eighteen years old,' I hear myself shouting, 'he died, actually died, for his beliefs, and you can stand there making excuses for his executioners ...'. Call yourselves Irish, I probably went on, before stomping off in a temper, utterly unaware of the extent to which I myself was, or was not, entitled to call myself Irish.

Like mine, like George Watson's (see p. xix above), my mother's cultural confusions were among the greatest blessings of her life. The literature of England, high and low, was for all of us a refuge, a source of pleasure and enlightenment, an inestimable resource. A bibliophile propensity overtook us early. 'Delight in books' was our unspoken motto. Without books, we'd have languished unconsolably. An unimaginable deprivation would have eaten away at us. Books were a necessity, not a luxury as our forebears might have regarded them.

We had our different areas of enthralment, of course, along with a good deal of overlap. My poetry-enthusiast mother really appreciated very little poetry after Yeats. With some exceptions, 'moderns' such as Eliot and Auden left her cold. She was more attuned to Keats and Shelley than the Byron of 'Don Juan'. And Tennyson: 'glamour', for her, meant 'The Lady of Shalott,' 'embowered' within her 'four grey walls and four grey towers'. Certain lines by James Ellroy Flecker, from 'The Old Ships' and 'The Golden Journey to Samarkand', made her hair stand on end. The exotic-narcotic cadences perfected by this poet easily overwhelmed me too, whenever I gave myself up to them: '...for Famagusta and the hidden sun, / That rings black Cyprus with a lake of fire ...'. Famagusta: it's a far cry from Lurgan jeers and brawls and backyards and chilblains and the waterlogged Head of the Plain. ... Then, my range of children's reading was considerably wider than my mother's had been (more was available in the 1950s), but both of us, at different times, were addicts of Greyfriars School and the incomparable doings of Harry Wharton and Co. She rather liked historical fiction of the Margaret Irwin–Jane Lane variety, about which I took a slightly snooty tone (it was different if it was *Irish* historical fiction, when the subject would win out over any perceived stylistic infelicity). She revered Graham Greene rather more than I did, while my detective novels – Christie, Sayers, Nicholas Blake – didn't hold much appeal for her. We both liked humorous verse, and local verse, and Scottish ballads, and poets of the First World War. With the last, though, I opted for Owen and Sassoon, and she for Rupert Brooke.

There was a personal reason for that. Her father had died a death as inglorious as Rupert Brooke's, in the same year and in the same part of the world, committed to the same cause. Frances Cornford's tribute to Brooke, beginning, 'A young Apollo, golden-haired ...' caught my mother's imagination. That the poetry of Brooke was saturated in Englishness didn't matter a jot: it was lyrical and elegiac and accessible, and composed in a spirit she found it easy to respond to. 'Just now the lilac is in bloom, / All outside my little room.' *It rhymed.* Also, and it probably wasn't even a conscious transference, I imagine a tinge of the glamour attaching to the person, and the poetry, of Rupert Brooke became associated, in my mother's mind, with her own dead father. Since she'd never known him, she was free to attribute to her missing father whatever traits she chose.

Not that she ever talked about him; no one talked about him, to me at least. I used to think my grandmother's silence on the subject of her husband's death betokened indifference: now I think the opposite was true. It was simply too painful to make a topic for casual comment. And the pain didn't go away as time passed: other pain got added to it. When I was growing up, I'd have found it hard to envisage my grandmother *with* a husband: she seemed essentially to stand alone, a bit aloof, not liking to be touched, slightly detached from the routines of our small household, of which she was a part. (My child's-eye view was faulty, of course; my grandmother's domestic and financial acumen contributed greatly to all our well-being.) As for my lost grandfather ... as far as I am concerned, he disappeared into a void, leaving virtually no tangible mementoes of his existence: no photos, possessions, autographs, marks of identification. Only the ring on my finger and the Dead Man's Penny in the drawer upstairs. No repeated anecdotes illumined his character or passed into family lore. As far as I know, only a solitary saying of his has survived, preserved in the memory of his second daughter. It relates to the children. 'Make them do as they're bid,' he would say, as infantile chaos threatened to overwhelm the house, 'make them do as they're bid.' It isn't much of a pointer to the texture of a life.

Nineteen hundred and fifteen. Within the close-knit, extended Lurgan family circle, my grandmother isn't the only person to suffer an annihilating blow. Catherine Harland had already lost her husband Terence Brady earlier in the year, and now comes the terrible news of the death of her oldest son. It may have been the double affliction that drove her to drink (as we've seen, above). But, at the time, like everyone else connected to the Edward Street William Brady family, she rallied and suppressed her emotions for the sake of the children. The newly fatherless children were the focus of everyone's attention. Catherine, the dressmaker, sewed clothes for them and sometimes had them for breakfast on their way to school. She made them porridge, which they hated, but were too polite to refuse. On one occasion at least, the porridge went into a pocket, to the detriment of the new, exquisitely worked clothes. ... Perhaps a resolve was entered into to ensure that all the young Bradys should thrive, in spite of everything. It didn't work entirely, but considerable goodwill was there. And the baby Nora in particular came in for a lot of cosseting and indulgence.

But my grandmother was defeated by Christmas. Between poverty and bereavement, she had no cause to love its overcharged atmosphere. I doubt if much of a festive spirit prevailed at 26 Edward Street, in the first year following William Brady's death, or later. A packet of sweets, a couple of oranges or tangerines in a stocking, was all each child could hope for. But again, an exception was made for Nora. The year she was five or six (she remembered), the entire family left the house on Christmas Eve and walked up the town to a toy shop to buy her a doll. I see them proceeding in single file, in their dark winter coats, like an illustration from an annual – *Blackie's Children's Annual*, say – the mother striding ahead and the straggle of daughters following, all for a stupendous purpose. The Christmas tree lit up with fairy lights in the town centre, the carol singers in the streets, would have added to the pungency of the occasion. In later life, I think, all of them to some extent made a thing of despising Christmas. But in that one year at least, a little of the magic of the season was vouchsafed to them.

My mother related another childhood incident, a grimmer one. She is still around five or six, and she has a bosom friend, a little girl of her own age: let's call her Bridie. Bridie lives nearby. Some streets away – Black's Court, perhaps? – in an unkempt kitchen house, lives a friend these two have in common, a motherless girl whose father and older sisters neglect her shockingly. We'll call this one Sheila. My grandmother does not approve of Nora's friendship with Sheila, due to the family's bad reputation. There is even a suggestion that Sheila's older sisters may supplement the family income by engaging in a bit of amateur whoring, bringing into play a dark and slatternly side of Lurgan life. But Nora sticks up for her friend, and she and Bridie are often at Sheila's house. It's a great venue for childish carry-on: no grown-ups to put a damper on things.

One day, a group of four or five small girls, including Nora and Bridie, has gathered for the purpose of play in Sheila's kitchen. At one point they take a notion to wash dolls' clothes. They are being serious and aping the domesticity of grown-ups. The clothes are duly washed in the sink with everyone lending a hand, and then hung up around the open fire to dry. Nora, wiping her hands on a dirty old kitchen towel, suddenly remembers she's promised to be home by a certain time, and needs to leave at once. The others try to persuade her to stay on. But she knows she'll be in trouble if she doesn't get back when she said she would. She lets herself out by the front door and runs through the streets, arriving out of breath in time for her tea. Some hours later comes the news that Sheila's house has burnt to the ground and everyone in it. Sheila, Bridie and the others – all burnt to a cinder. I don't know if Nora drew from this horrendous event a moral lesson about obedience, if she felt later that she, the survivor, had been singled out for some celestial purpose, if the Catholic faith made a way of assimilating and assuaging the tragedy. *I don't want to take a moral tone about it.* But it must have alerted her, at a frighteningly early age, to the unutterable fragility of existence.

No doubt my grandmother went down on her knees and thanked Providence for steering her youngest child away from an inferno. But Providence has yet a diabolical trick up its sleeve. Some time during the autumn of 1922, nineteen-year-old Lily Brady complains of abdominal pains. She becomes feverish. The pains escalate. A frenzy of anxiety engulfs the house. It's no small matter, in those pre-National Health days, to summon a doctor: but a doctor is sent for. He comes with his Gladstone bag and diagnoses a stomach ache. Has Lily eaten something that's disagreed with her? He prescribes some powders or pills and goes on his way. Some time later, before the horrified eyes of her mother and sisters, Lily dies of a burst appendix. Black days follow: the coffin, the priest, the rosary beads, the weeping relatives. And the terrible image in everyone's head: the back bedroom, the screaming girl, the fruitless efforts of those around her.

The date is 2 October 1922. Two days later, Lily is buried in Dougher Cemetery with the full rites of the Catholic Church. How was this death allowed to happen? I envisage my grandmother at this moment, aged forty-one and dressed in black, as a kind of '*bean caointe*' – keening woman – as in the *sean-nos* song which is rendered with such feeling by the great traditional singer Pádraigín Ní Uallacháin. The woman in the song is burying the last of her children – '*Suilfaidh me an rod seo gan lui na leapa, / Faoi mo Neilli beag mingheal 'ta sinte faoi thalamh*' ('I'll walk the roads without sleep or bed, / Since my sweet gentle Nelly is lying dead'). It's an Omeath song, but, Pádraigín Ní Uallacháin says, a version was current in south Armagh, and no doubt it would have migrated northwards. Not that my grandmother or any of her family would have known it. They weren't Irish-speakers; and, at the time, there wasn't much general interest in the heritage of Irish-language song. But there would have been an empathy with the strong emotion contained in the searing lines of 'The Keening Woman'.

Tragic Lily Brady went under the sod, and for ever after a steely silence was preserved on the topic of her life and death. It was almost as if she had never existed. Only the photo that came into her sister Eileen's possession testifies to Lily's presence in the world of factory work, huxters' shops, sectarian onslaughts, Sinn Féin activities, sisterly companionship and friction, St Peter's Church, flirtations with boys from round about, Sunday best. All the elements of intense, unexalted life. Lily's story, which can barely be imagined now, has to be fitted into what's known of early twentieth-century Lurgan, and also into a poor, or poorish, Catholic household, but one very conscious of occupying a notable position in the neighbourhood. Once the shock of sudden bereavement was over, the 'keening woman' image was not a thing my grandmother Sarah would have clung on to. She'd have hated people to associate her, or those belonging to her, with a stricken or ill-fated course in life. A needy comportment was not her métier. Within the limits of her environment, she went all out to create a sense of auspiciousness, an up-and-coming atmosphere. Perhaps it was the Blacker blood coming out in her, but what she repudiated utterly was the poor mouth. You wouldn't have caught her creeping off to the pawnshop with a shawl flung over her head, or borrowing anything from anyone. She stood on her own two feet. 'A great manager' was what her children said about her, looking back, and paying tribute to her resourcefulness in making a meagre income go a long way. No one in her care went hungry or barefoot, even if a lot of mending and making do went on.

I'm not sure if the two events are connected, but it's around the time of Lily's death, I think, that Sarah's youngest, Nora, is briefly sent to sleep across the road, in some supportive arrangement with a neighbour. Nora crosses the road to go to bed, and then returns home in the morning to eat her breakfast and set off for school. ... Am I right to read into this an instance of the impulse to protect this child from the worst of the anguish afflicting the disrupted household? I suspect a benign conspiracy, initiated by her mother, to spare the nine-year-old a too-close acquaintance with the devastating effects of death and despair. Nora is favoured, in this and other respects, in ways her sisters might have come to resent – as, indeed, at least one of them did. Between Nora and Eileen, now thrust into the position of oldest daughter, deep resentments combined with mutual

Eileen and Lily Brady (seated), *c*.1919

admiration and affection to create a complicated relationship. (When Eileen died in 1994, well into her eighties, my mother said it was the worst day of her life.) Nora's *friend* in the family was Kathleen, the closest to her in age; but for the whole of her life, her sister Eileen was among the people who meant most to her.

Once I'd gained an inkling of the circumstances surrounding this second tragedy in my mother's family[17] (information acquired not all that long ago), I held the doctor's incompetence to blame for the destruction of a promising life. I say 'promising', because that single existing image of Lily Brady shows an attractive, composed, intelligent girl, seated on a chair in some photographer's studio, while her considerably less well-adjusted sister Eileen stands grimly by her side. Eileen's expression suggests she's about to burst into tears, that she's having her photo taken very much against her will. It's clear that she would rather be anywhere else in the world than standing mutinously there beside her self-possessed sister. And in a way, this discontent with her lot was a marker for the rest of her life. Like my mother – and not, perhaps, like the two middle sisters – Eileen would have benefited from an education, but, after primary level, one was not available to her. Every step she tried to take to further her own interests was thwarted in some way. From an early age, she developed a sense that the world was against her. She developed, too, a good line in glares, some of which were directed half-humorously at those around her. Eileen had a formidable presence – and being aggrieved, pragmatic and good-natured all at once endowed her, at the very least, with an interesting personality.

I blamed the doctor for Lily's death: but it seems, at the time, it was fatally easy to confuse the symptoms of appendicitis with those of a lesser ailment. It was a matter of carrying out a cursory examination and hoping for the best. But you can't get away from the fact that a more conscientious or enlightened doctor would have got the sick girl to a hospital in time to save her life. She didn't have to die, but she did die, leaving a ruptured and grieving household behind her. That year, 1922, saw a deeper than ever repudiation of the follies of Christmas among the North Street[18] Bradys. The house was wrapped in darkness and lamentation. But gradually, very gradually, a slight degree of optimism about the future revived. It was tied up with Catholic neighbourhood solidarity, with continuing support from concerned relations, especially the large contingent of Brady cousins nearby (Sarah's sister's lot), and with the emerging scholarly abilities of the youngest child of the family, for whom the nuns of her primary school had high hopes.

The background to all the home-front adversity was a town awash in dissension and bigotry. The children going to Mass on St Patrick's Day were preyed upon by gangs of jeering Protestant contemporaries who tore the shamrock from their lapels. Reciprocal aggravations: I think of my great-uncle Jim Brady drilling Irish Volunteers up and down Edward Street under the noses of old-established enemies (how did he get away with it?). Irish Volunteers – but, as it happened, Great-Uncle Jim was a British Army veteran. His sister-in-law, my grandmother, was a Dardanelles widow. Poppy Day in the future put her in a quandary. Confusions concerning questions of loyalty and allegiance proliferated. When the Treaty was signed in December 1921 my grandmother thought something momentous had been achieved – only to be put right by her Tipping relations who were holding out for a united Ireland. She'd hung out a tricolour in celebration: but some of her half-brothers and their sons came to her home in a rage and told her to take it in to hell's gates out of that. There was no cause for jubilation: nationalists in the North had been sold down the river. The War of Independence – total independence – would continue.

Thinking about a particular period – the years between 1910 and 1920, say – and trying to place myself within a web of family and extended family connections, I'm brought up against so many diametric opposites that it seems a wonder I wasn't cancelled out before I got started. Pro-Home Rulers and anti-Home Rulers, Carsonites and Redmondites and revolutionaries, those for and against British Army enlistment, subversives and conservatives and (mostly female) minders-of-their-own-business, unequivocal and ambivalent supporters of the war effort.[19] ... The war effort. Here an extra anomaly of a personal character enters into the family history narrative. While my Brady grandfather was, with however many reservations, committed to fight on the side of the British, direct descendants of my Heller great-great-grandparents were fighting on the other, the German side. There's scope here for a stranger meeting than Wilfred Owen's.

However, if the end product of chance and interfusion (myself) adds up to a bundle of genetic and ideological inconsistencies, it's an admixture – in my case and everyone else's – for which there is a good deal to be said. It should (though it doesn't always happen) exclude the possibility of fanaticism and discredit the chimera of a 'pure' bloodline, of any coloration whatever. As I've said before – and I make no apology for saying it again – all of our bloodlines in the north of Ireland are very likely to be tempered by a bit of the other strain – whichever that is, and whether it pleases us to know it, or doesn't please us.

CHAPTER 7
A BAD LOT

'There was a man shot in the tram I was in,' said Colm.

'There was a woman shot stone dead on the other side of the street. There's a sniper on the mill all the mornin' and you daren't put your nose out the door.'

Shots crackled fiercely and the man instinctively ducked his head.

'Jesus, Mary and Joseph!' said the woman, blessing herself. 'That's near.'

Michael McLaverty, *Call My Brother Back*

Violence comes in cycles, say historians. But sometimes it comes *on* cycles.

Harry Tipping

It's worth taking note of the bicycle's role in the business of fostering revolution. All over Ireland, in the years between 1916 and 1923 (say), you might have spotted figures in trench coats cycling in all weathers through boggy back roads or mountain passes, up and down hills, dripping wet, sweltering in the heat, more often than not on borrowed machines with perhaps defective brakes, misshapen saddles or a buckled rim. They were all at it: Tom Barry living, before reliving, his *Guerrilla Days in Ireland*, Sean Treacy veering ahead with the 3rd Tipperary Brigade and going on to die by gunshot in a Dublin street, Dan Breen immersed to the hilt in his *Fight for Irish Freedom*. You had Ernie O'Malley pedalling past demesne walls with thoughts of iniquitous Big House people in his head and Pierce Ferriter's poems in his pocket. Past military road posts and fortified barracks he goes, on and on: east Clare, Waterford, Donegal, Monaghan, all the hill districts and scattered villages of west County Cork. On the roads of Cork, O'Malley might have met the student Volunteer O'Faolain, similarly mounted on a bike, on the same insurrectionary business, undeterred by the noise of machine-gun fire, the prospect of an army ambush or a convoy of Black and Tans careering round the very next bend in the road. And in his pocket, as likely as not, the poems of Yeats.

Sean O'Faolain's first collection of stories, *Midsummer Night Madness* (1932) is filled with the spirit of heroic, brutal and foolhardy undertakings in the name of Ireland free. It has old-style activists holed up in barns and outhouses, digging trenches, gathering information, dodging the enemy, scouting and skiting all over the countryside to more or less encouraging effect. Saturnine Volunteers hunched over handlebars possessed by a steely intent. And it wasn't, indeed, only men, young men, who cycled for Ireland. Carrying dispatches or ammunition, alerting IRA men on active service to dangers approaching, or hastening to lend a hand at some makeshift field hospital: these were ways in which the women of Ireland could involve themselves in the national struggle. Sean O'Faolain's future wife Eileen Gould, for example, was a courier operating between Cork itself and the shifting divisional headquarters in various locations to the west of the city. Cycling skills were required, along with skill at evasion and a steady nerve. And luck – which couldn't always be relied on. Eileen Gould was arrested and imprisoned (briefly) in 1923.

Irish republican women on bicycles might be said to constitute an offshoot, or a specialised section, of the cycling cult which began in the 1890s, and saw the 'New Woman' of that decade carried forward on wheels into a brighter, more expansive future. It required spirit and determination to progress from wobbling to freewheeling, but the end result was worth it. '...On a bicycle you feel a different person; nothing can come near you, you forget who you are. ... It [makes] life an absolutely different thing ...'. Miriam Henderson, in Dorothy Richardson's outstanding series of novels with the overall title *Pilgrimage*, speaks for a whole generation when she lauds the bicycle and its liberating effect. And in early twentieth-century Ireland, its association not only with personal, but with national freedom, gives it an additional éclat.

Sean O'Faolain's friend, fellow-Corkman and author Frank O'Connor, includes in his first collection (*Guests of the Nation*, 1931) a story about an eager girl entrusted with an IRA missive. *Bring your bicycle.* She does, donning gaiters and a stout woollen coat before cycling out of the city and into a warren of muddy back roads clogged with pot-holes. A sodden hay wain, an old woman leaning over a half-door, a boy driving a cart up a boreen: these pass her by like emblems of a country out of time, a country worth fighting for. And she, Helen Joyce, has a part to play in the fight. True, when Helen delivers her dispatch it's accepted off-handedly, as something of small consequence. But what odds – she's in great company, sitting in a 'safe house' by a blazing fire and listening to tales of blown-up bridges and hair's-breadth escapes. But then reality breaks in, in the form of a dead young Volunteer, shot through the chest and stowed in a car outside.

When I was sixteen or seventeen, I lapped up all such stories and reminiscences. The O'Connor/O'Faolain brand of realism, though, may well have sparked a misgiving or two in my head. Though I relished the artistry of their fictions – who would not? – and pungent Irish atmosphere, I'd have felt that the freedom fighters among their characters were entitled to rather more reverential treatment. No 'impossible young fellow[s], ... playing about with guns and explosives, ... letting on [they were] somebody of importance' would do me, thank you very much. No jeers and sneers and 'delight in devilment'. 'Two fine young fellows kilt outright – they're picking up the bits of them still.' 'Our cause is just' was more in my line – and any attempt to temper, or tamper with, the appropriately elevated tone, was flawed in my view from the word go.

But what did I mean by the 'just Irish cause'? As I've already made clear, I saw it – the glorified purpose – as an unassailable entity, allowing no scope for degrees of commitment, or differing forms of interpretation. It was embodied in resistance to injustice, pure and simple, injustice inflicted on the native Irish through eight centuries of misrule. Well, that was all I knew about it. I had the story of Ireland in outline, from Dermot MacMurrough on, and it was always and ever a question of might versus right. There was always a side to revere and a side to deplore, and I knew which was which. It was perfectly straightforward. Even when Irish patriots separated themselves into different categories, one of these categories remained head and shoulders above the others. It was a matter of fidelity to the truer objective, the undiminished ideal. Had I been alive in the early part of the twentieth century (say), I'd have followed the insurgents of Easter Week (or at sixteen I certainly believed I would), not the Redmondite British Army recruits. And after 1921 I'd have thrown in my lot with the anti-Treaty, not the pro-Treaty, faction.

When Frank Tipping came home following his years of service during the First World War, it didn't take him long to exchange his British soldier's khaki for a uniform more in keeping with his background and beliefs: that of an Irish Volunteer.[1] Frank's younger brother Gerry, late of the 2nd Royal Irish Fusiliers, followed suit. It was 1919, and the War of Independence was under way. The country, everyone agreed, was in a shocking state. The hopes of various factions, in the wake of the Great War, were far from being realised. A general election at the end of the previous year had seen Sinn Féin winning all before it in the South, unionists holding on in the North, and a cut-off portion of the country looking very much on the cards. In the effort to get things sorted out (an impossibility), frantic negotiations between all parties were taking place.

At 76 Edward Street, Lurgan, an intensely Irish atmosphere prevailed. It was high-minded, up-the-rebels territory. Four Tipping brothers – Henry and Mary Anne's sons Matt, Frank, Gerry and Jimmy – were full-fledged IRA men, adamant about the proper line to take. It had something to do with the way the country was run, with long-ago massacres, pikes-in-the-thatch, mass rocks, hedge schools, baton charges, guns, and shouts in the street. They were firmly in favour of their own wronged people. The youngest brother, Bertie, had joined the cadet branch of the Volunteers, the Fianna; and one sister, Lily, was in the women's section, the Cumann na mBan. All of them rode about on bicycles on republican errands as circumstances dictated, though other forms of transport weren't excluded from the picture, as we shall see.

Lily Tipping was brainy and go-ahead, and in later years enjoyed a successful career in various branches of nursing – medical, surgical, fever, etc. She had strings of letters after her name. Lily was enrolled with the Royal Rhodesian Medical Corps between 1939 and 1944, and won an international Red Cross medal for services to nursing. She'd trained as a basic nurse at Lurgan Hospital, completing her course in 1917, and then went on to secure all kinds of advanced professional qualifications endorsed by certificates. She became a midwife and a district nurse. But before credit and renown overtook her, Lily demonstrated her full endowment with Tipping mettle by devoting herself to the national cause. 'Nurse and gunrunner', articulated with a certain ironic admiration, is an appropriate tag for Lily in the eyes of her family-historian nephew Harry.

'Enterprising' is another word. Those were dangerous days, with – in Ireland – a plethora of wars to command people's allegiance and harry their nerves. Picture a spring morning in 1919 – say – and a couple of sturdy girls on the platform at Lurgan station awaiting the Dublin train. They are wearing, perhaps, high-waisted, belted, three-quarter-length coats over tailored blouses and navy serge skirts ending just above the ankle. Perhaps felt hats and walking shoes. And carrying canvas holdalls. They're not the chattering kind. A somewhat keyed-up air surrounds them, a sense of urgency. They are Lily Tipping and her friend Elizabeth McCusker of Brown Street in the town. ... The train judders up to the platform, Lily wrenches open the door of the nearest carriage, and the two of them step on board. As they settle themselves, rows and rows of backyards glide slowly past, washing strung on clotheslines blowing in the wind, then flash away into the distance as the train gathers speed. A moment of apprehension occurs at Portadown, perhaps: dear God, are these plain-clothes policemen getting on? *Who* is that military looking man on the platform who seems to be staring at us? Or later along the route: why is the train stopping in the middle of nowhere? But soon it jerks forward again, getting into a steady rhythm: past apple orchards filled with blossom, through the countryside where fortified bawns were built and atrocities committed, where detachments of ancient soldiery roved intent on badness. Past the aloof facade of Carrickblacker House, where direct descendants of Lily's direct ancestors lived their lives, and where bullets were fashioned in a time of disturbance to aid the Orange cause. On and on ... the Gap of the North is coming up, Slieve Gullion to the west, the Carlingford hills on the other side, all the wild and rugged terrain of south Armagh. Newry, Dundalk, the Boyne Bridge, Drogheda ... then Amiens Street station and running the gauntlet of beggarly children with their Dublin whines. On, at a steady pace, to where they've arranged to go, to collect what they have come to collect. ... Some hours later, purpose fulfilled, the two young women alight at Lurgan, the morning's innocent holdalls crammed with service revolvers, spare parts and ammunition, with maybe a cardigan or jumper folded on top to allay suspicion. These girls are part of a Cumann na mBan detachment whose work for Ireland is to fetch and carry home arms from Dublin – easy to get away with in the pre-border era, but nevertheless requiring a steady temperament, an ability to stay unfazed in the event of coming up against the Royal Irish Constabulary. To unsuspecting eyes, it must seem at the time that the town is filled with young day-trippers who have nothing better to do than travel back and forth between Lurgan and Dublin on the train.

I was determined to get Lily Tipping on to a bicycle, and – lo and behold – here she is on one, undergoing a nightly trial of strength by cycling between Bessbrook and Omeath (a journey of about ten miles), where a couple of wounded IRA men are dependent on her nursing proficiency. This clandestine engagement goes on for about two weeks. Lily's daytime job, at the Sisters of Mercy Convent in Bessbrook, keeps her busy ministering to ill nuns and malingering boarding-school pupils: when on earth, one wonders, does she find time to sleep? Skill and determination, the national cause and gritted teeth, I imagine, keep Lily going. Whatever the hardship to her, she'd tell herself, the two men in her care have worse, much worse, to endure.

The men are survivors – just – of the 'Egyptian Arch' debacle of 13 December 1920. A two-part operation was planned for that date, involving about two hundred IRA Volunteers: first one lot was detailed to burn the RIC barracks at nearby Camlough, and the second set to wait in ambush at the 'Egyptian' railway arch at Newry for army and RIC reinforcements rushing to the barracks' aid. It's the night of 12/13 December, dark and foggy and filled with intense activity. Trees are felled on both sides of the railway embankment to make a road block, and once that's done, selected Volunteers, poised to do killing, take up a firing position along the top of the arch. They are armed with guns and hand grenades, but only a limited supply. The bulk of their equipment rests out of reach in dumps on the south Down side of Newry, irretrievable at the necessary moment due to frequent RIC searches in the area. It's not an auspicious start to the night's work.

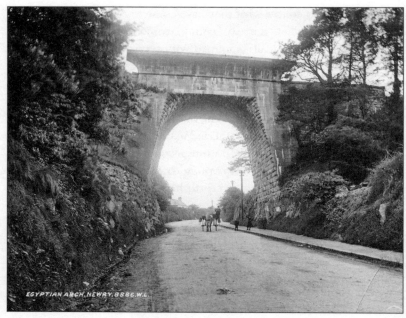

The 'Egyptian Arch' near Newry, where an IRA ambush was foiled in December 1920

Back at Camlough, Volunteers succeed in setting fire to the barracks,[2] but the fire is quickly extinguished and Verey lights set off to alert the Newry garrison (as the Egyptian Arch contingent had anticipated) to serious trouble in the village. South Armagh Commandant Frank Aiken calls off the barracks attack and commandeers a donkey to carry away an associate wounded in the leg. (I hope this useful donkey is well looked after.) At the same time, armoured cars and Crossley Tenders are speeding past the Egyptian Arch when the IRA roadblock stops them in their tracks. Grenades rain down on them but fail to explode, or explode uselessly in the roadway. Soldiers and RIC men scramble out of their vehicles and run for cover, dodging bullets coming from the top of the arch and swiftly retaliating with machine-gun fire which kills one Volunteer and seriously injures others. There's nothing for it but another IRA withdrawal, which takes place in difficult circumstances. Two wounded men are carried pickaback across the Cooley Hills (a distance of eight or ten miles) – first being hurriedly tended in a shepherd's hut by a couple of Newry doctors named Flood and Quinn. An appalling journey follows, before they're brought to safety at a hospice attached to the priory of the Charity Fathers at Omeath. This is where Nurse Lily Tipping comes in.

Lily Tipping figured quite strongly in my childhood, as someone approved of and cherished in the family. People talked about her a lot, about her time on Achill Island, County Mayo, as the first district nurse appointed there, about her years in Rhodesia and advancement beyond her stay-at-home siblings, about the pull of home that, nevertheless, brought her back in retirement to set up house with her widowed sister Monny (Lily was the only member of her family who hadn't married, and Monny was the only married one who hadn't had children, so they suited one another: oddities both). Small and sharp and ironical, Lily is a person of consequence and a frequent subject of conversation among her relations. What isn't mentioned, though, is the thing I'd have paid attention to, had I been listening: Lily's days as an out-and-out republican. For my parents' generation, by and large (and for the previous one), the political past is a fraught and dingy place better left unrevisited. We're in the '50s, '60s now, a world more peaceful and hopeful, closer to a fair deal for everyone, old-time grudges and angers fading away (or so it seemed). Fading away – but enough of a residue remains to agitate nationalists and reformists, in whose enlightened company I place my sixteen-year-old self. Continuing injustices stare us in the face wherever we look for them, and all down to the English and Orangemen.

I thought of Lily Tipping as a kind of aunt, but she was, in fact, my mother's cousin (though of an earlier generation). I never bothered to sort out the gradations of Tipping connections. There were so many of them – names constantly on my mother's and my grandmother's lips. I was taken to visit Lily a couple of times when she was old and I was nineteen or twenty – and if I'd had the wit to cross-question her, she, I am sure, would gladly have recalled her rebel days, wild nights in December and cycling through the countryside on a patriotic errand of mercy. Brave young women couriers and IRA auxiliaries I knew from books, but here was one, unacknowledged, on my own doorstep, so to speak.

Lily didn't have to go it entirely alone. Her young brother Bernard (Bertie), a prominent Fianna member at the time, is sent from his home in Lurgan to temporary lodgings in Newry, from which he emerges after dark to accompany his sister on her hazardous nocturnal journeys between Bessbrook and Omeath. It's up to him to see her safely back to the convent, once she's done whatever is necessary for her patients. In one case, Lily's ministrations aren't enough. There's nothing she can do – Volunteer Peter Shields is too badly hurt to survive. He is done for, even before he reaches the sanctuary of the Charity Fathers' hospice. He dies from his wounds on Christmas Day and, like the hero of Corunna, is buried darkly at dead of night. It's a sorrowful and macabre occasion in the hospice grounds, the torch-lit procession, the grave-digging Brothers, secrecy and haste. ... The other Volunteer, William Carr, has a leg amputated but recovers under Lily's care and lives on for many years.

The thing that alarms me most in all of this is Bertie Tipping's age. He is fourteen years old and should be at school, not pedalling all over County Armagh running horrendous risks. Or, if not at school, at least serving behind the counter of his father's shop. Didn't his parents have any say in the matter? I can't imagine his mother Mary Anne being overjoyed to see her youngest son set off on his bicycle for the train station en route to Newry and a dangerous mission. Of course, it is possible the parents were not in possession of all the facts. They may have believed that Bertie was simply paying a visit to his older sister, taking a break from his grocery apprenticeship. If a domestic conspiracy was taking place, though, his brothers were in it. His older brother Jimmy (1899–1976) is commanding officer of the Fianna *Sluagh* (Company) to which Bertie belongs. (Jimmy is interned at Ballykinler camp in County Down at this time – see below – but he'd have been kept apprised of events outside.) And Frank and Gerry are still at home and up to the eyes in subversive activity. Or, I suppose, it is just possible that Bertie went to Newry with his parents' full knowledge and blessing. 76 Edward Street was, after all, well known as a 'safe house' and this would require the cooperation of everyone in it. As a dropping and collection point for dispatches, the location of an arms dump and a temporary place of refuge for men on the run, the house sat there in plebeian Edward Street as a beacon of principled resistance.

And it's true that Bertie is no novice, so he isn't, for all his youth, in the ways of republican agitation. The previous year, 1919, Bertie had joined his brother's Fianna *Sluagh*, acquired a gun and a uniform, and, thus equipped, might often be seen cycling with fellow Fenians, through areas both friendly and unfriendly, as part of an IRA recruitment drive.

Also in 1919, Bertie is present and standing to attention at the great St Patrick's Day rally at Piper Hill outside Lurgan, listening to Darrell Figgis[3] deliver an uplifting oration. 'His noble voice re-echoed o'er the waters of Lough Neagh', avers an anonymous local bard roped in to commemorate the occasion. (Probably Aghagallon man Jimmy Devlin.) He also notes some important participants in the event:

> I saw Joe Burke and Tipping[4] as the first command they
> gave,
> I saw Dan Corr and Joe Maguire in those Irish ranks
> so brave.

By the summer of 1920, Bertie is a veteran of police baton charges and arms raids. He's entrusted with keeping guns cleaned and in working order. Along with his friends in the Fianna, he has attended lessons in the making of gunpowder (whew!), and been shown how to refill shotgun cartridges with buckshot. ... Lily too has acquired experience in secretly tending to the wounded long before her involvement with the Egyptian Arch casualties. People with RIC bullets in their flesh have been carried into her home by the back door, to be patched up by Lily and thereby enabled (some of them, at any rate) to get themselves to a hospital for more intensive treatment. On one occasion, Bertie and two local IRA men accompany one of these bandaged and shaken Volunteers on the train to Belfast and a hospital in the city.[5] Even before he makes the transfer from the Fianna to the IRA proper, which occurs in due course, a lot of responsibility is placed on the shoulders of teenage Bertie.

We're still in the summer of 1920 when Bertie receives orders to present himself at Lurgan station to meet his brother Jimmy coming off the Belfast train. From Jimmy he obtains a small travelling bag and nonchalantly carries it out of the station under the eyes of many who'd have gasped at its contents. (I don't know if Jimmy returns to Belfast straight away, without leaving the station, or if he accompanies his innocent looking brother through Lurgan's inflammable streets.) Is Bertie's heart beating wildly as he goes, for all his unconcerned appearance? Does he understand the risk he's running? In the current state of unrest, police and soldiers are constantly on the look-out for anything untoward, such as one youth picking up a bag from another – and in that particular bag, on that July day, are a couple of revolvers and a supply of ammunition. The revolvers may have come from Cork and are destined for a particular purpose. It is possible that one of these firearms holds a special significance for republicans which I'll recount in a minute. We are now approaching the well-documented Swanzy assassination in Lisburn and its terrible aftermath.

The story has often been told, though aspects of the affair remain surrounded by a certain haze and contradiction. In outline, though, it is clear enough. It begins in Cork,[6] with the murder of Tomás MacCurtain, lord mayor and officer in command of the city's 1st IRA brigade. It's 19 March 1920, the middle of the night. MacCurtain is shot in circumstances of extreme brutality at his home in Thomas Davis Street, in the presence of his pregnant wife Elizabeth and with five young children asleep in bed. (Or not asleep: the banging at the door and eruption into the house of men with blackened faces brandishing revolvers no doubt aroused them into a nightmare – every child's worst, most exorbitant fears come true.) After the killers have fled, the police and army arrive and turn the house upside down in a search for seditious material (weapons and documents). They find nothing. MacCurtain's personal revolver, concealed under the mattress of baby Eilis MacCurtain's pram, is overlooked. It is possibly this revolver, earmarked at once for a retaliatory purpose, that is briefly in the keeping of Bertie Tipping in Lurgan, before it is put to its designated use. Or maybe the story of MacCurtain's gun and its ultimate destination is purely apocryphal.

At the inquest into the death of the lord mayor, the coroner's jury brings in an unexpected and amazing verdict. Indicted on a charge of wilful murder are

> ... David Lloyd George, Prime Minister of England; Lord French, Lord Lieutenant of Ireland; Ian McPherson, late Chief Secretary of Ireland; Acting Inspector General Smith, of the Royal Irish Constabulary; Divisional Inspector Clayton of the Royal Irish Constabulary; District Inspector Swanzy and some unknown members of the Royal Irish Constabulary.

Those named become immediate targets for the IRA, though some are clearly beyond their reach. Of those who aren't, two of the specified 'unknown members' of the RIC are the first to die, shot on a tram car in Cork city. Their names are Garvey and Harrington, and they are popularly believed to be the people who fired the lethal shots into Tomás MacCurtain. The process of revenge is under way. Michael Collins himself, in mourning for his close friend and ally, has authorised these and further executions. District Inspector Swanzy is high on the condemned list, and for his own safety the DI is hurriedly transferred from Cork to Lisburn, a staunch wee Protestant town in the distant north. In the eyes of those facing republican implacability down South, Lisburn would look like a haven of loyalism.

But plans are afoot. Ulster and Munster are poles apart, but the whole of Ireland, between the spring of 1920 and the Truce of 1921, is undergoing 'the full voltage of British military oppression' (in the words of Sean O'Faolain in his autobiography *Vive Moi!*), and a complementary network of republican resistance is operating throughout its length and breadth. It isn't too difficult for IRA Intelligence to track the district inspector to his new posting. Soon the IRA has Swanzy in its sights. The Cork brigade claims the honour of carrying out the sentence, but, as the Belfast IRA reasonably point out, their Cork accents would make them conspicuous in the North. In the event, it becomes a joint operation, though with each party reluctant to accord too much credit to the other. 'This was a Belfast Brigade job,' claimed one of its members, Sean Montgomery, in an unpublished memoir,[7] 'the Cork men were guests.'

The Cork men thought otherwise. They were the primary activists in the business, according to them, with Belfast merely taking a secondary role. It was a Corkman, Sean Culhane, who fired the first shot at DI Swanzy as he left Christ Church Cathedral in Lisburn after attending morning service. The date is Sunday 22 August 1920. The gun in question, as I've indicated, passed into republican mythology as Tomás MacCurtain's own, miraculously undetected during the raid on his home on the night of his murder. (Ironically, the permit for this gun had been signed by Swanzy himself in the mistaken belief that it was going to a 'loyalist' in Cork city.[8]) It is possible that Sean Culhane had carried it with him on the train from Cork – risking its confiscation and his own detainment – or, on the other hand, that it had made its way north some weeks earlier, and been handed to Bertie Tipping in Lurgan to be kept until called for. Bertie has testified that the two guns he collected from his brother Jimmy were among those actually used in 'the Swanzy affair'.

Some time during that summer of 1920, Jimmy Tipping is installed in lodgings in Belfast which he shares with Jack (Sean) Leonard, a taxi driver originally from Sligo, and currently a Volunteer with 'B' Company, Belfast Brigade. The lodging house is in Bedeque Street off the Lower Crumlin Road, just opposite the Mater Hospital. The two young men are deeply involved in preparations for the coming assassination. The first time an attempt is made on Swanzy's life – on 15 August 1920 – things do not go according to plan. The DI gains a week's reprieve.

It's in connection with that first Sunday that differing accounts begin to obscure the actual course of events. But what I think took place was this. A bona fide taxi driver named George Nelson was hired to pick up four men on the Shankill Road and take them to Portadown. One of the men was Jimmy Tipping. The taxi, as instructed, then proceeded up the Springfield Road towards Hannahstown (not the Cave Hill Road as Sean Leonard later recalled it), and at a prearranged spot it was halted by three masked men carrying revolvers who sprang out of a hedge. The passengers then joined forces with the hijackers. Nelson was blindfolded and had his hands tied behind his back; he was then led across some fields to a barn where two men guarded him until it was judged safe to let him go. One of the IRA men standing guard over Nelson was Jimmy Tipping. In the meantime, the commandeered taxi on its way to Lisburn had come to grief: either a wheel flew off (one account), it simply broke down (another account), or the driver from Cork got hopelessly lost among the Antrim byroads. Or, a further account has it, Swanzy simply failed to appear at the appointed moment to be shot. Operation postponed.

Lessons were learned. (That's a joke.) The following week a similar ploy is adopted, but the non-bona fide taxi driver for the occasion is Sean Leonard (why didn't they use him in the first place?). Roger McCorley of the Belfast Brigade is already in Lisburn monitoring events, his colleague Joe McKelvey[9] having reported on the expected movements of the DI. As far as I am aware, Jimmy Tipping does not on this occasion travel with the shooting party to Lisburn, but stays behind in Belfast poised to help construct an alibi for the returning victorious executioners. (I am not sure how this works, but it does, at least for a time.)

Lisburn, Market Square, 1.03 p.m. An instant of shocked silence overtakes the Sunday crowds milling about the town centre as shots ring out, leaving Oswald Swanzy lying dead on the pavement, and his killers making a getaway as panic and confusion swiftly flare up. Shouts and screams contribute to the uproar as pedestrians stumble off frantically in all directions. The IRA men continue firing to ward off capture, like something out of a cops-and-robbers screening at the Diamond Cinema on the Falls Road in Belfast, but the only other casualties are a blackthorn stick shot out of the hand of an outraged pursuer, and the grazed leg of a Miss McCreight, who's managed to get herself in the pathway of a bullet. All the gunmen scramble into the waiting car, with Sean Leonard at the wheel, apart from Roger McCorley who nearly gets left behind in the shambles. He has to make a dive for it and as he does, his gun goes off, driving a bullet hole through the floor. McCorley is hauled to safety by his companions as the car speeds off in a manner not consistent with the rules of the road. Pursuit by police in a taxi is foiled by that vehicle losing a wheel as it goes too recklessly round a corner.[10] (There are a lot of flying wheels and bullets in this story – not to mention spokes in wheels.)

Leaving their pursuers far behind, and speeding out of the town towards the back road home, the exhilarated Volunteers reach Belfast without further ado. At Great Victoria Street station, the two Corkmen in the party board a train to Dublin, where, as arranged, they report to Michael Collins on the outcome of the mission and receive his congratulations. Their Belfast associates, Roger McCorley and another Volunteer named Tom Fox, walk away not too hastily and disappear into a district known to be sympathetic, leaving Sean Leonard still driving the cab in the city centre. As far as I can gather (accounts of the business don't always tally), he drives it to Tates Avenue off the Lisburn Road where a couple of supposed 'fares' – actually, Jimmy Tipping and an IRA man named Liam Devlin – are waiting to be collected and taken to Holywood and Helen's Bay to create a sense of an ordinary Sunday outing. In fact, the guilty taxi cab is flagged down and searched by RIC patrols both on the outward and the return journey, but on each occasion the searchers fail to spot the bullet holes which should have alerted them to something fishy. But the reprieve for a few of the northern Volunteers (like Oswald Swanzy's) is short-lived.

Looking back over what I've written about the Swanzy shooting, I'm slightly dismayed to encounter a certain flippancy of tone, as if the only way to treat the event is to be mildly cynical and sardonic. Is this appropriate? Two things I know, or think I know: had I been present in that street in Lisburn when the DI was gunned down, I'd have been as horrified and shocked by the bloodshed as anyone else. And – conversely – if the planning of this piece of retribution for the awful murder of Tomás MacCurtain had involved my cooperation to any extent, I'd have given it freely, regarding the proposed execution as a brave and necessary act to bolster the republican cause. Then, as now – I hope – I'd have drawn the line at exulting in anyone's violent death (well, apart from droves of Black and Tans or other hoodlum belligerents); but equally, I'd have condoned the tactics of guerrilla warfare or any other form of resistance to the current dreadful state of misery and terror throughout Ireland. Those whom Sean O'Faolain called 'the tremendously gallant few', the Irish freedom fighters, could have counted on my iota of advocacy, had I been there to proffer it. The shadowy allure of gunmen and patriots was a thing well understood by me. And yet – I have to acknowledge an impulse to dissociate myself from violence and mayhem, however appealing the cause (the Cause). At the risk of sounding like 'Outraged of Ballymurphy (or Ballymacarrett)' in the Heaney poem, 'Whatever You Say, Say Nothing' – ' "Oh, it's disgraceful, surely, I agree", / "Where's it going to end?" "It's getting worse" ' – I have to deplore destruction, destruction of life, livelihood, architectural treasures, aspiration for the future, homes, whole towns or anything else getting in the way of an undeviating certainty about a right course of action. But someone, you might argue, has to make a stand against perceived injustice and corruption, whatever it entails. Perhaps it's just a question of bravery and fidelity versus expediency, with myself at present in the middle-aged expediency camp, I don't know. But I do understand Louis MacNeice's interrogation of gunmen,

> ... who shoot to kill and never
> See the victim's face become their own,
> Or find his motive sabotage their motives.

If you take to the gun you can't afford to consider any clashing form of integrity, or allow complications to undermine your total dedication. And if, like Michael Collins, you're setting yourself up for future deification or vilification, it's just a way of perpetuating 'us and them'.

★ ★ ★

One thing the would-be saviours of Swanzy got right when they sent him North: Lisburn should have wrapped itself around the DI like an Orange sash. He *should* have been out of harm's way in a town so Protestant and partisan. And when it turned out he wasn't, all hell broke loose. Lisburn's loyalist population is handed on a plate a pretext for a pogrom against Catholics, all of whom are supposed to be tarred with the Fenian–Sinn Féin–desperado brush. Even as the successful killers, Corkmen Culhane and Murphy, are passing through the town on the Dublin train, they see from their carriage windows smoke rising from the first burnt-out 'Fenian' premises. In the terrible 'Swanzy' riots the town is wrecked and burnt as Protestants run amok, and nearly the whole of the Catholic population is driven out. Desperate Catholic refugees carrying whatever they could salvage make their way on foot across the hills to the (comparative) safety of Belfast – following the route of the getaway car a short time earlier – where St Mary's Hall in Bank Street provides a sanctuary of sorts. Days later, the charred remains of shops and houses, the mutilated streets of Lisburn, give rise to a topical comparison. Like a bombarded town in Belgium, it looks: Mons or Ypres or some other ravaged war zone.

Not all the victims in Lisburn are Catholic, indeed; no one can stop Protestant property from going up in flames in the general conflagration. (A lull occurs while internecine energies are marshalled. The social commentator Hugh Shearman had a memory of himself as a very young child in a car going quickly through the empty streets of the town. It was Monday 23 August. The following day, nearly the whole of Bow Street was burned to the ground.) ... But mob fury is directed against the town's Catholics – all innocent of complicity in the crucial killing – and few Protestant voices are raised in sympathy, or even in acknowledgement of their plight. Among those who do express concern and horror at the escalation of anarchy in the streets are the mother and sister of the murdered Swanzy: they are 'grieved beyond measure' by what has taken place in Lisburn – distraught, indeed, that the death of the district inspector should provoke such excesses of wreckage and infliction of terror. For them, it's an added affliction piled on top of mourning.

In 2008, the novelist Glenn Patterson published a book reflecting the kind of ancestral diversity common to most of us. *Once Upon a Hill* tells the story of his Lisburn grandparents, Catherine (Kate) Logue and Jack

Patterson, who were there in the thick of the Swanzy disturbances, one – perhaps – momentarily moidered and running the streets with the Protestant wreckers and looters, the other (possibly) crouching terrified in a cellar, while the noise and excitement of sectarian venom raged at fever pitch above her. Also in hiding in Patterson's putative cellar are Kate Logue's mother and her five-year-old daughter, the latter born out of wedlock due to Jack's opinionated mother, and her refusal to countenance as a daughter-in-law a mill girl and – worse – a Catholic. Glenn Patterson would like to absolve his grandfather Jack of any involvement in the uproar. He would like to think Jack's attention in the crisis was focused on the safety of his wife-to-be and his daughter. But he can't be sure how his grandfather acted – how anyone would act – in the heat of the moment.

Whatever he did, or didn't do, during those berserk August days of 1920, Jack Patterson was forgiven. Catholic, or half-Catholic Kate became his wife in due course, and their Protestant son, the oddly named Phares, Glenn Patterson's father. Jack described Kate as 'the best little woman in Lisburn', while as far as she was concerned, he was simply 'the best man that ever lived'. These mutual declarations of esteem were made years after the Lisburn cataclysm, when the town had long settled back into its workaday routines. Jack by now has succumbed to an evangelical onrush and got himself 'born again'. I'm not sure what religion, if any, his wife Kate professes – probably a low-key, adopted Protestantism – but she's held on to a remnant of her mill-girl aplomb and enjoys as much as anyone (as much as *my* grandmothers) that novelty of the 1960s home, television.

By bringing all of his novelist's skills and insights to bear on the subject, Glenn Patterson has produced the most vivid account I've come across of the Swanzy shooting and its aftermath. The incident is at the centre of his memoir. 'Love in troubled times' is the subtitle of *Once Upon a Hill*. It is not an overstatement.

> ... Earlier in the day the Belfast [Fire] Brigade had sent some of its units to assist, but it withdrew them again at seven o'clock after their hoses were repeatedly cut. The only check now on the arsonists was their own energy and ingenuity after more than thirty hours of destruction and, in a great many cases,

continuous drinking. On Cross Row ... Phelan's pawnshop was looted and burned ... so too was the ice-cream parlour belonging to Pietro Fusco. ... On Bridge Street McCourtney's confectionery and fancy bakery shop was wrecked. ... All of this though, and despite the enthusiasm with which they went at it, was really just a diversion from what had been the target since the crowd marched out of Railway Street and on to Cross Row the previous afternoon:'Sinn Feiners ... sympathisers of the murderers', or, very simply, Catholics.

Jefferson's timber yard went up in smoke, Glenn Patterson continues, so did Burns's fruit and veg. And adds: 'Poor Burns. Poor Lisburn and its fatal attraction to flames.'

The allusion is to 1707 when Lisburn was all but wiped out in an accidental fire. And back beyond that date to the burning of 1641 when the rudimentary town was under siege and defended against the Irish rebels by – among others – the Tipping sons of the earliest settler John. There were Swansys (sic) about the place at that time too: an ancestor of the murdered DI was christened in Lisburn cathedral in 1666 and went on to fight for King Billy at the Battle of the Boyne[11] (alongside William Blacker? – Ah, suppositions). Tipping, Swanzy, Blacker: 'Each individual's story spins complicated cobwebs of relationship.' I'm quoting here another fine Northern Irish writer, the essayist Chris Arthur, meditating in 'Water-Glass' on his home town, Lisburn. Looking back, he says: 'Before that initial cluster of 250 [i.e. the original seventeenth-century builders of the town] there were others, long forgotten, for whom this place was home. Their lives have vanished, their stories are untold, the chemicals that once constituted their fleshy presence have unravelled and dispersed and melded, wraith-like, with the anonymous substance of the earth they used to tread on long ago. Who knows what ghosts haunt the dust of Bachelor's Walk?'

Who indeed. Chris Arthur's perspective here is a bit too long for my particular purposes, but ghosts I can go along with. The ghosts of Warwickshire settlers revisiting the site of their first Irish dwellings; the ghost of Henry Munro re-enacting his bungled execution. And Oswald Ross Swanzy's wraith hovering over the place of his ancestor's christening and his own death. Ghosts of anonymous people trying to lead decent lives; ghosts of infuriated, intoxicated mobs. Coming up to the recent past and the days following 22 August 1920, Chris Arthur remarks bleakly and accurately: 'The worst violence in modern times was done by Lisburn's own people.'

Late in the afternoon of 22 August, taxi man Sean Leonard is arrested in Belfast in connection with the shooting.[12] Two weeks later, at his home in Lurgan, it's the turn of Jimmy Tipping. Charged in the same connection, 'he was subsequently removed under escort, and at a special court in Belfast was remanded on the capital charge,' the *Lurgan Mail* reported solemnly. In fact, no charge is brought against Jimmy (for lack of evidence) and he's dispatched back to Edward Street, only to be promptly rearrested and then interned without trial at Ballykinler camp in County Down. Here Jimmy sits it out for the next fifteen months, until, in December 1921, republican prisoners and internees are released in a general amnesty consequent on the Anglo-Irish Treaty.

A family myth, when I was growing up and beginning to take an interest in such matters, was that one of our Tipping relations was solely responsible for the assassination of DI Swanzy. He had fired the fatal shot. And the same relation, I believed in a vague but adamant way – I hadn't got the Tipping contingent at all clear in my head – had been tried and convicted and was actually languishing (I'm sure the word languishing came into it) in the condemned cell awaiting execution when – miraculous day – the Treaty supervened. I don't know when or how the truth got magnified, whether I did it subconsciously myself, or if it was somehow conveyed to me in this exaggerated form, aggrandisement having occurred spontaneously with the passage of time. Certainly I latched on to the Tipping/Swanzy overstatement. With a name like Craig, I needed all the republican clout I could get.

There were four strands to my family, indeed (taking grandparents into account), but the Wexford Letts only got a look-in, in those besotted days, due to a story of rather less substance than the Swanzy enlargement mentioned above. I cannot get it corroborated from any source I've consulted, but long ago when I was going about waving a green flag, I had a picture in my head of some innocent cousins on my father's side, bowling along a country lane in a pony-and-trap, and being shot dead by trigger-happy Black and Tans for whom *any* native Irish were suitable targets. Unlike the bedraggled Protestant refugees of 1798, whom yeomen took for insurgent-affiliated due to their unkempt appearance, these Wexford cousins weren't given a chance to proclaim their support for the British connection. If they existed, which I now think is doubtful. But where did the story come from? I can't have concocted it entirely out of thin air. Of course, there were many such incidents –

> From Cork on to Limerick, Clare and Mayo,
> Lies a trail of destruction wherever they go –

On the Limerick road, wrote Ernie O'Malley,[13] 'Three lorries of Tans and R.I.C. came up. They were shouting, singing and shooting off their rifles.' This was normal behaviour. And it is possible, I suppose, that those hypothetical Wexford Letts (or whatever their name was) were victims of this kind of lethal exuberance. Possible, as well, that the Protestant side of the family would wish, in the future, to dissociate itself from any alignment with rebel grievances.

For me, of course, the opposite was true. If – and it's a large if – the Black-and-Tan incident really happened, I could use it to reinforce my claim to an Irish identity. I could follow John Hewitt's take on the death of his Protestant great-grandmother in County Armagh, as recounted in his poem 'The Scar': she handed a crust of bread to a starving beggar during the Famine and, he says, for this act of charity, 'accepted in return the famine-fever'. And, he goes on, 'that chance meeting, that brief confrontation, / Conscribed me of the Irishry for ever'. The point being that the whole nation was subject to the same unifying calamity, with consequent undermining of sectarian differences. Well, that was a natural standpoint for a liberal humanist like Hewitt. But how you regarded the great issues in Ireland, of nationality, religion, allegiance and so on, was still for most people a matter of inheritance as much as instinct.

The Wexford Letts. But now another version of that apocryphal Black-and-Tan shooting has come to my attention, and it turns the whole business on its head. In the first place, it has nothing to do with the Letts. In the second place, the shooters in question were IRA Volunteers. ... You will remember my great-grandmother Marie Heller (see Chapter Five) and her employment by the upper-crust Mays of Belfast and Dublin. Marie had died back in 1891, but her children, including my grandfather William Craig, would have gone on taking an interest in the grand family with which their mother's fortunes were intertwined. A great-niece of the family named Winifred Barrington, a granddaughter of Olivia May's brother, was a casualty of the War of Independence. She was shot and killed while travelling incautiously in a car beside a Black-and-Tan officer.

The place was Coolboreen in County Limerick (*Cul Bothairin*, literally: small back road), the date was 14 May 1921, and the merry party, consisting of three young men and two girls, was returning in high spirits from a fishing expedition when the ambush occurred. The car, with a hated Black and Tan in the driver's seat, was sighted by an IRA man who alerted others to its probable route and sent them scurrying to the spot armed with rifles and shotguns. Winifred, wearing a riding outfit and an officer's cap, and looking game for anything, was seated next to the driver and actual IRA target, twenty-six-year-old Inspector Henry Biggs. By all accounts a bit of a tomboy, a VAD recruit during the Great War, and liked by everyone in the district – though no one, after her death, was going to say otherwise – pretty, twenty-two-year-old Winifred took a bullet in the chest and died shortly afterwards from shock and haemorrhage. She had tumbled out of the car and fallen into a ditch. Inspector Biggs, shot in the throat, fell out on the other side and lay in the road, dying. Further shots were fired into him before the Volunteers took to their heels. The three in the back of the car escaped more or less unhurt. It was later claimed that Winifred Barrington was mistaken for a man, due to the way she was dressed. When her identity was disclosed, one Volunteer shouted, 'If the bitch hadn't been in bad company, she wouldn't have got shot' – in other words, slap it into her. But the general feeling in the area, after her death, was one of sadness and dismay at the craziness of the world people inhabited and the tragedies it created. There was jubilation over the execution of Biggs, notorious for brutality and horrors of every kind inflicted on the Irish, but it was tempered by regret for the accompanying death of lovely, lively young Winifred Barrington of Glenstal Castle.

So: a fatal shooting during the Black-and-Tan war, an innocent victim, a distraught family, a Catholic church bell tolling mournfully as the funeral cortège passed by on its way to the Abington Church of Ireland cemetery. ...The event, widely reported, would soon have reached the ears of my grandfather's family in the North, and struck them forcibly due to their slight personal connection with the Barringtons. At the very least, they'd have been well informed about Winifred's antecedents. The

Coolboreen killing, at least for a time, would have loomed large among their preoccupations.

And as it faded, did a whiff of the surrounding shock and outrage get transmitted to me, a long way into the future, and in a distorted form? More likely I'd have effected the transformation all by myself. I'm reminded of Tom Dunne's relative pointing to Scullabogue as the site of a Cromwellian massacre of Catholics (see p. 80). Whatever horror had taken place, in whatever circumstances, it was down to annihilating enemy tactics, never a product of honourable Irish resistance. Or so we – Irish nationalists – were programmed to think. So I may have manufactured a spurious connection to *Irish* victimhood on the part of my Protestant family, out of the bare bones of Coolboreen. I don't know. It is at least a possible explanation for the supposed Black-and-Tan atrocity which no one among my father's relations will corroborate.

During the War of Independence and then the Civil War, things were different in the North. It's necessary to bear this in mind. Sean O'Faolain's 'tremendously gallant few', the rebel soldiers of the Limerick, Cork and Tipperary Brigades (among others), enjoyed a resource unavailable to their northern counterparts:

> The fight was carried through by those tremendously gallant few, darting here and there for an ambush, folding back into their 'normal' lives until they could get another crack at the enemy. They could not, it must always be said, have done anything without the silence, patience and loyal help of the whole people.

But for those operating from Belfast, say, more than half the people had placed themselves at the furthest imaginable remove from the republican ideal. It wasn't only the British who were the enemy, but the Orange population of the North – and for latter-day adherents of Wolfe Tone's philosophy it was important, and often impossible, not to be seen as a factionally motivated force. In the eyes of their enemies, Sinn Feiners were Catholic gunmen out to shoot Protestants, not soldiers of a putative republic defending their communities against loyalist incursions. Despite the example of Protestant nationalists like Bulmer Hobson and others, the old divisions would not go away; and at street level they assumed their most basic and virulent form: Prod versus Taig. When Bertie Tipping, for example, recalled cycling in his Fianna uniform 'through very unfriendly areas' of Lurgan, we understand the hazards he and his fellow-republicans faced on their way to and from political gatherings. Name-calling was the very least of it. And it's axiomatic that the threat to their safety didn't come from St Peter's parishioners.

In the city, 'the noise of shooting, / Starting in the evening at eight, / In Belfast in the York Street district' (Louis MacNeice's words) was a regular cause of alarm – and not only in York Street. People with miserable standards of living in acres of streets all over Belfast, each defined by its place of worship, had almost incessant bloodshed, assault and apprehension imposed on top of their everyday aggravations of poverty and exhaustion. The place was in turmoil. The years between 1917 and 1924 were marked by riots, raids and reprisals. Bigotry and discrimination on one side bred anger and disaffection on the other. It is hard to envisage the scale of the violence and vehemence, and consequent destruction, afflicting Belfast's more volatile quarters – or at least it was hard, during the relatively undisturbed middle years of the century, before the most recent phase of 'Troubles' brought it all sweeping back again, in an even more cruel and chaotic way.

A massive battle with paving stones, the death toll rising, St Matthew's chapel blazing, snipers sniping, this was Belfast in the early 1920s. 'The violence finally petered out ... eighteen people had died, about three hundred were wounded and there was a serious refugee problem. Most of the deaths had been as a result of shooting by the military. ... Ten of the dead were Catholic and eight were Protestant.'[14] All over the city, arms and ammunition are deposited with sympathetic households – in one instance, a Mills hand grenade sits boldly beneath a hat on a sideboard, and is still there at the end of an RIC raid, giving a literal application to 'keeping it under your hat'. There are hair-raising retreats over backyard walls, fake priests escaping with their lives in borrowed clerical garb, bicycles commandeered from passers-by – whether willing or unwilling – to carry handguns away in the aftermath of an ambush. To complicate matters, you find republican fellow-travellers among members of the RIC itself: those willing to pass on crucial information and even, on occasion, ammunition.

In Lurgan, the Tipping residence at 76 Edward Street is subjected to frequent raids by unambivalently orientated police and military. In

September 1920, for example, just after Jimmy's removal for internment, the house is raided once again – and once again reluctantly accorded a clean bill of compliance with regulations. Arrangements – Bertie Tipping's guarded expression – arrangements are always in place to safeguard any wounded Volunteer being treated by Lily, and any arms or documents secreted about the house, once word of an imminent raid is received. It is all very urgent and mysterious. Constant vigilance is necessary. Lower your guard for an instant, and horrors may happen. A neighbour, for instance, standing at the Tippings' door, and mistaken for one of the family, is shot and seriously wounded by an Orange sniper. Desperate times. The Sisters of Mercy Convent, just across the road from 76, is under threat from loyalists, and a nightly patrol, including one or two Tippings, is formed to guard the premises. They spend the hours of darkness being sniped at from an Orange quarter behind the convent, and never hesitating to return fire. The nuns in their beds have cause to be grateful for the shooting skills of their night watchmen. My mother, seven or eight years old at the time, is a primary school pupil attending the convent during the day. No doubt she gains kudos among her peers from pointing to her relations in the armed guard.

The life of those days, all its upsets and stresses, took its toll on the health of the mother of the Tipping family, Mary Anne Dowds. She died aged sixty in 1926. Five of her six sons,[15] and one daughter, were active in the republican movement, upholding all attendant forms of insubordination and exposing themselves to constant danger. From time to time, the sons would quietly interrupt their grocery work to engage in Sinn Féin business. Cutting telegraph wires to disrupt communications, holding up trains, raiding for arms, setting fire to bread vans ... all these form part of the learning process of soldiering for Ireland. Utterly divested of their anti-social aspect in the prevailing conditions, these activities contribute to the message being transmitted to the authorities: republicans mean business. Acts of destruction that would, in normal times, engender outrage in the naturally law-abiding (among whom I would place the Lurgan Tippings – well, most of them), are instead regarded as ethical strikes against a hated system – a system that deforms and derails the lives of ordinary people. The times aren't normal at all, and the naturally law-abiding are provoked into anarchy by having no democratic laws to abide by.

The Tipping brothers, apart from one, all saw the inside of prisons or internment camps. Matt, the oldest – born in 1890 – went to Scotland after the war. He got employment in the Glasgow shipyards; and while he was there, true to the family tradition, he joined the Glasgow Battalion of the IRA and quickly rose to prominence in it. (His future wife Jean Rice was already a member of the Govan Cumann na mBan.) I've mentioned above the miniscule overlap between my (peripheral) family history, and Glenn Patterson's – and I'm about to pinpoint an intriguing instance of a similar kind of convergence. There's a point at which the Tipping story intersects with that of another writer I esteem enormously – the novelist, essayist and critic Andrew O'Hagan.

Andrew O'Hagan's great book *The Missing* is an account of various kinds of disappearance, from his grandfather reported missing in action during the Second World War, to the girls enticed away and killed in Gloucester by Fred and Rosemary West. It's also a memoir of a Glasgow/ new town childhood, and it takes in aspects of an older city and a way of life experienced by O'Hagan's recent forebears. The early-twentieth-century O'Hagans were Catholic and – with that name – of Irish descent. Some of them gravitated naturally towards Sinn Féin. 'The history of Sinn Féin in Glasgow,' he writes, ' – that sometimes boiling community of Socialist-Catholics and Ulster Orangemen – has, for the most part, been erased from the city's account of itself. In the twenties, it was much more than a matter of one or two households and the zealous machinations of the families within. It was a faith – a bitter creed for some – scribbled into the very pavements around St. Mary's.' Not too far in spirit from Lurgan or Belfast, then.

In May 1921, O'Hagan says, 'something happened in the Calton, something involving the chapel of St. Mary's, and guns, and Sinn Féin, my grandfather and his uncle Francis, a confectioner.' What happened was an attempt to extricate a couple of high-ranking IRA prisoners, one of them a seasoned gaol-breaker, from a black van, heavily escorted, on the way to Duke Street Prison. The driver of the van was a Constable Thomas Rose.[16] His colleagues were named Stirton, MacDonald, and Johnston. Suddenly, like something out of a cowboy film, groups of men erupted from alleys and closes, firing revolvers; Inspector Johnston was hit and died on the spot; Stirton received a shot to the wrist and dropped his gun. Pandemonium overtook the streets. The IRA men might have brought it off, but failed in the attempt because the van doors jammed, securing the prisoners inside. Everything depended on split-second timing: no scope for snags. They abandoned the operation and scattered in all directions. 'It was a matter of seconds, that's all it was, and they'd all disappeared.'

O'Hagan goes on: 'There was one young man, a witness observed, a stout, dark-haired fellow stuffing a revolver into his pocket as he strode away. He was as pale as a sheet. Very white, this young man, as he made his escape. He got away through Cats' Close, a thin, uneven passageway which cut through the tenements behind High Street.' I have it in my head that the person he's describing here is Matt Tipping, Matt who led the unit involved in the fracas, and fired the shot which struck Constable Stirton in the wrist, disabling him. Later in the afternoon of 4 May the arrests begin, and Matt is rounded up along with others; so is Andrew O'Hagan's great-great-uncle Francis. Matt is held in prison for three months but never charged, and on his release – having lost his job – he returns to Lurgan with his wife Jean. They set up a grocery business of their own in Edward Street, and – in 1929 – become the parents of my cousin Harry Tipping.

On 4 September 1921 Michael Collins is in Armagh city addressing a huge rally of his constituents[17] and assuring them of his opposition to any expedient leaving northern nationalists in the lurch.[18] At the same time, he attempts to play down the fears of unionists by telling them they won't be coerced. I am not sure how he reconciles the two assertions. As he leaves Armagh, his car is stoned by Orange diehards who clearly don't believe a word of it. Throughout the day, Collins is protected by a guard of honour, made up from active service units in the district. It includes a couple of Tippings. Perhaps it's one of these who itches to respond to the Orange provocation by firing shots above the heads of the stone-throwers, and has to be restrained by Collins: I don't know. The entire Lurgan Company is present for the occasion and entrusted with the roles of bodyguards, escorts, sentries and so forth. They're in the thick of it. Cumann na mBan is well represented too. Lily Tipping is in the crowd with her box camera, and gets a good shot of Collins as he engages in his customary oratory. (Lily's photograph eventually finds its way to the National Museum in Dublin, where it still is.)

A Tipping *not* in the middle of the Armagh rally is Jimmy, whose sojourn at Ballykinler camp has another three months to run. It is making him a veteran of rough treatment. A book on internment in Northern Ireland, by the author and civil rights activist John McGuffin, was published in 1973. McGuffin spent a lot of time in Lurgan talking to Jimmy about things the ex-internee recalled from the fraught 1920s, his time in that grim enclosure of barbed-wire fences and manned sentry boxes, of poor food and constant aggravation. And republican camaraderie of course, with parades, exercise and education classes geared to reinforce ideological commitment – all organised by the prisoners themselves. For all the details he supplied, though, Jimmy isn't named in McGuffin's book; no doubt he chose to remain anonymous, at a time when ancient conflicts were undergoing a horrific replay. Jimmy's lawless past, had it been raked up in public, might have endangered the quiet days of his seventies, adding to the agony of seeing the whole bloody business start up again. Jimmy had done his bit for Ireland and possessed three medals awarded by the government of the Republic to prove it: Na Fianna Éireann Jubilee medal, Truce Commemorative medal, and Irish War of Independence service medal with bar.[19] (Two of his brothers, Matt and Gerry,[20] were similarly honoured, and granted small military service pensions following De Valera's Irish Constitution of 1937.)

In the enterprise of keeping down the Tippings and their ilk, the British government is succeeded in 1921 by the new Unionist administration which quickly passes a Special Powers Act enabling it to carry on interning.

In the early hours of 26 January 1923 comes a loud persistent hammering on the door of 76 Edward Street. It's the RUC on the trail of the Tippings. The whole street is roused by the disturbance. Sleepy faces appear at upstairs windows; some neighbours give a weary shrug and go back to bed, while others stand at their front doors in a hostile mode taking note of aggressive goings-on. Special constables stomp through the Tipping house while the rudely awakened family emits defiance in the front kitchen. Present in their night clothes – or wearing hastily donned shirts and trousers – are all six of the brothers, along with their parents Henry and Mary Anne, and their sister May. It's not, indeed, the first time the house has been raided – successfully or unsuccessfully – but on this occasion, they all maintain at the time and later, there is nothing untoward in any corner of the premises.

The RUC has a different story. Policemen pounce on a round of .455

revolver ammunition stowed in a pocket of Henry's overcoat hanging in the hall. Henry, open-mouthed, has no idea how it got there. Nor has anyone else. Some seditious papers are then spotted poking out from behind a row of books in the front room. 'What's this? What's this?' Everyone denies all knowledge of these items, provoking derision in the searchers. Mission accomplished, the police snap a pair of handcuffs on the wrists of brothers Frank and Gerry, and bundle them into a waiting Crossley Tender. 'Dear God,' murmurs distressed Mary Anne once again, falling back on a Lurgan mantra, 'Dear God this holy day and hour.'

Arms and ammunition were distributed among sympathetic households in the town, including my grandmother's. She kept a supply of weapons in a sideboard in the kitchen, and breathed a sigh of relief each time a detachment of police officers passed her front door by. It didn't always happen that way. Once, alerted by some sixth sense to an impending incursion, she mustered sufficient presence of mind to dump the things into a shoe bag and hang it from a nail outside a back window, saving the stash for future use and herself from a load of trouble.

The family at 76 had considerable experience in keeping their own arms supplies from falling into the wrong hands, so it seems odd they'd have been so careless at the time of the January raid. Of course, they insisted the items were planted by the raiding party, but whether or not this was so is impossible to tell. You can take your choice about whom to believe: the police seeking a pretext to detain the Tippings, or the Tippings wishful to cast the RUC in the worst possible light.

The police under Lurgan District Inspector P.J. Ferriss achieve their purpose, whether legitimately or fraudulently, with regard to at least two members of 'this very undesirable family'.[21] Frank and Gerry are on their way to the cheerfully named Larne Workhouse Internment Camp. Gerry, never the most robust of the brothers, falls ill with rheumatic fever in this terrible place, and is moved to a hospital attached to the Crumlin Road gaol in Belfast. After a month or so of hospital treatment, he's released unconditionally on medical grounds, but worries that people may think he signed some kind of undertaking renouncing his republican beliefs. 'I suppose there will be terrible rumours about how I got out,' goes a rueful letter to Frank at Larne Workhouse, 'but my answer to them all is: our cause is just and holy; yield not to coercion; our day shall come;[22] and God is with us. Take out of these lines what you like and they are the terms I brought to freedom with me.' No tergiversators among the Tippings.

In July of that year, Frank is transferred to the prison ship *Argenta*, where his brother Jimmy is already ensconced in one of the eight metal cages which form accommodation on the boat. The *Argenta*, moored near Carrickfergus, makes the workhouse seem desirable. Potato skins are mentioned in several accounts as a main part of the diet there. Meals, such as they are, are eaten by inmates sitting on the floor. Tables and chairs are banned, lest they should get smashed up for makeshift weapons. Whatever nightly escape routes the prisoners envisage evaporate with the coming of day. As in Ciaran Carson's poem, 'The Ballad of HMS *Belfast*', which ends:

> And then the smell of docks and ropeworks. Horse-dung.
> The tolling of the Albert Clock.
> Its Pisan slant. The whirring of its ratchets. Then everything
> began to click:
>
> I lay bound in iron chains, alone, my *aisling* gone,
> my sentence passed.
> Grey Belfast dawn illuminated me, on board the prison
> ship *Belfast*.

How did Jimmy Tipping arrive on the prison ship *Argenta*? An incident of 23 May 1923 provides the answer. On that Sunday morning flames are spotted rising from a building near Derrytagh South Bog not far from Lurgan. Also spotted at the same time are seven or eight young men cycling for dear life away from the scene of the outrage. The unoccupied building set alight, supposedly earmarked for a new police barracks, is the property of a family named Turkington. Towards it, under cover of darkness, had come the same young men on bicycles laden with petrol cans, guns and homemade explosives. Despite this dangerous equipment rattling along the rough road, no one gets hurt, or at least hurt very much. According to a report in the *Lurgan Mail*, Mrs Turkington and her son, who live nearby, are held at gunpoint while the burning operation goes ahead. It can't have been pleasant for them, but their new building doesn't suffer irreparable damage and they don't die of fright. Asked to attend an identity parade some time later, the Turkingtons fail to recognise anyone in it – although, says J.P. Ferriss apropos Jimmy Tipping, 'I am satisfied the Turkingtons knew him if they wished to say so.'

They don't wish to say so, but it makes no difference as far as Jimmy's presumed guilt is concerned. Picked up in yet another night raid on 76 Edward Street, along with his young brother Bertie, Jimmy is taken away in police custody en route to the *Argenta*. 'He is undoubtedly a leader, and a dangerous one, and should be interned,' the grim Mr Ferriss states unequivocally in his report to the Minister of Home Affairs, Sir Richard Dawson Bates. At the same time, sixteen-year-old Bertie Tipping finds himself summarily installed in Derry gaol. 'He [Bertie] seems to be about the worst of the lot,' goes another withering note to Dawson Bates, who perhaps by this stage has had his fill of the family. But he hasn't heard the last of them.

The *Argenta* internees latch on to anything and everything to keep their spirits up. As Jimmy writes to his brother Gerry (still in hospital in Belfast):

> Frank is transferred here and is my bedmate on this old boat. All the boys are delighted to hear of you getting on so well. Frank and I are doing our best to get Bertie here and expect to succeed. I can see you at your breakfast 'Moyah', it must be great. Tell the Miss Tennysons they have my best regards.
> – With best love from your brother Jim.

But despite their efforts Bertie stays where he is, and an alternative plan on the part of the authorities, to dispatch Frank and Jimmy to Derry – '[They are] both dangerous men – they would be safer in an ordinary prison' – is vetoed because 'it would make a large collection of this very undesirable family' in the one spot. Concern for Bertie's well-being continues – even his father Henry writes a letter pleading for clemency on account of the boy's age, and his usefulness as an assistant in the grocer's shop – but nothing comes of it. The next thing is a postcard from Jimmy addressed to his sister May in Lurgan, which sparks a slight panic among the prison authorities, sending a flurry of communications flying back and forth at every level. After thanking May for a parcel she'd sent – most of whose contents had reached him, he says, bar an item or two confiscated by the censor – and requesting his usual 200 cigarettes and a string of rosary beads, Jimmy wonders if anything has been heard from Bertie. Then comes the sentence causing alarm and affront. 'The Governor of Derry Gaol should be notified,' writes Jimmy, 'to the effect that, should Bertie be ill-treated in any way, he will not be forgotten.'

Jimmy's postcard is read with horror by the warden on the *Argenta*, who promptly dispatches it to the Ministry of Home Affairs. Did Jimmy really write it with his own hand ('It would be well to obtain a specimen of this internee's handwriting', goes a solemn suggestion), and is the implication really as sinister as it seems? Letters go forth to the Derry governor warning him to be extra vigilant, to the inspector general of the RUC, to the county inspector, Armagh, to the sceptical DI Ferriss in Lurgan – who at last gets the thing in some kind of proportion. 'I have no reason to fear that any of the Tipping family at present at large would molest the Governor of Derry Prison,' he assures his superiors shaking in their shoes. 'No doubt the Tippings are a bad lot, but in my opinion the reference … to the Gaol Governor is a bit of bluff.' His opinion is listened to. The postcard finally reaches its addressee. No action is taken against Jimmy on account of it. But all three of the Tipping brothers are kept in custody until December 1924, and then only let go when a general release of internees is decreed.

Things are changing in the world of Irish affairs, or at least the emphasis is shifting. With De Valera's about-turn in the South, and the 'Protestant State' consolidated in the North, the nationalist population of towns like Lurgan continued to seethe, indeed, but seethed more quietly. Fewer eruptions of fighting occurred in the small rough streets. Worn out, perhaps, with all the rioting and destruction of the early 1920s, rival factions snarled and grimaced, but kept their distance from one another, on the whole. Threats to 'burn out' this or that sectarian quarter mostly came to nothing.

At the same time, the causes of disaffection were, if anything, on the increase. It was hard for northern Catholics and nationalists to be happy with their lot. They were constantly told they were rogues, dupes and outsiders. Forms of social, religious and indigenous inferiority were pasted over them. Nevertheless – harking back to the seventeenth century – they believed the country was rightfully theirs.[23] They subscribed to a highly charged version of history. It was, of course, a story of wrongs inflicted and – in the teeth of persecution – patriotic values upheld. The republican Tippings (and others) saw a certain kind of moral obligation staring them in the face, and acted upon it. Not to have done so would have branded them as spineless and spiritless. If their actions brought down an old house on their heads in the form of internment and other tests of endurance – well, so be it, they would grit their teeth and endure the lot. There were side benefits, of course: exhilaration, a terrific sense of purpose gingering up the prosaic side of life, being in the thick of things as they slipped away from weighing tea or totting up bills to subvert the state.

Perhaps the instinct to engage in undercover activity was imprinted in their genes. Before they were Protestant, some of the English Tippings were Catholic and imprisoned in the Tower on account of it,[24] 'comitted,' a contemporary report goes, 'uppon Suspition of treason'. Plots and counter-plots fizzed about their heads in the pungent Elizabethan underworld of conspiracy and duplicity. A James Tipping crops up in the 1580s taking a minor part in the Babington affair, and in another, stillborn endeavour to shoot a poisoned arrow into Queen Elizabeth as she walked in the garden. The removal of Elizabeth was essential to the plans of English recusants. James Tipping and his brother John, three centuries and more before their Lurgan namesakes, believed in the possibility of a different kind of social hierarchy, the overthrow of Protestantism and restoration of the Catholic nation, and risked their lives in the effort to achieve it. They held a genuine belief in the justice of the Catholic cause, unlike the many government agents who infiltrated the cabals to the detriment of the plotters. Torture and imprisonment loomed, a consequence of double dealings on the part of informers. The Tower, the *Argenta* ... here comes a cliché but I can't resist it: *autre temps, autre moeurs.*

John Tipping ... hmn. What if – and *here* comes an enormous speculation – what if the husband of long-ago Katherine Rose was not a Stratford man at all, but an ex-conspirator on the run from London to Warwickshire? All right, he'd have had to be nineteen or twenty years older than his bride, but that's not an impossible circumstance. (Or perhaps he had a son, another John.) And yes, I know it's ridiculous to conflate the Babington conspirator and the cutler, on no firmer evidence than the coincidence of their names, but I offer this bit of nonsense for what it is worth.

In twentieth-century Lurgan, time is passing. The leaves of the trees in Lurgan Park turn golden-brown and russet, and then the trees are bare. The lake freezes over, and children slide and slither with enjoyment along North Street. Spring: cherry blossom, daffodils, balloons and hop-scotch. In summer comes the smell of new-mown grass, hay wains and endless sunny days, and a cool breeze blowing from Lough Neagh. ... All of the Edward Street brothers marry and raise families, and over the years enjoy considerable prestige in the locality on account of their darkly glamorous, freedom-fighting past. Republicanism didn't go away, and never would go away, but old-style republicanism was on the wane – though it had a burst or two of reinvigoration before the end of the 1950s (when I was affected by it).

In Lurgan, for example, partisan passions were reignited in the run-up to the general election of 1935. Electioneering meetings, the *Lurgan Mail* reported in its strange decorous prose, 'were full of interest'. So they were. One (unionist) in Market Street, was addressed by the Conservative and Unionist candidate Sir William Allan to the usual cheers and boos. Another (republican) drew an equally large and voluble crowd to Edward Street, where the speakers included 'Madame Gonne MacBride' in her old-fashioned attire. After the meeting, on Tuesday 12 November, Maud Gonne is hastily spirited away to Bertie Tipping's house in Lake Street, where she's arranged to spend the night.

In the early hours of Wednesday morning, something occurs. Police and B Specials surround the house. By crossing the border, Maud Gonne has contravened an exclusion order made against her some time ago (I'm still quoting the *Lurgan Mail*). Roused up by the furore, Bertie and his wife attempt to instil a sense of urgency into their distinguished (and blasé) visitor, but the doughty veteran of many republican campaigns simply snaps her fingers at the RUC and all its works, turns over in her bed and goes back to sleep. It's some time before the recently wed Tippings can get her out of the bed and into her clothes. Her stately descent to the hallway is no doubt a cause of relief to the somewhat nonplussed constabulary, who haven't the knack of dealing with female firebrands and muses. Politely conducted to a car and driven to Newry under police escort, Maud Gonne – not yet exactly old and grey and full of sleep, despite her early rising (and although she's not far short of seventy) – is then safely deposited on the proper side of the border. (On her journey north, Maud Gonne had cannily bought only a one-way ticket, knowing she could rely on the RUC to see her safely home.)

On polling day (Thursday 14 November), says the *Lurgan Mail*, 'there were large numbers of voters waiting to record their votes, including a large contingent of people who had been at early morning Mass in St Peter's Church'. Ho-hum. At the town hall, the report goes on, somewhat cryptically, 'it was alleged that a young man, a supporter of the unionist cause, interfered with some girls and excitement ensued'. In the ensuing excitement, 'the police found it necessary to draw batons and chase a crowd of about a thousand up High Street'. Here you have an instance of bitter Lurgan recidivism. It's no good expecting elections to be conducted sedately. The unionist candidate will win the day, of course, but Sinn Féin means to give him a run for his money. Think Belfast in the docks area in 1857, the Brickfields in 1864, the streets filled with noise and fear. Heads struck with bottles and batons, seasoned rioters dispersing and disappearing, weary policemen slumped over their riot shields at the end of the night ... all these features of endemic instability make an Ulster picture to dishearten ameliorists. 'From every entry and from every lane, / The brickbats and stones in showers they came.'[25]

The Orange young man who 'interfered' with the – I assume green – girls turns up in Edward Street being battered by a mob: from this predicament, I am pleased to say, he is extricated by Gerry Tipping who finds himself unable to stand idly by while harm is done to a fellow human being, of whatever colouration. Gerry, by some means or other, gets the offending youth to the safety of the tally rooms in Jordan's Factory (the property, you will remember, of Gerry's grandmother's relations – though I doubt they'd be falling over themselves to acknowledge the kinship). Ructions over, 'by 11 p.m. the crowd had dispersed and the usual normal conditions prevailed'. Whatever 'normal' means.

Jimmy Tipping – ex-felon – at various times is host in Lurgan to General Tom Barry of *Guerrilla Days in Ireland* fame (an old friend), and to Major Vivion de Valera, oldest son of the Irish president. The days of real poverty, recklessness and raids-by-night are over, for some of the family at least. They just get on with their lives. All prosper, to varying degrees. Photographs from the summer of 1935 show a merry quartet,

Jimmy, Bertie, Bertie's wife Annie and a friend, on holiday in Kerry, all looking at ease on horseback as they trot exuberantly through the Gap of Dungloe. Back in Lurgan, Frank invents an automatic egg-packing device and patents it (not that it nets him a fortune, alas). And when the time arrives for Matt, Jimmy and Gerry to apply for formal recognition of their services to the Republic, they are able to muster a lot of support from people willing to speak on their behalf. All the relevant documents are in the military archives in Dublin, and I don't propose to quote from them – well, apart from the following exchange, which I include as a riposte to the unionist view, the 'troublesome youths', 'bad lot' assessment of the authorities:

Q.   They were a great family, the Tippings?
A.   They were.

CHAPTER 8
THE IMPORTANCE OF
LOCAL KNOWLEDGE

... Never go by Cupar Street, my father would warn me, and I knew
this was a necessary prohibition without asking why, for Cupar Street
was one of those areas where the Falls and Shankill joined together
as unhappy Siamese twins, one sporadically and mechanically beating
the other round the head, where the Cullens, Finnegans and Reillys
merged with Todds and Camerons and Wallaces.

Ciaran Carson, 'Question Time'

A time arrives when the fatherless Brady family of Lurgan receives a
boost. Nora becomes a day girl at a top-notch convent. She is plucked
out of her primary school classroom, where rote-learning, chilblains,
snatters and blockheadedness are the order of the day, and deposited
on top of a hill, in the select surroundings of Cornakinegar, and
with optimum advancement anticipated. She can't believe her good
fortune.

It's 1924 or 5, and a one-time industrial school for boys, formerly an
imposing Victorian mansion called Irishtown Hill House, has changed
its function once again and opened its doors to fee-paying, day- and
boarding-pupils. Girls this time, of impeccable Catholic standing, better-
than-average brains, and (it is hoped) susceptibility to the school spirit.

The elevated setting reflects its upward orientation in terms of social class and holiness. Our Lady's Secondary School, soon popularly known as Mount St Michael's, Lurgan.

The school's earliest intake isn't quite sufficient to meet Ministry of Education requirements, so to bump up the numbers a year's free tuition becomes available to poor, or poorish, primary school pupils of an appropriate disposition and intelligence. Some of these extra pupils are recruited from the convent in Edward Street, and a shining light among them is champion speller, grammarian, reader and general knowledge wizard Nora Brady, a child so good at answering she's got beyond her primary-grade teachers. When Nora's mother is summoned and the proposition put to her, she grasps it with both hands: *anything* to prolong her youngest daughter's schooling is a godsend. She's not the kind of mother who hurries her children into paid employment to enlarge the family income. Education is the key to a brighter life, she knows that, but until this moment advanced education has had no more relevance to her own situation than pie in the sky. Now, at last, it seems, the pie is in a dish and being borne towards her. And really, it's no more than her due. The Bradys, like the Tippings, think well of themselves, they always have, but scrimping and saving has imposed a kind of martyred aspect on them. And my grandmother understands that it's not enough just to trudge through life, taking blow after blow and still find the heart to laugh and joke – you need some extra ingredient, some source of grace or well-being, to balance the hard times.

So here is Nora in her navy-blue-and-white Mount St Michael's uniform – acquired at goodness knows what cost in exertion or privation – plus all the grammar-school accoutrements: satchel, lesson books, hockey stick, sheet music, drawing block, pens and pencils and what-have-you. And so much invested in the probable outcome of all this! The whole family rallies to make the most of the opportunity, for Nora and themselves. Those already working help with additional costs. As she leaves the house each morning, stepping out buoyantly for her new school, Nora carries the weight of everyone's expectations on her unassuming and unbowed head.

The pressure is enormous, but what makes it bearable, more than bearable, elating and enchanting, is the way she fits into the new environment, like the subject of a restored birthright in a fairy tale. From the minute she sets foot in Mount St Michael's, Nora has a sense of being in her element. It was the biggest thing that could happen to her. The little world of classrooms, corridors, bells, nuns, lessons, japes, bosom friends, games, nature study walks to the shores of Lough Neagh; the glorious convent grounds complete with lawns, fir trees, pines, beeches, hockey pitch and tennis courts ... all this enfolds and sustains her. It's a place apart from rainy, sect-ridden Lurgan, a refuge from a home still reeling from the death of Lily, and attendant sorrows. ... Her charming, tentative sister Kathleen, who married after the war and made a new life for herself in the south of England, was loth to recall those days of the 1920s and 30s, summing up the whole period as 'not a very happy time'. That was all she had to say about it. But for Nora it was different. Nora is going places – or so they all believe – and everything is geared to help her along the way. She is shielded, as far as possible, from the effects of depression and deprivation – just as I, in my turn, am shielded from harsh realities such as a less than adequate household income, and intermittent parental discords.

When I was young and unaccustomed to proper seaside holidays, my mother and I would often go to Dublin on the train. She had cousins there of whom she was very fond, the Ellen Brady tribe whose Lurgan childhoods were entwined with hers and her sisters'. They, the cousins, had migrated southwards with their family at the start of the 1930s, and at the same time my grandmother, with *her* family, had upped sticks for Belfast. What provoked this double exodus in opposite directions from Lurgan I don't know. (The Tippings stayed put.) But contact between the scattered cousins was maintained at a high level. When it came to our Dublin trips, my mother's and mine, in the late 1940s and '50s, it might be just a day's excursion, or we might stay overnight with Josie, Anne, Clare or Maureen; or even as long as a week. And every time the train from Belfast slowed on the outskirts of Lurgan, my mother would raise her arm and point to a four-square, grey building atop a hill, 'That's my old school.' A jumble of emotions including pride, affection, wonder, reverie and wryness were intermingled in that simple statement. It is heartbreaking now to contemplate. I had no idea. I'd nod and smile, without paying too much attention. It was no big deal. Everyone of our sort[1] had an old school somewhere. Didn't they? At five or six, enclosed in my nutshell world, I was as ignorant as could be of the vast implications surrounding my mother's status as an old Michaelonian.

An old Michaelonian – but hold on a minute. Didn't I say my mother's scholarship was only tenable for a year, just long enough to give her a taste of heady grammar-school life, before the prize was snatched away, and her pre-Michaelonian destination of mill or factory reinstated? Yes, but Nora did so well at the school that the nuns were reluctant to lose her – a shame to curtail a promising academic career – and prayers were offered up for a way round the impasse. As a consequence – perhaps – *someone* had a brainwave. The suggestion may have come from the school, or my grandmother may have thought of it herself, but the upshot of all the cogitations on Nora's behalf was the widow Brady getting into her best clothes and marching her daughter Nora, in her trembling-in-the-balance Mount St Michael's uniform, off to the High Street offices of the fledgling British Legion.

The British Legion came into being in 1921 to help ex-servicemen, war widows and their dependents. It was funded partly through the 'Poppy Day' appeal, and high on its agenda was the education of dead soldiers' children. And here was one who fitted the bill, stepping smartly into the office with all her glowing recommendations accompanying her. An unassertive but steadfast child, she must have made a good impression on top of her mother's resolute, no-nonsense demeanour. Between the two of them – and with Nora's teachers' strong backing – they make out a good case. The British Legion officials agree to shoulder the burden of Nora's school fees.

So she's back at the school on the hill for the start of the autumn term of her second year (Form C1). Hardly anyone knows what a close-run thing it was, how easily young Nora might have vanished into a different milieu of factory hooters and boisterous behaviour in the street. Her place in the class is assured, and her essays go on being read aloud by the English teacher as models of composition and insight. All she has to do to keep educationally afloat is to pass her Junior, and then her Senior Certificate examination in every subject – which she does, though not without fuss and anxiety surrounding the maths papers in both exams. If no one twits Nora on account of her scholarship status, it's possibly because her friends are not aware of it: I've written elsewhere[2] about the kindness of nuns who included Nora in the bill-distributing ritual at the end of term, to save her embarrassment, having carefully placed inside her envelope a slip of paper with the words 'No charge'. I think it's unlikely, indeed, that a gulf was apparent between the few scholarship pupils and the rest of the school: whatever their backgrounds, these were *all* provincial Catholic girls, all more or less unworldly and uncouth, vigorous on the hockey field and unabashed by their County Armagh accents and country faces. It wasn't uncommon for one or two to appear in the classroom in twisted black stockings or a slovenly gym-tunic, and come in for a wigging on account of it.

It's true that my mother, like the scholarship heroine of Winifred Darch's *Heather at the High School*,[3] might have based her anticipations of her new life on the treatment meted out to Lancashire ex-council schoolgirl Betty Barton (in the weekly paper *The Schoolgirl's Own*) on her arrival at snooty Morcove ('Scorned by the School' was the title of the opening episode). Also like the eponymous Heather, she'd have found the reality to be different. But a wish to remain securely one of a group, not differentiated from her peers in any way, would have kept my mother silent about her home circumstances.

There were, of course, other reasons besides a fear of snobbishness for keeping the British Legion connection dark. The word 'British' didn't go down too well in republican Lurgan, with its illicit tricolours and Easter lilies as emblems of disaffection. I'm not sure how much of the true state of affairs was divulged by my grandmother to her Tipping relations (some of whom, as we've seen, were interned for anti-government activity around this time). Two of these, indeed, were themselves ex-servicemen; but all that, Salonika and Sud-el-Bar, was obliterated by subsequent overwhelming, countervailing commitments. They, the Tippings, might have taken a critical attitude to *any* dealings with the British. On the other hand, they could have understood that something was owed, and could legitimately be claimed, by Irish families bereaved by the First World War. 'Good for you – take whatever you can get' might have been uttered, commending my grandmother's gumption. Or: 'You'd no call to go crawling to those imperialist bastards.' One or the other, I can't say which.

But no ideological considerations can deflect my grandmother's drive to secure the best possible outcome for her daughter Nora. Whatever needs to be done, she will do it, and reconcile in her own mind any conflicting obligations arising from her actions.

As for Nora – her romantic nationalism survives the acquisition of a non-Irish source for her school fees. And at the same time, her romantic

'Great War' obsession flourishes. 'If I should die, think only this of me ...' runs through her head – though perhaps with 'Ireland' substituted for 'England' in it. It doesn't matter very much; it's the slant of the poem that's important, the high-flown self-sacrificial stance, not the specifics. Also, Brooke's poem chimes with the notion of self-suppression, the unimportance of the individual, purveyed by nuns – one reason why it's taught in Form C1's English class.

The Mercy nuns of Our Lady's Secondary School aren't greatly perturbed by the state of the country. Violence and alarms in the streets hardly impinge on them in their house on the hill (unlike their counterparts in the town centre). They like being Irish, of course, but only in so far as Irishness is conflated with Catholicism. They bask in their remoteness from pagan ways. And the aim is to instil in every pupil a similar aspiration to Hibernian holiness.

Every facet of the social world of Mount St Michael's is bolstered by religiosity. Hymns in the morning, hymns in the afternoon, prayers before class, holy water fonts all over the place, 'Tantum Ergo' in the school chapel, 'pious objects' in everyone's possession, Missionary Society, sodalities of all sorts, virtue and modesty, the Blessed Virgin Mary, Benediction, the annual Retreat, lectures by priests on 'The Suffering that Mortal Sin Gives to God'. A garden party for past and present pupils begins with everyone kneeling on the ground, nuns, teachers, visitors and all, heads bowed, to receive a blessing from a local Monsignor wearing a kind of fur-trimmed cape over a short white muslin dress with a deep lace border, and a long black skirt buttoned down the front. And a silly hat on his head to boot. And an intense solemnity surrounding the proceedings, with never a maverick schoolgirl to nudge the person next to her, causing the both of them to choke back an irreverent outbreak of giggles.

Well, as far as I know. I'm envisaging a deferential gathering here. If all the pre-war girls of Mount St Michael's were bursting with suppressed rebelliousness, they'd have controlled themselves and put up a front of angelic behaviour. It was what they were trained to do. The whole Holy-Father-Reverend-Mother-Corpus Christi-Virgin-Mary gallimaufry had worked its effect on them. It would be the most shaming thing in the world to be taxed with a spiritual deficiency. They had all been got before the age of seven and had swallowed the Church and all its ploys and edicts. The Catholic way of life could hardly have been more fundamentally taken for granted.

(Taken for granted: but quite a high proportion of the school community has a name suggesting a different ancestry and affiliation. Holmes, Rodgers, Harrington, Berwick, Black, Walls, Forrest, Warren, Hinds and – yes –Tipping.[4] And many others to offset the *fior-Gaedhalach* contingent, the O'Boyles, O'Hagans, Raffertys, McQuillans. And all of them lumped together under a cloistered designation. Products – like all of us – of ancestral mixing-and-matching, these girls have all come out unequivocally in a sectional mould. ... Take any classroom in the North, for that matter, and no doubt you will find a similar denominative mix. My own class at St Dominic's High School in the 1950s, I remember, contained Waters, Commerton, Drummond, Buckley, Glover and so on, alongside O'Callaghan, Caffrey, O'Hagan, Devlin, Quinn, Mageean.)

And these particular Mount St Michael's lambs of the flocks of Catholic Ireland are immensely privileged, so they're told, by being in receipt of an education extended well beyond the official school-leaving age of fourteen. They're assured of it over and over, and they believe it wholeheartedly. They are being prepared for a life of service to God (eyes turn upwards and hands are pressed together prayerfully at the idea) – ideally, as nuns or missionaries or something ostentatiously vocational; or more likely – second-best – as Catholic housewives and mothers in some substantial Ulster suburb of new-built houses with garages and lawns. Whichever it is, underpinning the rest of their lives on earth will be that unassailable faith acquired at birth and cultivated thereafter as assiduously as Lord Emsworth's prize-winning pumpkin.

A full immersion in Catholic immaculacy will make each Mount St Michael's girl a better person, and the social ethos of the school will make her a better class of person. (So the received wisdom goes.) She's in a position to look down her nose at the brawls, shawls, catcalls and all the bitter routines of the streets. Walking home in the centre of a group of mildly sky-larking friends, through the gathering dusk of a winter's afternoon, light fading across the rooftops of Lurgan, my mother can feel secure about her place in the world. And, later, she can reminisce self-deprecatingly about those charmed days, inspired, maybe, among other things, by that fleeting glimpse of the sacred spot from the Dublin train, 'There's my old school.'

None of this, the nuts and bolts of a Mount St Michael's training, is very much in the spirit of interdenominational accord. Catholic exclusiveness, like its Protestant counterpart, is a strong feature of the times, the period between the early 1900s and the 1960s (say). Despite the measure of inadvertent integration mentioned above – Harrington/O'Hagan – the integrated school is a thing of the future, as every sect holds fast to its own version of divine revelation.

They know they are right. And no school rebel arrives out of nowhere to pose a challenge to the system, or disrupt the decorum of highly regulated corridors and classrooms. They are all good girls at Mount St Michael's. They are silent at times when silence is enjoined on them, and meekly proceed in crocodile formation to wherever they're summoned by a ringing bell. My mother in particular conforms to the school code and sails through the whole five- or six-year course. ... Move forward thirty-odd years, and you find the same is not true of her only daughter whose career as a Dominican schoolgirl in Belfast can be summed up in a storybook title complete with exclamation mark, *Expelled*! But that's a generation closer to the inevitable undoing of the convent system, and an event which in some ways prefigures the last gasp of nunly autocracy. My mother shows no comparable tendency to look for trouble – at least, until she suddenly throws caution to the winds and marries a Protestant (albeit a convertible Protestant). Ah – you can hear the Sisters of Mercy sigh – here comes an infusion of bad blood; and so it is proved, with regard to the daughter of the marriage. But Nora still has quite a way to go before this impulse of exogamy overtakes her.

She has a whole university course to get through. Her amazing progress doesn't stop at Mount St Michael's. Queen's beckons, though not without an obstacle or two along the way. First come the dreaded maths papers – scraped through, with a sigh of relief. Then, having moved from Edward Street to North Street in Lurgan (some time after Lily's death), my grandmother – as I've said – for some reason gathers up her family and sweeps them north to Belfast, to a dingy house in a street off the Stranmillis Road called Sandhurst Gardens, one of a group collectively known as the River Streets. The phrase 'damp Lagan fogs' comes to mind, again, courtesy of Maurice James Craig[5] and his poem imploring the Lord to be kind to Belfast. These Stranmillis streets slope down to the Lagan and consist of small terraced red-brick houses with miniscule gardens in front and back yards running along an alleyway behind. Indeed the new habitation is very convenient for Queen's

University once Nora gets there; but first comes her final year at school and an arduous train journey every morning from Great Victoria Street station all the way to Lurgan, and back again in the afternoon. (I don't think boarding was an option for her, and neither was a change of school at this late stage.) Some pressing reason must have underlain the leaving of Lurgan, no doubt about it, but what it was I have no idea. The two families, as I've said, the David Bradys and the William Bradys, decamped southwards and northwards at the same time. It didn't have a beneficial effect on Nora's school career, but neither did it knock her off-course entirely. More work, more adjustment, greater concentration, that's all there is to it. She sits her Senior Certificate examination, passes it, and is accepted by Queen's.

This was a vastly more significant achievement than it is at present. Nowadays, third-level education is a right of everyone; but university students were a privileged minority, in those intoxicating, irrecoverable inter-war days. They were a small, high-spirited, but basically hard-working and tractable group, which suited my mother down to the ground. It was a wonderful time for her. She brings to Belfast her notebooks filled with cherished verse, and her tentative self-assurance (assurance nurtured in Lurgan by nuns more helpful than those of my experience). The gracious and expansive university milieu seems like an extension of the well-sited, well-loved school on the hill. Both are, and aren't, Nora's natural habitat, and gain in piquancy from the anomaly. It's just a short step from each, no more than a mile or so, to the crowded and straitened family home with its tiny scullery and mangle in the yard.

And here is Queen's in all its splendour, a refuge of calm in the heart of unruly Belfast. Its carved stone, diamond-pane windows, its buttresses and battlements, all suggesting permanence and pageantry, a ceremonious attitude to life. Looking ancient – though it is, of course, only Victorian. Here are the lawns, the quadrangle, the panelled Great Hall, the gowned figures lending an air of formality to the scene. And here is Nora-from-North-Street acquiring a university sensibility, with her books tucked under her arm and her air of purpose. Here she is during a break between lectures, seated on a bench in the cloisters with a bunch of male and female friends around her, and a medical student – I'm sure he's a medical student – acting the clown in the background. Girls are at a premium at Queen's in the 1930s, when they make up only a quarter of the student population, and hence come in for a lot of gossip and joking attention. Especially if they're at all pleasing in appearance.

My mother led an active social life at Queen's. This is plain from a clutch of letters from admirers which she kept to raise her spirits in grimmer post-war days. Jack, Joe, Jim, Sean and Frank were the writers – all unknown, all vanished into the maw of time. She'd sometimes mention, in sorrow and disbelief, a handsome university friend – maybe one of the above – who ended life with his head in a gas oven. But sorrows and tragedies were figments of an unimaginable future, back in the charmed '30s with its Shakespeare and Keats, its dress patterns garnered from magazines and run up in cheap material to wear at the weekly 'hop', its lovely Queen's Elms building where women students congregated. Unlike her contemporary John Boyd, or the slightly later Robert Greacen, my mother was not dissatisfied with Queen's. She was not disposed to criticise its professors. The need to take notes during lectures didn't aggravate her. Professor Savory wearing riding breeches under his academic gown was not a figure of fun as far as Nora was concerned. She hung on his every word. Everything to her was new and exhilarating then: autumn leaves swirling round her feet in the Stranmillis Road, the steamy Palm House in nearby Botanic Gardens, the keyed-up atmosphere of the examination halls.

The Boat Club Hop, a 'rugger' match, a dance 'up Islandmagee way', a 'Happy Tea' – whatever that is – Rag Day, the student magazine *PTQ*: all these are entered into with gusto. 'I hope you were not scolded for staying out late on the night of the dance,' writes Jack (or Jim). And again: 'I am glad you suffered no ill effects from your "debauch".' The mind boggles: whatever can he mean? This is my stainless mother he's addressing, she of what he calls 'the supercilious eyebrows'. 'Debauch', indeed. Did Nora drink a glass of Babycham? I refuse to entertain the possibility of any more exorbitant impropriety. During my own inflamed student years (and later), I had to protect my mother from the things going on in my head (and not only in my head). Hers was a more innocent generation (or so everyone likes to believe about their predecessors). It was infinitely more shockable. So – no debauched goings-on in those days, thank you very much.

But the wretched Jim (or Jack) won't leave off. 'I'm sure we could do famously if we were laid out somewhere along the Lagan,' he suggests. Well! I had thought the Lagan towpath as a venue for wanton behaviour was a discovery of myself and my contemporaries. And here it is fulfilling the same function back in the days of (supposed) piety and decorum. ... Does Jack's Lagan idyll ever take place? I don't know – well, I assume it does, but my mother at twenty or twenty-one is really an unknown quantity to me. As for Jim/Jack: his medical student bawdiness keeps bursting out (so to speak). In his letters to Nora he alludes to the John Donne poem, 'On His Mistress Going to Bed', and at the same time hopes to provide her – if she'll let him – with abundant saucy anecdotes to entertain her grandchildren. And adds: 'You'll never know how near I was to writing 'our' grandchildren.' What I know is how near he came to writing me out of existence in the process.

But what went wrong between my mother and her undergraduate suitor (and other suitors about the place)? That's a story that can never be told: the facts are missing. For all her relish for learning, Nora becomes an exile from academia, by her own act and choosing. When she comes to marry, some years on, she opts for a person adept in banter and gregariousness, a singer in the John McCormack mould, of a lively temperament and unexalted means of livelihood (he works for the Ulster Transport Authority fitting together parts of trains). Against the odds, it proves a happy alliance in many respects. ... It's just my grandmother I can't help feeling sorry for, with another thundering disappointment to add to her life of hardship and stress. After all the sacrifices, all the aspirations invested in Nora, she has *not* fulfilled her unspoken obligation of marrying into the professional classes, and thereby bumping up the Brady family's social position. Not that her mother, my grandmother, holds this dereliction against her. Whatever Nora decides is right in her mother's eyes; or so she persuades herself. (This attitude, transmitted to the following generation, prevails in relations between my mother and myself, possibly to the detriment of my behaviour. Many actions of mine that should by rights have infuriated her, are excused or even applauded due to her absolute commitment to my well-being – lovely for me, of course, if not ultimately conducive to a sterling character.)

I don't know why my mother's university sojourn didn't lead to a different outcome. The social life of Nora and her sister Kathleen is centred on Queen's for a time ('Remember me to K. and tell her how nice I thought she looked on Friday night last,' writes J.), and then it isn't. They go their different ways. Nora is the first to marry, followed by Kathleen who meets an Englishman, a soldier stationed in Northern

Ireland during the war, at my Craig grandparents' house at Dunmurry, and with whom she emigrates to Wickford, Essex, settling in a bungalow the newly-wed pair calls Lismoyne, in honour of the location of their first encounter. In the meantime, I have come on the scene and am growing up to question none of the choices made by my elders, none of the circumstances of my intriguing life (intriguing to me). It is just the way things are. It takes a long time for the thought to enter my head that my parents are perhaps not entirely on the same wavelength, despite a shared sense of humour and a good many friends in common. It's something to do with one being a reader and the other not, one committed to sociability and the other more to social responsibility. Does the Protestant/Catholic divide come into it? Not at a fundamental level, I think, but perhaps the differing traditions and family settings do in some way work a bothersome effect. I'm not complaining: the marriage endows me, I believe, with an ancestry which is, at the same time, implicit in most of our Northern Irish backgrounds, and unusually explicit in my own case. ... But I wonder a bit about the paths my mother *didn't* take, the kind of life she might have led with someone of a comparable upper mobility, a co-religionist or a fellow schoolteacher.

Like one of those besotted Queen's undergraduates, for instance. 'It was very pleasant to hear that both you and I had passed that Scholastic Philosophy examination,' writes another of Nora's holiday correspondents (more sedate than Jim/Jack, who jokes in one letter about getting drunk and proposing to a barmaid in Derry, while on a mission to offload the magazine *PTQ*). Scholastic philosophy – hmn. The phrase ushers in a fact of university life at the time. Religious segregation. Students were either Protestant (overwhelmingly) or Catholic, and a minimum of intermingling occurred. My mother, of course, knocked around with a 'Catholic' set: a Celia Lenaghan, Frances Kelly, Maureen McKavanagh, Maureen McKenna, Maureen Harbinson, Honoria Smyth, whose future thankless task is to teach *me* arithmetic at St Dominic's High School, Maire Casement, another future Dominican teacher whose English lessons will constitute the highlight of my dodgy school career.

The scholastic philosophy course was available to Catholics only.[6] The department, says Marianne Elliott, had come into being 'in response to a successful campaign to create separate Catholic teaching programmes in controversial subjects'.[7] In the 1930s, scholastic philosophy was the province of Father Arthur Ryan (later Monsignor Ryan), an amiable and cultured professor by all accounts. Many of the current batch of undergraduates would end up as teachers, and the aim was to make them fit to teach in Catholic schools – and thereby perpetuate religious differentiation. Ah me. Few integrationist voices were raised at the time.

The blame for this situation need not be apportioned solely to Catholics. Take Riddel Hall. This otherwise admirable hall of residence on the Stranmillis Road was unambiguous about its orientation. When it opened its doors in September 1915 – incidentally, the year and month of my grandfather William Brady's death in the Dardanelles – it might as well have placed a banner across its seemly facade bearing the words 'No Taigs'. It was set up explicitly to make a home-from-home for female *Protestant* students and teachers of Queen's University, Belfast. ... Have I struck a note of criticism here with my outraged italics? All right, I know in one sense I'm applying standards of the present to institutions of the past. I know they did things differently then, and that it suited each sect to adhere to its own network of ideology, support and social organisation. I'm aware that in ordinary people's minds, attachment to one sect, and repudiation of the other, was bound up with integrity, not bigotry. Bigotry was an attribute of the back streets, the very stupid, or those in high places with an axe to grind (e.g. the 'Protestant' government of the day). For everyone else, it simply made for an easier life to abide by the rules – the 'Protestant' rules, or the 'Catholic' rules, whichever you'd been born to. Abide by the rules – and never bother about contributing by your line-of-least-resistance to the upkeep of apartheid.

Hindsight, that useful commodity, may allow us an amended moral attitude, but it shouldn't encourage automatic condemnation of people who actually did a lot of good, like the two Misses Riddel (though I've got another bone to pick with them, or their relations, in a minute). This pair of well-off, high-minded sisters put up the money to build and endow Riddel Hall, thereby aligning themselves with the cause of women's education in Ireland, and saving generations of clever young women from the miseries of bleak bed-sitting-rooms. Yes, indeed, only good Protestant girls from the country need apply for Riddel Hall accommodation – nevertheless, at the time, the new hall of residence represented an amazingly enlightened and generous action on the part of the two old benefactors (aged 84 and 78 in that year, 1915). We can credit the sisters with a feminist, or proto-feminist, attitude of mind, if not with ecumenical leanings.

But who were these Riddels? Miss Eliza and Miss Isabella[8] were among the youngest of the ten children born to a Belfast hardware merchant named John Riddel and his wife Annabella Charley (yes, of the same linen family that employed my grandfather William Craig as a groom, and founded the school attended by his children in the 1920s). John Riddel had died in 1870, but his sons took over the business and prospered and at some point the family acquired a substantial mansion called Beechmount House. The odd thing about Beechmount House was that it was on the Falls Road. Well, not the historic Falls of popular imagination, with its down-at-heel terraced rows of houses, its cobbles, backyards, factories, street games and disaffection. Beechmount House stood well back from the redoubtable road itself, on high ground in the shadow of the Black Mountain, the Cave Hill clearly discernible to the left, the whole of Belfast spread out beneath it, stretching away in the distance to the shipyard gantries. (It still stands in the same spot, but its function has changed, as we shall see.) ... Or maybe the eponymous beech trees screened out the view of grim glum Belfast, I don't know. Here the very plain looking, unmarried Riddels lived on and on, in elevated style, until the last of them, Eliza, died in 1924.

If you'd lived in the district around the turn of the twentieth century, you might have seen, like an image from another world, Samuel Riddel and his sisters driving down the Falls Road in an open carriage, clip-clopping along while you drew your shawl more tightly around you against the japs from the gutters, or raised your dingy old cap from your uncouth head. There they went, noses in the air, 'like proper royalty', as it seemed to local footsloggers at the time, awestruck by the unimaginable luxury of *Protestant* existences. ...When the people impressed by Riddel hauteur were themselves old, in the 1950s, they'd talk about elements of the past, including Beechmount House and its occupants, and captured the interest of Ballymurphy boy Joe Graham (a future local historian[9]). The phrase stayed in his mind.

Beechmount House, for all its seclusion, wasn't happily situated. It *was* the Falls Road. Isabella Riddel missed the worst of the flaring 'Troubles' by dying in 1918, but the last years of her sister Eliza were filled with distress and apprehension, fear of what the world was coming to. Terrific skirmishes, violence, shouts in the streets. The news is appalling, day after day. And some of it very close to home. For instance: in May 1921 an ambush of police and B Specials takes place near the Ballymurphy brickworks on the Springfield Road. Fourteen men of D Company, armed with handguns and grenades, wait behind a hedge in anticipation of a police tender. ... Here it comes, round a bend, the IRA men open fire, the police retaliate, the ill-prepared Volunteers run out of ammunition. A quick getaway is in order, and the keyed-up republicans go tearing and stumbling across a succession of fields, over a stream, past a clay pit, skirting a small council estate, through a gap and into the private grounds of Beechmount House, out of breath, dodging behind the trees and heading pell-mell for the Beechmount Drive entrance, past the gate lodge and so out on to the safe haven – comparatively safe – of the main Falls Road. And Miss Eliza and her servants cowering in the drawing room. We're reminded of the moment in Elizabeth Bowen's novel *The Last September*, located at the other end of the country, near Mitchelstown in County Cork, when a man in a trench coat, intent on Ireland's business, hurries past the heroine Lois in her own demesne. It's 1920, the Black-and-Tan war is under way, and nineteen-year-old Lois is susceptible not to the romance of the republican cause, but rather to the allure of the great house (a stand-in for Bowen's Court).

'Demesne': it's too grand a word for the grounds of Beechmount House, all thirty-one acres of it notwithstanding. You can't altogether detach the house from its environs, the dusty, rundown terraces, street lamps coming on in the evenings and a fine rain falling on patches of waste ground, the pigeon-fanciers' lofts, the mongrel dogs, the fifteenth-of-August bonfires, the front-parlour shops selling honeycomb and yellowman, the pubs with spittoons and sawdust on the floor, the Mountain Loney with the wee tin church halfway along it, the Brickfields and back fields and sectarian murders perpetrated up sinister alleyways, the half-built houses at the top of the Donegall Road drawing swarms of Catholic refugees. The last intimidated out of their homes in 'mixed' areas, and not lending an uplifted tone to the mid-Falls district. And people in Catholic dress all over the place, priests and nuns and first communicants and what-have-you. And the future Father Ryan of the Scholastic Philosophy Department at Queen's University growing up in a three-storey house on the front of the road, with iron railings separating it from the street, and large bay windows with looped lace curtains proclaiming an attachment to the middle-classes.

As we've seen, the Riddels drew the line at Catholics, so they did. Well, we shouldn't blame them too much for failing to rise above the orthodoxies of the day. It's different, though, when a piece of prejudice gets inscribed in a formal document. We've all heard of clauses in wills prohibiting a person of this or that persuasion from acquiring some specified property at the legator's disposal. It seems the deeds of Beechmount House contained a similar proviso against a future Catholic ownership. The estate was never to be allowed to fall into Papist hands. ... At any rate, this was the received wisdom at Catholic-street-level. It was firmly believed all over Beechmount, the Whiterock and St James's. If it's true — a large 'if'[10] — it is uncertain whether the Riddels themselves, or their predecessors, were responsible for the exclusion order. Again, if it's true, the framers of this bit of sectarian baiting had reckoned without Papist astuteness. ... Enter Daniel Mageean, Bishop of Down and Connor from 1929 until his death thirty-three years later. Mageean had long had his eye on Beechmount House, and when it came on the market around 1932, he arranged to buy it for the Church through a Protestant intermediary. Well! If we accept this story, it is hard to decide who comes out worse in the dodgy transaction, the authors of the initial reprehensible clause, or the bishop scheming to overturn it.

The phrase that comes to mind is 'turning in their graves'. Appropriated for Catholic Belfast, the house exists for many years as a hospital-cum-old-people's-home. Eventually it is taken a stage further and gains not only a Catholic, but a Gaelic overlay. At the present time, renamed Ard na bhFea,[11] it is flourishing as an Irish-language school. Alas, the house and surroundings have undergone unsightly renovation. Bits subtracted and added on. Car parks and sports grounds where a shady beech grove once held sway. A 'leisure centre', God help us, in place of the original gate lodge. The trees incessantly sinned against by concupiscent trespassers of the 1940s and '50s — all gone.

The moment of greatest consternation for ghostly Riddels and their ilk occurs in the summer of 1954, at the height of Father Peyton's transatlantic 'Rosary Crusade', when vast numbers of telling-their-beads enthusiasts swarm all over the grounds of Beechmount House in an intense affirmation of Catholic identity. Oh holy, holy, holy, lord. ... And where am I, while a portion of my home territory is thus devotionally deranged? Not on my knees in the midst of the praying Mass going, 'Hail Mary, holy Mary', that's for sure. I am not and never was a shining light of churchly exhibitionism. You would likely have found me in the back garden of 551 Donegall Road reading *The Mystery of the Hidden House* or *The Reluctant Schoolgirl*. Happily – though I accepted the obligations of being a Catholic child – I was not subjected to excessive religiosity in the home. I never knew a thing about the great Rosary Rally going on just a stone's throw away from our sunlit garden, and, if I had, I'd have taken scant interest in it.

What did engage my interest, up to a point, was the high stone wall running along the Falls Road end of Beechmount House grounds, all the way from the Giant's Foot Road to Beechmount Drive. For some reason, I was drawn to oddities and anomalies, and it was certainly odd to find a one-time gentleman's residence, complete with gardens, in this part of Belfast. At eleven or twelve, on my way to and from school, I would pass this wall four times a day. In my mind I endowed the house beyond the wall with a gothic aspect far removed from the plain reality. But I never ventured up the long curved drive to see the place for myself. And once I understood it was an old people's home I ceased to be intrigued by it. By this stage, of course, Beechmount House was well and truly incorporated into the Catholic Falls, with a nunly and priestly aura about it, and hand-wringing and woe for the wraiths of the Riddels.

When Riddel Hall for female students came into being in south Belfast during the First World War, a warden was appointed to oversee its arrangements. The first and most distinctive warden was Ruth Duffin, a relative by marriage of Miss Eliza and Miss Isabella.[13] She was thirty-six years old at the time, and connected backwards through her ancestor William Drennan to the 'United Irish' movement and the entire ethos of liberal, Protestant, nineteenth-century Belfast.

William Drennan. I've referred to him earlier (see p. 93) as an old Irish separatist, but it's possible I was over-simplifying things with this unequivocal tag. Yes, he founded the Society of United Irishmen in 1791; but later in the decade he disengaged himself from conspiracy and rebellion. In the run-up to the 1798 centenary celebrations, Dr Drennan's son, John Swanwick Drennan, co-opted his father for the unionist cause. At the same time, William Drennan remained an object of veneration for the extreme nationalist contingent. And both parties were right, in a way (which tells us something essential about northern politics). It depends on where you place the emphasis.

William Drennan, New Light Presbyterian, United Irishman, author of the stirring ballad 'The Wake of William Orr', had always held a place in the pantheon of radical Irish patriots, as far as I was concerned. He was up there with Emmet, Pearse and Tone. ... Then, towards the end of the 1980s, as a participant in the newly founded John Hewitt Summer School, I sat in a lecture hall at Garron Tower on the Antrim coast, and listened to poet-and-academic Adrian Rice restore a measure of complexity to the ironed-out, romantic-Irish version of Dr Drennan. Ultimately, Rice claimed, Drennan's social ameliorism and egalitarian standpoint had raised him above 'the diehard dogmas' of the factions of Orange and Green. He'd have wanted no truck with any outraged rabble. He was a social reformer, and once certain reforms were enacted he'd have ceased to be an agitator to any degree, and upheld the status quo. That was how it seemed to William Drennan's son (himself a doctor, a poet and a man of eighty-two at the time of the 1798 centenary celebrations). But Irish nationalists and Parnellites (we're still in the 1890s) took a contrary view. Total separation from England, they maintained, 'was the ideal taught by him'.[13] Drennan's own lines, 'The cause it is good, and the men they are true, / And the green shall outlive both the orange and blue', were constantly on their lips. Thus, you had rival factions laying claim to the larger portion of William Drennan. I would like to detach him from both of them, Green and Orange alike, and reinstate him as a symbol of integration. For whatever is or is not debatable about Dr Drennan's political convictions and private beliefs, one thing is certain, he supported full social rights for Catholics, having identified this lack as a grievous abuse of power. He threw his weight behind the cause of Emancipation (and died before it was achieved). A reasonable and moral Presbyterianism – which Dr Drennan[14] professed – precluded going along with any form of discrimination on grounds of creed or caste.

And here is his great-granddaughter,[15] a hundred years on, attached to an institution excluding Taigs from its intake. (I'm sorry to go on about this exclusion policy on the part of Riddel Hall – and I've already acknowledged its commonplace, non-threatening aspect at the time – but there's a certain irony here which I can't resist noting.) However, if she missed out on her ancestor's ecumenicalism, Ruth Duffin inherited something of his poetic ability. With her sister Celia Duffin, she brought out a couple of collections of verse in the 'fairy fiddler', 'quare wee house' mode – the vernacular manner interspersed with some lofty and archaic stuff. There were, at the time (1890s–1920s), quite a few prosperous Protestant women poets – 'Moira O'Neill', Helen Lanyon, 'Elizabeth Shane', Florence M. Wilson, and so on – who found their subject-matter in countryside lore and Ulster folk emblems, homing in on a mythical spot where pagan Ireland and Catholic peasant Ireland joined forces with Ulster Scots. You know the kind of thing – 'He played by the braes o' Comber, / A quare wee lift o' an air; / It stirred the childer from slumber / With its notes so sweet an' rare ...' – verse, according to the critic Terence Brown,[16] that 'treats of an aspect of Ulster rural life that has a significance for many Ulster people's self-understanding'. So it does, or so it did, and occasionally it rises to a stupendous indigenous piquancy, as in Florence Wilson's 'The Man From God-Knows-Where' with its button-holing opening lines: 'Into our townlan', on a night of snow, / Rode a man from God-knows-where'. You have to read on, for the story and the local ideology. The year – the resonant year – is 1798; and then it's 1803 and a crowd has assembled outside Downpatrick gaol to witness an execution. The poem is written in homage to an exemplary *Presbyterian* steadfastness and integrity. William Drennan would have relished its drift, and probably his great-granddaughter did too, though her own verse eschews any political content whatever. The Carbery/ Milligan brand of defiance is as alien to her as a pawnshop on the Lower Falls.

There's a single poem in which Ruth Duffin's literary reputation resides, and it's called 'The Fairy Piper':

> Who hears the fairy piper play
> Beneath the secret hill,
> Though he should wander worlds away
> Shall hear that music still.

This crystal-clear offering makes an appearance in my mother's brown-paper-covered, personal anthology of cherished verse, along with Helen Lanyon's 'The House of Padraig' and Ethna Carbery's 'The Spell-Stricken' (and John Clare and Thomas Hardy and Yeats and Keats and Shelley and Browning and Tennyson and Wilfred Owen ...). But she'd hardly have known that its author was going about her duties as warden of a girls' hostel just across the road from Sandhurst Gardens, in a building housing many of Nora's fellow students – with whom she probably wasn't acquainted. I doubt if she ever set foot in Riddel Hall. Its Protestant ambience (here we go again) would have struck something of a jarring note. But on the other hand, I think, she wouldn't have known or cared about the religious affiliation of any of the poets, local or otherwise, who made it into her hard-backed notebook. ... I find it slightly odd that so many Ulster poets of the day – town-bred for the most part – should wish so much to immerse themselves in the trappings of picturesque Ireland, all bogs and boreens and banshees and baloney. (I'm not trying to strike a superior note here: I lapped the whole lot up, all the holy wells and rushy crosses and boys-from-the-Rosses, no less than any other indigenous-emblem addict.) And the dour Ulster, not to mention manse backgrounds of some, make for an added irony. ... Of course, exponents of an Ulster pastoral verse form were by no means entirely Protestant, or female, or even Big House people: think of Cahir Healey and Cathal O'Byrne, for instance. Or Joseph Campbell, head and shoulders (in poetic terms) above the rest. One of my mother's university friends married a poet of this lilting type, John Irvine, who, like John Hewitt, fell under the spell of local place names: 'Limavady, Cloonnagashel, Donaghedy, Carrowdore ...'. Indeed, I believe the huge black pram from which I surveyed the activities of St James's Avenue and the Donegall Road was a gift to my mother from this Mrs Irvine – but the friendship must have lapsed, for I never got to know the pair. I liked his book *By Winding Roads*, though, with its William Conor dust jacket showing a donkey-and-cart, and lively illustrations. It was bought in Mullan's bookshop in Donegall Place, and it sat on a shelf in our sitting-room for many years. It's on one of my own bookshelves now.

The summer of 1937 comes, and, with it, the chancellor's garden party at Queen's University, a day filled with sunshine and excitements, at which a row of sweet girl graduates is photographed for a local paper. 'Degree day smiles', the caption goes: twelve joyful faces, the whole row linking arms and each of them putting her best foot forward, as if about to break into a triumphant quickstep. Happy days. And my jubilant mother among them, wearing her graduation gown like a badge of honour, all confidence and exuberance.

Graduation day at Queen's, 1937. PC's mother is first left, in the front row

She'd have considered herself enrolled in an up-and-coming
minority of women graduates, but alas, the promise of that early hard-
won achievement was not to be fulfilled. It had something to do with
the times, the years of economic depression, downbeat Belfast, a glut of

Leaving the censorship office at Stormont, *c.*1944. PC's mother is on the right

women teachers on the market, no clerical or professional connections
to put in a word. It is distressing to think of applications going out and
out from 31 Sandhurst Gardens, and leading nowhere. ... Then, at last,
comes a series of ill-paid, stand-in appointments, some as far afield as
Ballymena or Ballynahinch. Nora's work is to fill in for a teacher of
English indisposed for a term or two, or a nun in the grip of a nervous

breakdown. Well, it's a way of gaining teaching experience. ... Then she gets married and cuts herself off even further from the prospect of full-time employment. Once you're married you have to stay at home, says the Catholic church. You have to stay at home and procreate. That is your role in life. But then the war comes, and things change slightly. It's not until 1943, however, that my mother secures a full-time job: in the censorship office at Stormont. Or, the Postal and Telegraph Censorship Department, to give it its full title. 'The work of Censorship has played an invaluable part in the concealment from the enemy of vital plans and preparations, in the detection and suppression of enemy espionage propaganda and other subversive activities, and in the enforcement of the many regulations necessary to sustain and extend the national war effort.' I'm quoting from a certificate of commendation presented in 1945 to 'all ranks of the Censorship staffs' – all now redundant – whose 'zeal, diligence and skill' are duly applauded.

This is my mother's contribution to the war effort: reading soldiers' letters and blacking out bits of them. I think she enjoyed it: the companionship, the sense of national urgency and the monthly pay cheque. And work as easy to her as falling off a form. My father continues in his employment with the Ulster Transport Authority at Duncrue Street. Their gurgling infant, meanwhile, is left in the care of her grandmother and aunt. They have all (myself excepted) lived through the terrible blitz on Belfast of 1941, when huge portions of the city were obliterated and temporary morgues set up in St George's Market and the Falls Swimming Baths, where stunned survivors come to identify the dead. Something happened at Beechmount,[17] I believe: the nearest the bombs approached to the Donegall Road. I can't remember any of it, of course; but I was told stories about the lot of us huddled under the stairs when the sirens went. Or, in summer, joining distraught hordes streaming up the Mountain Loney towards the sanctuary of a hawthorn bush. By this stage in the war it must be plain to all reasonable people that England's difficulty, in this instance, is also Ireland's difficulty, that the hellishness of Nazi Germany is worse than the devilry of Stormont.

This wasn't always the case. The minute war was declared, its bearing on Irish affairs was assessed rather differently by diehard republicans. Stories abounded of lights being left burning deliberately on the Falls Road, in defiance of the blackout, to guide Nazi bombers – proxy Sinn

Féiners in the eyes of some – on the way to wipe out a detested regime. It didn't work out like that, indeed, but the effect of such perverse wisdom was to reinforce Protestant misgivings about the 'loyalty' of the entire Catholic population. It's just another nail in the coffin of interdenominational accord.

'Them sons of whores,' wails a hurt old woman in Brian Moore's 'blitz' novel *The Emperor of Ice-Cream*, 'them bastards done it on purpose. They brought the German.' 'Who?' asks Moore's ARP[18] protagonist, Catholic Gavin Burke, understandably a bit bewildered by this tirade. 'The Fenians, the IRA,' comes the snarled reply. 'Them's the ones who done it. They should be hung, every one of them, aye, and a fire lit beneath them.'

Brian Moore's novel (his fifth) was published in 1965, and it draws very closely on his own experiences as an ARP recruit in the early days of the war. Like Gavin Burke's, his action caused affront to his Catholic nationalist family. 'Gracious God,' (exclaims Gavin's Aunt Liz in the book), 'did I ever think I'd live to see the day when my own nephew would stand in this room dressed up like a Black and Tan.' Immediately – though they're not addressed in the novel – genealogical complications enter in. Pro-Sinn Féin Aunt Liz is an invented character, but Brian Moore's real-life aunts, his father's sisters, were the children of a Catholic convert; the family's ancestry included a strongly Protestant Ballyclare and Ballymena strain. (And the further back you go the more sectionally tangled it gets; but that, as I've reiterated, is probably true for most of us.) By the early twentieth century, though, the Moores had become as Catholic as Corpus Christi. Exorbitantly Catholic, but another twist of fortune had placed them in a house directly opposite the main Orange Hall in Clifton Street, Belfast – giving Brian and his seniors and siblings a grandstand view, each Twelfth of July throughout the 1920s and 30s, of Orange pageantry and braggadocio. And perhaps engendering a soupçon of atavistic empathy, as the Belfast parade in all its pomp assembled beneath their eyes.

The Emperor of Ice-Cream is probably the finest novel to come out of the Belfast blitz, Belfast's encounter with terror and destruction coming in from outside, not – for once – home-brewed. The resulting cataclysm should have fostered solidarity, an all-in-it-together orientation. In some ways it did, while German bombs rained down on Prod and Taig alike. Few on the ground would have demanded information about a bombed-out person's religion before lending a hand. But, instinctively and insidiously, the old sectarian bogey came poking through the new awareness of a common predicament. You get the Clonard and Holy Family parishes, for example, congratulating themselves on counting low numbers of Catholics among the people killed in the April 1941 blitz[19] – the blitz placed fairly and squarely by Moore's old Shankill Road shawlie (above) at the door of the IRA. 'Them's the ones who done it.'

'All very wearisome and very perplexing,' as Benedict Kiely remarked on the subject of Belfast bigotries. Nevertheless – writing in 1945[20] – Kiely sensed the presence of 'new ideas, generous ideas ... ideas as energetic as the inspiration that built the factories, deepened the river, marked the black water with the shadows of tall cranes and leaning gantries.' He was being a bit over-optimistic, but the times allowed it. The war was over. People of a liberal bent held the same belief in a new advancement, a society – at last – decisively non-sectarian. Surely to goodness, thought Brian Moore, the just-past global conflict had put Belfast's squabbles into perspective: how, in the modern world, could the Orange-and-Green monster go on exerting its baleful influence? Alas, we know the answer. The snake was scotched, not killed. Even while he tried to consign it to the past, Benedict Kiely remained miserably conscious of 'an uncouth, vicious thing that comes to life at intervals to burn and kill and destroy'. Inherited spites and hatreds proved as indestructible as Grendel before the advent of Beowulf. Periods of apparent calm and reason were doomed to fall apart, endlessly. As I write, in July 2011, Belfast nights are filled with the noise of petrol bombs, rubber bullets, crashing vehicles, shouts, screams, smashed paving stones, half bricks, broken glass, running feet.

Wearisome is not the word. We've seen it all before, in the Pound, Millfield and Docks area in 1857, Sandy Row, Brown's Square seven years later, the Brickfields, Donegall Street, the Shankill Road, Divis Street, Short Strand, Willowfield, Lancaster Street. The noise of shooting, 'Starting in the evening at eight, / In Belfast in the York Street district', assaulted the infant ears of Louis MacNeice. John Hewitt remembered night after night seeing the sky 'lit with fire'. By 1922, he says, 'We knew of and accepted violence / in the small streets at hand' – as the longed-for, vividly imagined 'tolerant and just society', receded further and further into the distance.

★★★

Wartime members of the IRA were in something of an anomalous position: not Nazi supporters, indeed (unless they were mad), but still implacable opponents of Britain and its Stormont adjunct. Many IRA men chose to ignore the war and its implications as far as possible, sticking instead to the old republican strategies of drilling, parading, attacking police targets and raiding for guns. A lot were rounded up and interned, and for this and other reasons the organisation was not highly effective at this time, or, indeed, greatly revered as a resistance movement. There wasn't, for instance, much sympathy for a Volunteer from Bombay Street who was hanged at Crumlin Road gaol in 1942, following the shooting of a policeman (a policeman bearing the not exactly unionist name of Paddy Murphy).

I don't think my mother experienced any nationalist qualms on account of her war work in the censorship office. To bolster her decision to accept this employment, she might have held in mind an image of her father in the earlier war, a soldier in a British uniform meeting his death in the Dardanelles. She probably had Rupert Brooke or Francis Ledwidge running through her head on the way to the office. (In the days when the office is being wound up, she brings her two-year-old to be admired by her Stormont friends and colleagues. I have no recollection of the occasion.) I am sure she understood that changed circumstances can call for previously unthinkable adjustments to an ingrained set of opinions. In matters of politics or allegiance, she was never inflexible. She had praise for those who acted in accordance with some reasonably formulated principle, like her Tipping relations. Going further back – and if she'd known about them or it – she might even have understood the Blackers' *de haut en bas* commitment to civic order as filtered through paternalistic obligations. Calm, order and good prospects for the future were the breath of life to her.

At some time during 1938, I think, my grandmother had moved house for the last time. With Kathleen and Nora, the daughters still at home,[21] she moves from Sandhurst Gardens to the Falls Road end of the Donegall Road. It is a slight step up in the world. The new house is semi-detached, with two bay windows, a gate and a paved path leading to the stained-glass-panelled front door, over which a sun curtain is suspended during the summer months. The house stands on a corner, and a garden extends round the side and into St James's Avenue. It boasts a privet hedge and iron railings (soon to be requisitioned to help win the war). A gate for tradesmen – coalman, milkman, refuse collector – is let into the side hedge. It is painted green and shuts with a snib. A stub of a long-gone tree still sits in the front garden, and a sally tree grows between the side wall and the hedge. A trellis structure separates the front garden from the side, and to this, in season, is hooked an infant's swing. A yard, a shed and a wooden garden seat on the back lawn complete the lower-middle-class picture. Inside the house, on the ground floor, are three rooms: the front room known as the sitting-room, a living-room called the kitchen, and a tiny kitchen called the scullery. Three bedrooms and a bathroom upstairs represent a new luxury. It seems like a good place to live. The house is rented from a Dan McGinley who, with his brother Joe, runs a grocer's shop at the top of the Donegall Road. It will be my home until I reach the age of twenty and decamp to London.

It's to this house that my mother brings her new young ex-Protestant husband towards the end of 1941. The whole area – St James's, Whiterock, La Salle, Ballymurphy, Rodney Parade – is intensely Catholic, with its focal point in St John's Chapel on the Falls Road. On this place of worship almost the entire population converges on Sunday morning, with Mass taking place at hourly intervals between seven o'clock and twelve. (Only very infirm or lazy people leave it until twelve.) The exceptions to this weekly display of denominational fervour are the few Protestant families dotted about the district who keep to their own devotional routines. These, however, are not otherwise separated from the life of the community. Certainly such families have no interest in presenting themselves as a beleaguered minority. We have two in our avenue, St James's Avenue, Twybles and Smiths, who experience no discord on account of their beliefs. True, they keep to themselves, but then so do most of us. We have pretensions in our area. Some of the younger generation subscribe to the high-quality monthly *Collins Children's Magazine* – which is not to say we'd never be caught taking a sneaky look at the *Beano*. Solicitors and shopkeepers and teachers live here. Neighbours are not constantly in and out of neighbours' houses, after the manner of the riff-raff of the Lower Falls, thank you very much.

Fast forward to 1971 or thereabouts and an appalling phase of the thirty-year 'Troubles'. Some rearrangement of residences has taken place, not for the first time in Belfast's history. Protestants no longer feel safe or comfortable in a Catholic district, or the other way round. A few house exchanges are effected amicably, between acquaintances of different beliefs, but more families of the 'wrong' persuasion are intimidated out, threatened with arson or injury or, at best, ostracisation. Walls are daubed once more with the old offensive slogans: 'Taigs out'; 'Burn all Prods'. It's a bad case of recidivism. After a few – a very few – hopeful years, the sects are once again up to the oxters in vile primordial muck.

Around this time, my father has an alarming experience on a Donegall Road bus. At a certain point beyond Maguire and Paterson's match factory and the old Bog Meadows (recently appropriated for the start of the M1 motorway), the whole St James's Catholic ethos gives way to a pumped-up Protestantism. It's a feature of the area between the Donegall Road and Tate's Avenue known as 'the Village'. Village lads – ha! – for amusement of an evening, assemble at a bus stop below Celtic Park: the first 'Protestant' stop on the route towards the city centre. The assumption is that anyone already on the bus will be Catholic and therefore fair game. My father is caught unawares in this way on one occasion, and surrounded on the upper deck by a gang of youths hell-bent on bodily harm. Where has he come from? Where is he going? Who were his parents? What street is next to Kitchener Street? What team does he support? What flag does he venerate? (Or words to that effect.)

Fortunately he is able to supply the right answers (right for the circumstances). He is coming from the greyhound racing at Celtic Park, he says, and is on the way home to loyalist Dunmurry. He simply walked up, not down, to catch the bus at the closest stop (otherwise he'd have missed it). His name is Craig. In the garden of his house, orange lilies are planted to bloom in season, and a Union Jack is faithfully displayed on the Twelfth. One of his own sisters lives in Tate's Avenue. An uncle was a dignitary of the Orange Order. He gives the name of the lodge: St Nicholas LOL 264. All true – but not the whole truth. He is, in fact, on the way to visit his mother and his sister Ruby who still live at Lismoyne. The flag and the lilies are matters of fact, and so is Uncle Freddie's Lodge. What's expediently omitted from the account, of course, is his marriage to a Taig, his own conversion and actual place of residence just yards away from the priest-ridden Falls. No matter: his Protestant credentials see him through. He's allowed to go on his way unharmed, and is lucky to wangle it, things being what they were at the time.

I'm reminded of the poet Ciaran Carson's 'Question Time',[22] which partly consists of a fraught exchange between the narrator (Carson himself) and a gang of youths (Catholic this time) who intercept him as he cycles into the Falls Road from the direction of the Shankill.

> *You were seen coming from the Shankill.*
> *Why did you make a U-turn?*
> *Who are you?...*
> *You were seen. You were seen.*
> *Coming from the Shankill.*
> *Where are you from?...*
> *What's the next street down from Raglan Street?*
> *Coming from the Shankill ...*

Carson had innocently embarked on a cycle ride through his childhood haunts which included the Shankill Road library with its stock of Biggles books. But that was a different time. The world is now inhabited by vigilantes who perceive any incursion into their territory as a threat. 'Coming from the Shankill' denotes a sinister intent. 'The questions are snapped at me like photographs.' But for Ciaran Carson, an Irish-speaker born in Raglan Street on the Falls, the answers are child's play. (His Orange great-grandfather he keeps under his hat.) Yes, he knows what street was next to Cape Street, and the names of the people who lived there. Yes, he can tell exactly the relation between Stockman's Lane and Casement Park. He's not, after all, a suitable target for assault.

> I am released. I stumble across the road and look back. ... I get on my bike, and turn, and go down the Falls ... feeling shaky, nervous, remembering how a few moments ago I was *there*, in my mind's eye, one foot in the grave of that Falls Road of thirty years ago, inhaling its gritty smoggy air as I lolled outside the door of 100 Raglan Street, staring down through the comforting gloom to the soot-encrusted spires of St Peter's, or gazing at the blank brick gable walls of Balaklava Street, Cape Street, Frere Street, Milton Street, saying their names over to myself.

CHAPTER 9

'THINGS WERE BAD FOR A LONG WHILE BUT NOW WE'VE TURNED A CORNER'[1]

Where can it be found again,
An elsewhere world, beyond

Maps and atlases,
Where all is woven into

And of itself, like a nest
Of crosshatched grass blades?

Seamus Heaney, from 'A Herbal'

The mad, bad times began in earnest in 1969. But things had already been simmering away for five decades and more, while active insubordination on the part of northern nationalists waxed and waned. With the civil rights movement and People's Democracy idealism of the mid 1960s, an interlude of hopefulness occurred. 'And the next thing, suddenly, this change of mood,' wrote Seamus Heaney in his poem 'From the Canton of Expectation'. An exhilarating exercise in social observation, this poem encompasses a new purposefulness which is overtaking the old subdued state of subterranean affiliations and kinship of the disaffected.

> Once a year we gathered in a field
> Of dance platforms and tents where children sang
> Songs they had learned by rote in the old language.

There's a photograph in the Bigger collection at the Ulster Museum of a feis in Glenarm in 1904 which is an exact visual equivalent of these lines; Heaney, as ever, is spot on. He is also, at the same time, harking back to that 'hidden Ireland' of the eighteenth century postulated by Daniel Corkery – the concept of a vanquished people holding on to their cultural resources in their own language, and indeed glorying in the sense of invisibility, or at least inaccessibility, this confers on them, rather like Mary Norton's Borrowers: tiny people living side by side with those of a normal size, and going about their business almost completely undetected by them. The 'subject people stuff' (to quote another phrase of Heaney's) does indeed contain a large element of resignation, or at best a muted defiance, and it's this sense of demoralisation that's about to be dispelled, according to the poem 'From the Canton of Expectation'. It's goodbye, all at once, to 'the guardian angel of passivity', as an age of assertiveness, with demands for fair play, is ushered in. Aside from its universal application, which enables it to be read on more than one level, I take it that this poem has a specific point of reference: to the 1947 Education Act,[2] and the confidence and articulacy it bestowed on many of its beneficiaries. Readers alive to the Northern Irish context to the poem won't be slow to pick up its pungent allusions.

I'm not sure exactly when it was that the opinion first began to circulate about the civil rights movement having its origin in the enhanced political know-how of the first eleven-plus generation. But before long this reading of the situation had become a commonplace among social historians. Ideally (if rarely in practice) education entails exposure to liberal ideas, and a natural corollary of this is commitment to justice in the social sphere – and would-be ameliorators in Northern Ireland in the late 1950s and early '60s didn't have to look too hard at the society they inhabited to identify its more egregious biases and disgraces. Decades of discrimination, the misuse of power, ingrained bigotries: if you possessed the smallest degree of consciousness, these couldn't help but hit you in the face. One of the earliest effects of widespread education was to foster a critical attitude to such enormities, once they were perceived as such, along with the will to do something about them. To place yourself on the side of the angels, you had to be committed to freedom and democracy (however you chose to define these concepts).

It wasn't long before a catalytic alienation, an honourable outrage, was brewing at Queen's University – and spiralling out into the community at large to generate a kind of buoyancy, an anti-sectarian optimism the likes of which had not been seen in the North since the 1790s (though that particular eighteenth-century 'dream of grace and reason'[3] came to a bad end also, as we know). Education, albeit on a smaller scale, was at the bottom of United Irish agitation: the following are the words of the satirist James Porter's[4] 'Squire Firebrand', in a *Northern Star* of 1796:

> O! How times are changed and all for the worse. Your Catholic emancipation – your Sunday Schools – your Charter schools – your book societies – your Pamphlets, and your books, and your one hell or another are all turning the people's heads, and setting them a-thinking about this, that, and t'other.

Thinking about this, that, and t'other is the first stage in devising a programme for reform, and the better trained and informed the thinking activist is, the more forceful and overpowering will that programme be. Among those people conscious of being in a socially disadvantaged position, and not handicapped by any deficiency of intellect, the drive to obtain an education has always been strong – this was as true of bookish English labourers, artisans and the like, as it was of those eighteenth-century Irish pupils coming in winter clutching their sods of turf to keep a fire going as they crowded into one hedge-, barn- or makeshift schoolroom after another; though the latter contingent, no doubt, had the sense of acting in defiance of an unjust authority to bolster them up. If you, as a social group, are actually forbidden an education through an iniquitous edict from above, your natural inclination, if you have any spunk at all, will be to seek one out as assiduously as possible. Hence the innumerable sites of hedge schools all over the Clogher Valley (for instance), dating from Carleton's day – hence too all the classical allusions inserted into Irish-language poems of the eighteenth century: '...Are you Helen for whom many were destroyed, / Or are you one of Parnassus' nine fair maids ...?' etc. Learning so hard-won simply cried out for some form of expression.

Move forward a couple of centuries, and – all over the United Kingdom – hordes of scholarship pupils (myself included) are gaining whatever advantages a grammar-school education can provide. In England, the process contributed to the making of many a socialist and free-thinker; but in the peculiar circumstances of Northern Ireland, with denominational disabilities imposed alongside those of class, the position was rather more complicated. But the upshot in one area, as I've indicated, was a burgeoning radicalism at Queen's University, as eloquent student-protesters-against-the-system, such as Eamonn McCann, Bernadette Devlin, Michael Farrell, John Hume, Austin Currie and others, rose from the ranks. They had all arrived at Queen's via the eleven-plus/university scholarship route.[5]

They had arrived, some with no bother at all, others with more of a struggle as obstacles rose up to confound them along the way. Some, non-arrivals, fell foul of hidden social pressures geared to sabotage the scholarship scheme. If these weren't hidden they were blatant, and might produce a discouraging or, on the other hand, a bracing effect. Defiance was as sterling a way as any of responding to denigration. The eleven-year-old Eamonn McCann, the minute he set foot in St Columb's School in Derry, was cornered by an insolent priest and quizzed about his home address. 'Where do you come from? Rossville Street? Oh yes, that's where they wash once a month.'[6] Seamus Deane, another of the brainy Bogsiders infiltrating St Columb's, encountered a similar superciliousness at the school: 'The welcome was not exactly stunning. I discovered that I was an Eleven-Plusser ... in the opinion of some teachers, a low type.' These two stuck it out, but others, victims of St Columb's 'unofficial but widespread snobbery', threw in the towel.

I was not a victim of snobbery, but of a churchly severity, as I've related in *Asking for Trouble*. Queen's was the place for me, I thought in my eighteenth year; but instead I had been diverted to a different establishment: art college. As a field of study I had life-drawing, etching, illustration, in place of the more appropriate English or Irish studies. But was I downhearted? No. Somehow I adapted to the new routines; well, it was a relief to have done with school, at least a school as uncongenial as my last one had proved to be. And the slightly bohemian art college atmosphere was exhilarating, even if I didn't participate in it fully. If I hankered after Queen's, it was only a peripheral hankering. Art school had its own form of liberal thinking – though it had more to do with style and sex than sectarianism. If I went around asserting my Irishness in the intervals of applying paint to canvas, I don't think too many people were impressed. (They weren't impressed by the painting results either.) They'd have relegated me, on this account, to the fusty, rather than the avant-garde brigade.

I did get acquainted with some Queen's students though, and briefly became a crusader for a type of socialism which seemed to offer a way out of the sectarian impasse we all deplored. Under the influence of Eamonn McCann, I went from door to door in east Belfast canvassing on behalf of the Northern Ireland Labour Party (without conspicuous success); and in his company too I visited the home of ex-shipyard-worker-turned-playwright, Sam Thompson, whose *Over the Bridge*, first performed in 1960, created such a significant brouhaha in Belfast. This play, described by its author as 'a plea for tolerance', was first accepted, and then rejected, by the Group Theatre, as the Group's pusillanimous board succumbed to misgivings about the probable effect in Belfast of its controversial content. *Over the Bridge* concerns trade unionism and bigotry in the shipyards of Harland and Wolff. Bigotry, of course, was not confined to the shipyards, but by focusing on a particular setting, one he knew inside out, Sam Thompson was presenting in a nutshell the city's outstanding defect. (We remember James Douglas renaming Belfast 'Bigotsborough'.) It proved too much to stomach for people blind to its likeness to life. The Group Theatre washed its hands of it; and a spate of resignations followed as the play's supporters got their backs up in their turn. Eventually, *Over the Bridge* was staged at the Empire Theatre, without its fundamental drift being watered down. It was directed by James Ellis, who also acted in the play; and one of the principal roles was taken by J.G. Devlin, father of my old schoolfriend Fiona Devlin (see p. 5–6). The entire cast of *Over the Bridge*, and everyone connected with it, Protestant, Catholic, Dissenter or whatever, could congratulate themselves on upholding the principles of tolerance, verisimilitude and freedom of expression. And, contrary to the Group Theatre's dismal prediction, the play's initial staging didn't cause offence leading to chaos in Belfast. Instead, it proved a tremendous box-office success.

I was not seated in the audience at the Empire Theatre when Sam Thompson's play set people a-thinking about this, that, and t'other.

At the time I was in my last year at school, attending the Assumption Convent in Ballynahinch where I vacillated between different ways of promoting an equitable society, and chafed under the school regulation enforcing scraped-back hair. In my daily doings I assumed the cultural high ground by speaking Irish assiduously; at the school, I took on the mantle of a would-be rebel by earnestly discussing with one or two like-minded girls the possibility of setting up, among the fifth- and sixth-formers of Ballynahinch, a branch of Cumann na mBan (the female section of the IRA). I rather lost heart for this enterprise on learning that my principal, indeed virtually my only, supporter in the plan, had gone away to be a nun. So the only outlet for my clandestine instincts was the collection box for the Political Prisoners' Dependents Fund which I carried through the streets of drab Beechmount and drabber St James's, as an adjunct to the above-board pools-collecting on behalf of Gael Linn, to which I was also committed. You will see that, despite my lack of a religious temperament, a lack I'd been aware of from an early age, I was living and moving and having my being in Catholic Belfast, with its rituals and rigmaroles, its delusions and exclusions and aggravations. I was vehemently on the side of all of us in an inferior position in the unionist state. I was also continuously undergoing chagrin at not being paid enough attention by whatever boy I wanted to pay attention to me at the time. It seemed being Catholic, and semi-fluent Irish-speaking, and up to the eyes in republican dissent, were fixed points in my otherwise fluctuating sense of identity. It took art school, I suppose, to liberalise my idea of liberalism. There was more than one way, it seemed – the Irish-Ireland way – of achieving an advanced persona for yourself. You could adjust your emphasis by going all out to shock hidebound Belfast (the student way), or by enmeshing yourself in international, not just national, causes (the 'Ban-the-Bomb' way). You could exhibit a proto-feminism by refusing to wash up the dishes in male student friends' disgusting flats. You could involve yourself in enlarging the scope of Belfast politics by supporting the non-sectarian Labour Party. I did, as I say, briefly throw in my lot with the last; but it wasn't, for me, a natural departure. The world of politics was not my sphere.

Sam Thompson. When *Over the Bridge*, that polemical play, ran into trouble with the Group Theatre in Belfast, the hero of the hour – one of the heroes of the hour – was actor/director James Ellis. He was there, a driving force, at every stage of the play's rehabilitation. His support for Thompson was unwavering – and it continued after the playwright's death in 1965 following a heart attack in the Northern Ireland Labour Party offices in Belfast. Both the author and the actor had placed themselves within a tradition of dissent in the North running against the sectarian grain. The *Over the Bridge* controversy, with its implications for the future, was a defining moment in the life of Ellis, no less than that of Sam Thompson.

The future. Here is a cemetery-set piece from 2010, which somehow embodies the confusions and crotchets, obstinacies and fiascos of Northern Irish affairs. Picture a pouring wet morning in late July, and a group of about fifty bystanders assembled in driblets under huge umbrellas at the top end of Belfast's City Cemetery. The occasion is the rededication of Sam Thompson's grave, with a new headstone 'erected by his friends', and inscribed with a line from Sam Hanna Bell, 'His was the voice of many men'. Appropriately – as it seems – the now elderly Ellis has been invited over from England to perform the unveiling and deliver a short address applauding the achievement of his long-dead friend.

We are a motley lot, standing in our raincoats waiting for Ellis to arrive and the ceremony to begin. The Black Mountain looms over the scene, with mist swirling about its summit and the Hatchet Field looking within easy walking distance. Forrest Reid, in his novel of 1915, *At the Door of the Gate*, remarked the way the cemetery ground rose steeply, 'its green surface broken by innumerable white and grey monuments, and threaded with dark trim paths'. He mentions how 'the hard silhouettes of a few cypresses, and the softer outlines of the trees in the park alongside, stood out against a pale blue sky'. And beyond (he adds), 'yet quite close, was a dark low range of hills, the air from which blew down, fresh and cold'. Today the sky is overcast, not pale blue, but otherwise the cemetery is much the same as it was in Forrest Reid's day (as long as the late-twentieth-century housing developments remain out of sight). We have, as I say, arrived from all directions, and from all walks of society. Sinn Féin is represented by Danny Morrison who has organised the event as part of the West Belfast Festival, ex-Lord Mayor Tom Hartley, and Gerry Adams himself who draws up at the graveside in a swish black car, and proceeds to hand around sweets from a paper bag. The old Labour movement in Belfast gets a look-in in the person of Brian Garrett – solicitor and Sam Thompson's literary executor – along with my friend

Anne Devlin, daughter of Paddy Devlin the great Belfast socialist and trade union activist. If she's here on behalf of her dead father, though, Anne is also present in her own right as an acclaimed short-story writer and playwright; along with her contemporary and fellow-playwright Martin Lynch, she imports into the gathering a touch of thespian glamour. My other Devlin friend – not related – now Fiona Coyle, also stands obliquely for the world of the theatre (via her father), and at the same time affirms the ethos of the burgeoning Irish-speaking population of Andersonstown. All of us, in our different ways, are here to honour the memory of Sam Thompson and the anti-sectarian ideal he stood for. Some of us are Catholic, by birth or conviction, some Protestant, and more, probably, subscribe to no religion at all.

Standing by the Thompson graveside with its pre-unveiling covering still in place, I'm struck by the way nearly all of the people present can be assigned to various ideological and cultural categories – allowing for overlap and interfusion, of course. And some of these categories are at odds with one another. Gaelic-socialist-republican-integrationist-theatrical-literary. ...The last brings me to the third Devlin present, Marie Heaney, who's accompanied by her Nobel Laureate husband Seamus. The Heaneys are in Belfast because Seamus is performing at the West Belfast Festival later in the day, reading some poems and talking about the headmaster, Michael McLaverty, of the school he, Seamus, taught in, in the days before fame overtook him. And they, the Heaneys, like the rest of us, are in the City Cemetery defying the damp to pay tribute to the author of *Over the Bridge*. His 'plea for tolerance' is in the thoughts of all of us. 'Shipwright, playwright and trade unionist', Michael Longley wrote in his poem 'The Poker' ('In memory of Sam Thompson'), 'Old Decency's philosopher ...'.

Another exponent of 'old decency' is James Ellis, who duly arrives at the microphone set up under a kind of makeshift tent affair. 'I haven't brought any notes or anything,' he begins. 'You'll have to forgive me, this is just an impromptu speech. Off the cuff.' Encouraging murmurs follow this announcement. 'Good for you, Jimmy.' 'You're all right, Jimmy.' 'Yes,' the famous Belfast actor goes on, looking round with an unexpectedly blank expression on his face. 'It's great to be here among so many distinguished people. Especially Seamus Heaney.'

Well, fair enough, I think. Given the occasion, it was Sam Thompson's due to be mentioned first; but clearly Ellis has caught sight of Seamus in the gathering and feels he has to acknowledge his presence. Now he's got that out of the way, no doubt he will get to the point. But it doesn't happen. Slight ripples of unease run through the crowd as we hear a strange assertion coming from the microphone, to the effect that it is an honour, 'a great honour for me to be here unveiling the grave of this famous poet, a Nobel Laureate, the greatest poet Ireland has ever produced. A great prose writer as well ... great eloquence ... I have signed copies of all his books ... a great poet ... Seamus Heaney ...'.

The acclaimed actor is in no danger of running out of words, but he seems to be attending a different ceremony to the rest of us. What is going on? We find out later that James Ellis has a mild condition requiring medication to keep him in a balanced state, and in the hustle and bustle of flying into Belfast that morning the medication was overlooked. Hence the unexpected oration which has us standing transfixed under our dripping umbrellas, torn between embarrassment, bemusement and an urge to burst out laughing (which no one does). Glances are exchanged denoting bewilderment and consternation. The only one who has the presence of mind to do something is Anne Devlin, who bravely steps across to James Ellis at the microphone, takes him by the elbow and apologises for butting in. 'Tell us about Sam Thompson, Jimmy,' she urges. 'It's important to remember that you are here today because you as an actor took Sam Thompson's banned play *Over the Bridge* and fought to get it on. That showed such courage as an actor, to do that for a writer, for a play that was banned. And it inspired me as a playwright, because I learned that culture was a form of resistance. And that is why we are here today.'

She's done her best, and more than any of us, but her intervention produces only a kind of benign puzzlement in the single-track speaker. It required a tremendous effort on the part of Anne to try to save the situation. ('My legs are about to give way under me,' she whispers, resuming her place in the crowd.) But no sooner has she left the enclosure than 'Seamus Heaney' starts up again. 'A great honour ... the eloquence of this tremendous poet ... Seamus Heaney's grave ...'. God knows what is going through the mind of poor Seamus as he stands there having to hear himself being consigned to a burial spot in the City Cemetery long before his time. He catches Anne Devlin's eye and shakes his head. He tries to efface himself behind the broad back of Gerry Adams. Eventually, though, as the inapposite elegy rambles on, he sees there's nothing for it but to intervene himself. He takes the microphone, thanks James Ellis for his comments, and wrenches the ceremony back on track with his customary grace and gumption. James Ellis, still looking not quite himself, apparently sees no discrepancy between the person standing beside him, alive and well, and the 'great poet' he's had dead and buried a minute earlier. He just seems politely bewildered by all these interruptions. And when Heaney, composed as ever but no doubt disquieted by the occurrence, returns to his place in the audience, blow me if James Ellis doesn't start up again. 'Great honour ... the grave of this great poet ... Seamus Heaney ...'. ('Jimmy was not to be diverted,' observes Seamus ruefully, later.) At this point the organisers give up, the dogged Heaney devotee is led away, still muttering, '... great poet ... grave ...', and the show is over. It's not long, however, before Ellis's usual civility and acumen are restored to him. The incident is just a blip in the long and productive association between actor and playwright. It's been unnerving but with an edge of comedy. And the heroine of the hour is Anne Devlin.

Anne Devlin's classic story 'Naming the Names' is the best account I know of the making of a terrorist. Her protagonist Finn (Finnuala) McQuillen belongs to the burnt-out people of the Falls, victims of an Orange onslaught in August 1969. Finn's grandmother is rescued from her house in Conway Street off the Falls Road, carried to safety in the arms of a neighbour, while the houses of other neighbours blaze around her. Stones and bottles are hurled at fleeing 'Fenians' by a crowd of arsonists at the top of the street. Some time later, Finn walks into 'a house in Andersonstown of a man I knew' and asks if there is anything for her to do. 'And that was how I became involved.' Later again, following the murder of a judge's son, Finn is arrested and interrogated in an interview room by members of the RUC. Asked incessantly for the names of her republican associates, she repeats like a mantra instead the street-names of the pungent old, disaffected Falls. 'Conway and Cupar, David, Percy, Dover and Divis. Mary, Merrion, Milan, McDonnell, Osman, Raglan, Ross, Rumania, Serbia, Slate, Sorella, Sultan ...'

This deeply humane story carries considerable resonance. Obliterated streets, mutilated neighbourhoods, harm done, causes good and bad and inescapable, come within its parameters. Who could witness horrors inflicted on unoffending people and not wish to retaliate, as Finn does in the story? And once you're committed, you're committed. Some distancing mechanism from evil effects takes over. ...Where did 'Naming the Names' come from? A work of fiction, it is very far from being Anne Devlin's own story. In 1981, her family unwillingly abandoned the house in Andersonstown where they had lived for fifteen years. Their exodus was due to violence, or the threat of violence, from ruffian elements of the Provisional IRA who disliked Anne's father Paddy Devlin's principled, and outspoken, refusal to condone the hunger strikers in the Maze prison. Hence some of the behind-the-scenes overlap and dissociation prevailing at the City Cemetery gathering, as indicated above.

However, as I've said, everyone attending the Thompson rededication could be classed as subscribing to liberal values, of whatever variety. And what the lot of us were up against, at the time we got going as would-be progressives, was the old inherited, ingrained and iniquitous 'Bigotsborough' mindset. And this mindset was embodied in a big way in an awful autochthonous figure. Here is an image from 1962. A current annoyance of one or two zealots is the notion that somehow the BBC in Belfast has become a hotbed of popeheads. Fuelled by the wrath of God, these religionists assemble in Ormeau Avenue wearing overcoats not designed for aesthetic appeal, and carrying placards alerting passers-by to the fact – which may have surprised them – that the BBC is the Voice of Popery. 'We Protest Against Roman Catholicism in the BBC,' thunders one of these placards, 'In Ordering Refusal of Protestant Protests Against the BBC's Submission to ROME IN ULSTER.' I don't know what brought on this particular choleric outbreak – not very succinctly, indeed tautologically, articulated; but it made an occasion for the Reverend Ian Paisley to leap on a soap-box outside the BBC, and go into denunciatory mode while emulating his roaring nineteenth-century predecessors such as the Reverend Henry Cooke (a bygone cleric every bit as black as he was painted).

Paisley was the new watchword, among us sceptics and reformers, for utterly abhorrent attitudes. Larger than life, a figure of fun, a cartoon Covenanter, yes; but also a purveyor of poisonous doctrines, a dangerous throw-back and demagogue. 'That noisy preacher,' John Hewitt called him, adding another epithet: 'old-fashioned'. Paisley stood for everything that was wrong with Ulster. The travel writer Dervla Murphy, who visited Belfast in the mid 1970s[7] and attended a Sunday sermon at Paisley's 'Free

Presbyterian' church on the Ravenhill Road, felt, as she watched him perform, that she was 'in the presence of pure evil'. And not without cause. 'We must attack the people – the people who represent the anti-Christ in our midst! Be violent for Christ's sake': this was among the calls to arms assaulting the congregation's ears. Incitements to hatred filled the air. Disbelief and despair filled Dervla Murphy.

My friend Douglas Carson, a Protestant liberal soon to become a radio producer with the Taig-ridden BBC, and his friend Erskine Holmes, equally liberal, took one look at Paisley's antics at the time and joined with the bulk of the populace in consigning the blazing cleric to some abysmal realm of sectarian malevolence and indigenous benightedness. Paisley was the millstone round liberal Ulster's neck. He was going, if he could manage it, to drag the whole province down. ...Years later, in a conversation with Douglas, I listened to him express a rueful amusement, shared by me, at the way things unfold. 'Who'd have thought,' he said (or words to that effect), 'that one day Erskine would be driving the one-time bugbear of all of us through the battlefields of the Somme; or that the same Paisley would sit with my wife and myself in our front room drinking tea and talking knowledgeably about art and books.'

Douglas went on to describe an occasion, a funeral at May Street Presbyterian Church, at which Paisley was also present. The one-time scourge of popery, it seemed, was pleased to draw attention to May Street's ecumenical past. It was, he said, the only Presbyterian establishment in the city in which a Catholic Mass had once been celebrated. This happened in the 1920s, when the then incumbent, the Reverend Alexander Wylie Blue, had offered it as a temporary facility to a local Catholic priest whose own church was destroyed by arson. It was a brave and neighbourly thing to do – and the odd thing was that Paisley appeared to approve of the gesture.

At some point – I am not sure when – the Reverend Ian Paisley emerged from his time warp and went from maleficent to avuncular. What brought about the colossal change I don't know, but it's possible that Sinn Féin had a hand in it. Following his very public show of camaraderie towards Martin McGuinness, Paisley could hardly assume the old-fashioned demonic mantle again. Or, as commentators trying to make sense of Paisley in the past had surmised, it may have been a case of a split personality, with the more agreeable portion finally winning out over the rest. He remains larger than life – but perceptions of him have become enlarged in their turn, to take account of complexities and contradictions (my mantra) in Northern Irish life.

Between the innocent ameliorative impulses of the early 1960s and the slaughterhouse strategies of the following decade, a great gulf opens up. An unprecedented change of atmosphere occurred. Violence and the threat of violence underlay everything, and a concomitant laxity in everyday activity came to the fore. While politicians and others in positions of power desperately sought to contain 'the situation', fighters on the ground, fellow-travellers, and, indeed, large sections of the populace, veered between bleakness and implacability, and a full immersion in a kind of dance-of-death furore. A tit-for-tat killing frenzy overtook the North. Housing estates all over the province got into the grip of a pulverisation mania. Things were torn apart. The old Ulster decorum became a laughable figment of an unimaginable past. And the worst occurrence of all was the alignment of paramilitary and criminal activity, to the point where the two became one and the same thing.

The journalist Kevin Myers was based in Belfast during the 1970s, and has recorded his shocking experience of the city in a memoir, *Watching the Door* (2006). It's a vivid account of the badness of Belfast, gangs and bangs and guns and torture and lamentation, with copious sexual shenanigans thrown into the mix. (When churchly restraints went by the board, they departed with a vengeance.) Myers watched Belfast disintegrate around him. His profession sends him hot-foot to the scene of every atrocity, every place of perdition. And he manages to get himself on the wrong side of everyone, so that the whole of Belfast seems out to get him. His book takes the form, by turns, of unnerving comedy, terrorist imbroglio and bedroom escapade. It presents a version of a Belfast gone berserk. And however much he jazzes up its scenes of depravity, Belfast remains for English-born, Irish-affiliated Myers 'an evil place'.

Was this true? Others, like the poet Carol Rumens, came to Belfast braced for the worst, but found instead leafy suburbs, gardens, cedar and larch and fuchsia, places where 'peace, and love, and money, are made'. Places where ordinary people got on with their ordinary lives, disregarding as far as possible the grim backdrop; where burnt-out cars and shattered buildings were emblems only of a distant derangement. Well, fairly distant. There were reverberations. Many standpoints were shaken. The breaking point for a lot of liberal-minded people occurred at the moment when dissent became accommodating of carnage. Republicanism was then seen to have parted company with idealism.

Sometimes a small occurrence was enough to tip the balance in a previous sympathiser. For example, I date my mother's disillusionment with romantic Ireland and its freedom-fighting partisans – I date her disillusionment to the moment when, with disgust and exasperation, she watched a couple of gun-toting whippersnappers, twelve or thirteen years old, hanging around by 551's back gate in St James's Avenue. (She'd gone into the garden to hang her washing on the clothesline.) The two swaggering juveniles were flaunting their weapons and glorying in the sense of aggrandisement thereby conferred on them. 'Mine's bigger than yours,' she may have heard one claim, accompanied by giggles. And, 'That's the IRA,' my mother snorted later, in sardonic mode. (And yes, I'm bearing in mind young Bertie Tipping and his involvement in illicit activity of the early twentieth century – but I believe, or choose to believe, that a structure and discipline existed at that time very far in spirit from the dislocated '70s.)

Imagine you're a Catholic housewife living in Belfast in 1970, and your sense of justice is constantly violated by one instance of discrimination after another. Your children coming home from school are attacked by thugs from a different school, while your co-religionists are burned and blasted out of their homes. You have statistics concerning Catholic unemployment and belittlement at your fingertips. You're Catholic by upbringing, and allied with that portion of the populace nurtured on a litany of wrongs, while actually undergoing ever more colossal wrongs – though your own lineage, if you cared to look at it, is far from being an ethnically unbroken story. ... This, at least, is true of the two young women whose experience of unionist inclemency I'm about to relate. (Not that being Catholic in the church-going sense is paramount in the evolving political standpoint of either. That's not what the conflict is about. It's about social justice, and putting a stop to terror in the streets.)

One of these young women is my cousin Margaret, my Auntie Eileen's daughter, and of all of us Blacker descendants, the one who is most in line with the Tipping tradition. The other, whom I called Olivia[8] in *Asking for Trouble*, is my old school friend and fellow-Dominican-convent-expellee. These two have found themselves living next door to one another in Andersonstown, and quickly become friends. They have in common membership of the People's Democracy student-run body, and a burning aversion to the way the state of Northern Ireland is run.

There are protests everywhere. In the news is the attack on a republican funeral by a Protestant mob who tear the tricolour from the coffin and carry it away in triumph into their own back streets where it's set alight. Police monitoring the funeral move in to make arrests, but not of the aggressors. They swoop instead on young males wearing black berets and what are later described as 'army style' jackets, these garments supposedly proclaiming membership of an illegal organisation. (No one doubts that this is the case, but what gets the goat of concerned observers is the partisan nature of police and army responses.) Black berets, combat jackets: add a guard of honour equipped with hurley sticks, and the thing goes from a funeral to a quasi-military parade. Or so it seems to those who attach a provocative rather than an emblematic significance to the hurley sticks.

Not everyone takes this view. A particular cause of anger is the Special Powers Act and the way it facilitates unwarranted arrests like those noted above. People passionate about justice are constantly inveighing against this Act which is not perceived to operate in an even-handed way. When the black-beret-hurley-stick contingent comes to trial, a 'Special Powers' protest by disaffected women is set to take place outside the Chichester Street courthouse in Belfast. Among those intending to join in the protest are next-door neighbours Margaret and Olivia. In a gesture of defiance against the system, they will wear a version of the jackets invested by the Royal Ulster Constabulary with an insurrectionary significance. A number of hurley sticks, sardonically brandished in the hands of some as 'offensive weapons', will complete the protestors' tableau – though, if trouble ensues as it is almost certain to do, it is possible that this satiric touch will succumb to the needs of the moment and lose its symbolic edge.

Indeed, what Margaret and Olivia find when they arrive at the spot on the appointed morning in February, is a minor riot already in progress. Two rival crowds, mostly women, have assembled on opposite sides of the street. They are Protestants fully in favour of arresting and trying IRA suspects – the more the better – and their Catholic, or quasi-Catholic, counterparts, incensed by the onslaught on their legitimate gathering, and not slow to respond to traditional insults. It isn't long before dirty Fenian gets and bloody fucking Orange bitches are jammed together in a wild indigenous fracas. Police intervention doesn't achieve a lot. Screaming women hurl themselves on two policemen, enabling a few of their captured friends to break free and disappear into the crowd. Another woman being taken into custody is suddenly bashed in the face by a huge white plastic handbag wielded by a roaring opponent, towards whose assault on their captive the forces of law and order turn a blind eye. Olivia and Margaret, looking on with a measure of bemusement and understanding the impossibility of staging the proposed 'peaceful' demonstration, decide to make themselves scarce.

At this point things take an alarming turn. Olivia is carrying a bag containing three hurley sticks which are poking out at one end. A large rough female in the crowd, catching sight of the sticks, starts shouting and pointing: 'There's another couple of them bastard Fenian scum. Tear the fucking faces off them! Don't let them get away!' Before they *can* get away an inspector appears by their side and informs them they're under arrest. A small local drama involving factions and overreactions is about to be played out. The two women are taken to a nearby police station and charged with behaviour contributing to public disorder, and with being in possession of the ubiquitous 'offensive weapons'. Along with twenty-nine of their fellow would-be demonstrators, some of whom are exhibiting a degree of truculence, they're stripped of their outer clothing – clothing retained as evidence, and later described by the trial judge as 'having a military or a paramilitary connotation in the particular circumstances of Northern Ireland' – and, once solicitors have been contacted and bail arranged, sent home without adequate protection against the freezing cold of a Belfast February.

Certain instinctive actions of the Royal Ulster Constabulary were apt to cause outrage in the bitter past, when the force's reputation for impartiality was not high. The way they would jump in any cat-and-dog situation was easily foretold. The courthouse protest and its chaotic outcome was witnessed by a number of lawyers, Protestant and Catholic, who later issued a statement condemning police leniency towards the attacking faction, not one of whom ended under arrest. Indeed, 'the RUC mixed jovially with the unionist crowd',[9] the statement averred. Its conclusion, that 'legislative reforms are but an empty formula when the administration of justice by the police and courts is so blatantly one-sided and unjust', was not referred to during the subsequent trials.

Nevertheless, you can read into this statement the faintest possible note of hope for the distant future – beyond the cataclysm – when a change of heart, or at least a change of orientation, will come into being. The uncouth, vicious thing deplored by the novelist Benedict Kiely (see p. 233), with its *raison d'être* in killing, maiming and destruction, isn't itself quite dead in the North at present, perhaps, but it's only a shadow of its former sectarian self.

Neither my cousin nor her friend believes they will wind up in prison following the abortive courthouse protest. They enter the courtroom, when their case comes to trial, expecting a fine and rap on the knuckles. What they get instead is a sentence of six months in Armagh gaol. The trial has proceeded in accordance with the guiding principles adumbrated above. Why were these women arrested in the first place? Because, said the officer in question, 'in my opinion the hurley sticks were offensive weapons, and in combination with the jackets, likely to cause a breach of the peace'. (Never mind that 'a breach of the peace' was strenuously under way before they came anywhere near the place.) When Counsel for the defence wants to know 'why all the arrests were carried out on one side only', he gets a somewhat evasive reply:

> 'I did not want to escalate the situation so I only made arrests where a breach of the peace seemed likely.'
> 'You did not consider that remarks shouted by the opposite side were likely to lead to a breach of the peace?'
> 'There were slogans and counter-slogans and cat-calls and jeers coming from both sides.'

There were indeed, so there were, but to say so doesn't explain the heavy hand clamped down exclusively on one side of the Chichester Street battleground. And for some of the protestors anyway, 'sides' were beside the point. When it comes to Olivia's turn to give evidence, she is asked straight out: 'Was the purpose of the hurley sticks offensive?' 'Certainly not,' comes the sturdy answer. 'We merely intended to use them as symbols.' 'You did not consider that they might be offensive to the Protestant faction?'

'I was protesting against legislation that affects everyone,' Olivia declares. 'I do not consider that I belong to one particular religious faction.' It's the thin edge of a socialist-feminist-republican wedge, the voice of a new liberal Ulster, People's-Democracy-derived (though not, alas, the voice of *all* the courthouse demonstrators, some of whom are stuck fast in the old denominational sheugh). And much good it does her. 'Six months,' the judge pronounces; and Margaret the same.

Shortly before the end of Margaret's prison sentence, I accompany her father, and my mother, on a visit to Armagh. 'The incongruously handsome women's prison', to quote the poet John Montague[10] is situated in the town itself, on the south side of the Mall.[11] Built between 1780 and 1820, facing Francis Johnston's courthouse, it is one of the great public buildings of Northern Ireland. But architectural concerns aren't uppermost in any of our minds at the time. The building is not looking its best. A few days previously, the Provisional IRA had blown up a couple of cars belonging to prison warders in retaliation, they said, for the ill-treatment of those locked away inside; and broken glass and debris from the explosions are strewn about the place. All the prison windows facing the Mall have boards nailed across them.

The prison's forbidding entrance is furnished with a peephole through which we are scrutinised before being admitted, by a wardress, into a large tiled hall with a number of archways leading off it. Seated on a couple of chairs against a far wall are two impassive fat women wearing bedroom slippers and slowly consuming enormous ice-cream cones. Male warders stand about jangling bunches of keys. 'Surreal' and 'oppressive' are words that spring to mind. The whole interior of the place is dank and gloomy. Whenever we venture a comment during the twenty minutes or so we're kept waiting – which isn't often, as we're somewhat unnerved and apprehensive – our voices resound off walls imbued with extremes of ancient tension and distress. A constant ringing of bells makes you wonder which miscreants are being summoned to perform what punitive undertaking. Well, I'd hardly expected the atmosphere to be encouraging, had I. But I don't like the way you are made to feel you are downgraded as a human being simply by association with your particular inmate. And what makes it all the more aggravating is the fact that our inmate has committed no crime in the first place.[12]

A sour-faced female warder – 'screw' – arrives and conducts us through the hall and into a small courtyard. We walk in silence. Pleasantries are not exchanged. Suddenly Margaret appears from another direction, accompanied by a wardress of her own. My poor cousin is clad in a shapeless green gingham skirt folded over at one side, a pink blouse and a thin navy cardigan. These are prison-issue clothes, distributed to inmates on arrival at the gaol, and after a strip-search has been carried out. Underneath the terrible outer garments are large blue knickers elasticated round the legs, and a patched-up bra with different cup sizes. Black laced shoes and brown lisle stockings augment the austerity picture. Margaret does not seem low-spirited, though, despite the awful circumstances. Her robust approach to life has stood her in good stead. She's been able to shrug and go through the experience, deriving from it whatever benefits she can. Unlike a number of her fellow-prisoners, she hasn't given way to violence (smashing up her cell) or hysteria. She's acquired a certain skill in sewing shirts and mailbags, in wall-, floor-, and lavatory-cleaning. Prison life is just an ordeal to be got through, days ticked off on a calendar pending the moment of release. It is also a republican rite of passage, aligned to the old resistance-and-endurance model which has long kept revolutionary aspirations on the go.

She relates an anecdote. A fifteen-year-old girl on the way to a remand home is offered a cigarette by one of the so-called 'IRA women'. 'But I'm a Protestant!' the girl exclaims, reluctant to accept the gift under false pretences. Makes not a whit of difference, she's assured, as she lights up reluctantly, still nervously anticipating some awful Fenian trick about to be played on her.

Go back nearly two hundred years, and you find Margaret's ancestral connection William Blacker attending a different institution of Armagh – the Royal School, dubbed 'the Eton of Ireland' – and, in accordance with the current system of fagging, being appointed to the role of 'slave or valet' to the future Earl of Longford, then Tom Pakenham, whose shoes he has to keep polished to the nth degree. Polishing shoes, brushing trousers, burnishing buttons, preparing meals, smuggling in ale ... these schoolboy tasks, 'purgatorial' as they were, were nothing compared to a singular bit of horseplay devised by the aforesaid Pakenham and endured by the young Blacker. The former would oblige the latter to sit on the top stair of the main staircase, bind his wrists to his ankles, seize him by the feet and drag him downstairs, bump, bump, bump, step after step to the bottom, whereupon young Pakenham would laugh uproariously

Orangemen waiting to attack civil rights marchers at Burntollet Bridge, 1969

at young Blacker's discomfort. A curious rite of passage – but never mind, William said wryly, looking back on those days in Armagh, such treatment toughened him up for life's assaults and affrays (which would shortly include the famous affray at the Diamond). And, if the flaming 'Orangeisms of after times' were still largely a matter of amorphous stirrings, a distinct political style and anti-democratic bellicosity is getting drummed up at Armagh's Royal School, where teenage William (elevated to head boy) is a leading light of the Loyalty Lads, a school society devoted to all the implications of its broad-orange-ribbon badge. ... A long, long, hell-bent march is getting initiated, and one of its ultimate destinations is a high ridge above the River Faughan near Dungiven in County Derry, where a line of rogue Orangemen, armed with sticks, boulders and nail-studded cudgels, waits to descend like cartoon savages on an unfortunate procession of civil rights upholders on the way to Derry. The date is 4 January 1969, the place Burntollet Bridge, and terrible scenes of mayhem and bloodshed are about to be enacted – all with the connivance of local B Specials and regular police.

The waylaid Derry marchers are battoned, slashed, kicked, pummelled, knocked unconscious and hurled unmercifully down the slope and into the shallow river. Those still on their feet scatter wildly in all directions trying to evade the onslaught. Frances Molloy, who was present at the time, later published a novel[13] (engagingly written in a County Derry dialect) which includes an account of her own experience of Burntollet (via her narrator Ann McGlone):

> As a was lyin' there ... somebody that called me a fuckin' Fenian bastard started te kick me an' rain blows down on tap of me way some heavy implement that a could feel but didn't risk lookin' up at. ...Then somebody musta come te save me ... for a heard another voice, just as the blows stapped, sayin', are ye tryin' te murder hir, ye cowardly bastard ye, can't ye see that she's only a wain? Me attacker then set te the man that was tryin' te save me, an' the man that was tryin' te save me said te me in a wile urgent kine of a voice, if ye can manage te stan', get up now for god's sake ... an' get outta here quick.

She goes on, 'It musta been a miracle, but nobody got killed that day an' soon after we got across the bridge, cars an' ambulances started arrivin' from both directions te help the marchers an' bring the badly injured te hospital.' Nobody got killed, and nobody got arrested either. 'The polis,' says Frances Molloy, 'knew damn well who the culprits were because they could be seen, laughin' an' chattin' te many of them, on the very best of terms, while the ambush was on.'

The verdict on this memorable episode issued by Captain Terence O'Neill, still holding on as Prime Minister of Northern Ireland, is as follows: 'Some of the marchers and those who supported them in Londonderry itself have shown themselves to be mere hooligans, ready to attack the police and others.' Whew!

The people carrying out the Burntollet ambush probably thought they were ingratiating themselves with their hero Paisley – if they thought at all – and also with one of Paisley's henchmen, a Major Ronald Bunting, who stood behind, supported and directed the wreckers and stone-throwers as their vicious project got under way. There is, however, evidence to suggest that Major Bunting cleared a way for some of the injured marchers, once he understood the thing he'd helped to set up was liable to end in murder, and felt his humane instincts kick in, however late in the day. (Better for those to kick in, than brutal, 'Papist-trampling' boots.) Or it may have been thoughts of his son that came into his mind and checked his Protestant militarism, at this critical moment. I don't know if Ronnie Bunting junior was actually among the Burntollet marchers,[14] but he was, at Queen's University, a prominent member of the People's Democracy group; and his subsequent career would take him as far as possible from the loyalist precepts cherished by his father.

Yes, by one of those indigenous twists beloved of historians and others, the younger Bunting was a convert to socialism and republicanism who became a founder-member of the Irish National Liberation Army, and met a violent end in 1980 when a UDA death squad was sent to his home in Turf Lodge, Belfast, to assassinate him. (He himself had been implicated in the London murder of Airey Neave.) He was thirty-two. He is listed on a roll of honour of republican dead in the Springfield Road, Belfast, one of a very small number of 'Protestants' to be so commemorated.[15] But his father, Major Bunting, had him buried in the family burial plot, in a final gesture of paternal affirmation. Poles apart as they were in political orientation, it seems that each of them, father and son, accorded some respect to the principles the other chose to live by. Major Bunting said of his son, 'I saw him as a man who was virtuous and high-minded, and who had a keen sense of social justice and who fought oppression and injustice wherever he saw it.'[16]

What happened at Burntollet Bridge shows sectarian rage running out of control. The Orange assailants – throwbacks – are, in their own view, defending 'their' territory against a flaunting invasion by a crowd of students, 'Popeheads', socialists and republicans. 'Where's your Pope now?' they sneered. 'Get your Pope now and he'll help you.' They believe their actions are justified – but it's not the way the event is seen by the rest of the world, with photographic and eyewitness evidence testifying to an alarming propensity for stoning and beating on the part of certain scions of Protestant Ulster.[17] It's Benedict Kiely's monster springing to life again. It's the clearest possible indication that things will have to change, that abhorrent energies will have to be worked off, once and for all. Not that people really believed, in the midst of the cataclysm, that change would come, but come it did – though only after years of carnage and destruction on a scale unimagined by even the most pessimistic observers of the start of the Northern Irish Troubles.

My wonderfully sympathetic mother had scant cause to be grateful for many of the routes my life drifted into: unapproved byways, cliff-edge paths. If these were at odds with the comfortable and conventional circumstances she'd have ordained for me – if she could – not one word of criticism on account of my waywardness did I ever hear from her. She managed to accommodate, and even to relish, my vintage-clothes mania ('Sure who's like her ...'), my hennaed hair, even my freelance existence and consequent financial insecurity. (I was happy as an occasional author, book reviewer, and flea-market aficionado, and that was enough for her.) Not that anxiety on my behalf ever left her, and I'm now appalled that I didn't take the trouble to present my daily doings as something more palatable than a source of maternal agitation. But one thing, at least, she must have been thankful for: that I was safely ensconced in London and well away from indigenous perils such as the Derry march and its Burntollet outcome. As a person susceptible to the socialist and radical excitements of the day, I might easily (in my mother's view) have opted for any foolhardy and dangerous gesture available at any time to underscore a reformist point. She'd have dreaded to hear I was half-drowned and battered – like some of my acquaintance – or in Altnagelvin Hospital nursing a broken head.

Our house in the Donegall Road, however, was not at a satisfactory remove from riot and disorder. From a front bedroom window we witnessed scenes of disruption, my mother and father and I, as a bus blazed in the roadway before our eyes; as a commandeered car was rammed with shocking violence, back and forth, back and forth, into a factory wall a hundred yards away, until the wall began to collapse; as soldiers erupted on the scene, leaping from their armoured cars equipped with riot shields and tear gas; as all the inflamed of St James's dispersed and regrouped, using local knowledge to good effect. It was early in the morning of Monday 9 August 1971, and we'd been roused from our sleep by an ominous noise: women parading the streets banging bin lids together to alert the neighbourhood to a state of emergency. Operation Internment was under way.

The day was strange. A minor riot continued to unfold on the patch of waste ground backed by the factory wall against which the reckless driver had smashed his stolen car. Unaccustomed noises filled the air: shouts, bangs, clashes, distant gunshots, stones hitting riot shields, pounding feet on asphalt pavements. Two of the last belonged to a young priest in a black soutane, holding up his skirts as he pelted up the road towards the junction with the Falls – 'By jinkers, that fellow can run,' my father exclaimed admiringly – a priest later shot dead in the act of administering the last rites to another victim of the turbulence. The day was strange, and a nervous apprehension held us in its grip as our once sedate neighbourhood succumbed to an access of anarchy. I thought of our quiet avenues, our old neighbours keeping themselves to themselves, cultivating tidy flower beds in their small gardens, library members, car owners, good housekeepers, emerging for Mass on Sunday mornings decently clad in old-fashioned dress. Where had it all gone?

I feel I am a part of the current exorbitant events, and also that I am not. I can watch and deplore the advent of uproar, outrage after outrage, from a good safe distance. Well out of it. Soon I am back in London, my summer holiday over, back with my Welsh-painter husband, my black cat, my stop-gap proofreading job, the Portobello Road, the National Film Theatre on the South Bank. My parents have no such escape route. They have another five years of being in the thick of it, bomb blast and murder and terror and savagery, five years before they will move to a quiet spot on the County Down coast and put a bit of distance between themselves and the maelstrom. And in the meantime, my mother's teaching is constantly interrupted by factors unconnected with the classroom. Bomb scares abound. Large portions of the day (she tells me) are spent standing shivering in St James's Road, as the school is evacuated yet again following another telephoned alert. Once, the army co-opts members of staff to scour the school for a putative explosive device. They're set to searching lockers, cupboards and cloakrooms, not really knowing what they are looking for, or what action to take if they find it. Normal life has to be fitted in around abnormal circumstances. Two of my mother's pupils blow themselves up in separate incidents, when their bomb-making skills prove lethally insufficient. Everyone's nerves are kept at breaking point, with no respite. A car backfiring in the distance is enough to send the whole class diving for the floor, leaving the teacher standing at her rostrum facing rows of empty desks. Topical excuses for failures of diligence are the order of the day: 'Miss, I couldn't do my homework with the bullets whizzing up and down the hall.'

In the summer of 1999 we came to live in Antrim, transferring ourselves from pleasant Blackheath to a hundred-and-sixty-year-old, three-storey stone-built house with an overgrown garden. It was the month of the Long March – implacable Protestant Ulster on the move from Derry to

Drumcree, in support of immemorial 'civil and religious liberties' which seemed in jeopardy once again, and in protest against continuing IRA atrocities. On our first night in the empty house we heard, in the distance, the sound of Orange drums, conjuring up an ancient intransigence and history of bad blood. (Conjuring up for me, as well, at another level, an irresistible ancestral elation.) What had we come to? Just down the road, on the way into Antrim town, was the railway bridge where an earlier march, bound for Derry via Burntollet, was attacked, jeered at and jostled by stirred-up loyalists of the town. In the other direction lay Donegore Hill, an eldritch hill, once the rallying point for United Irish rebels heading for defeat (but what a storied defeat!) at the Battle of Antrim.

Drumcree, in County Armagh, the destination of the present 'Long Marchers', is rich in associations too. It contains a church at which one of those ubiquitous frock-coated overbearing Blackers once served as rector; and it's the place where the notorious Garvaghy Road stand-off testifies to the persisting nature of the Northern Irish squabble. Teeth and claws perpetually at the ready. Orangemen might have agreed not to march down the Garvaghy Road to the annoyance of local residents; local nationalists might have agreed to let the Orangemen get on with it, in a spirit of goodwill. But neither of them does anything of the sort. A chance for the tonic gesture, bypassed yet again.

As I've said elsewhere,[18] our house, Ashville House, was built for a minister of Antrim First Presbyterian Church, a Reverend Charles Morrison, Belfast- or Saintfield-born, Inst-educated, for whom Antrim did not prove a hospitable incumbency. Negative emotions, for the Morrison family, must have been attached to the town. The minister offended a portion of his flock through some unspecified misdoing (sexual or financial), and soon it became expedient for a move to be made. The Reverend Charles was appointed Principal of Arnold Theological College in Hackney, North London, and there, no doubt, life for the uprooted Morrisons assumed a settled and punctilious character, far from the stresses of dour Antrim town.

Back in Ireland, though, was the burial place of two young sons of the family, a circumstance no doubt adding to the country's fraught associations. One of these boys died (here, in this house) in 1846, possibly from some Famine-related illness. Every part of Ireland has its Famine stories, its emblems of historical woe. I think of my infant great-grandmother, Ellen Jordan, wrapped in a shawl and carried in her mother's arms for sustenance to an Armagh soup kitchen; I think of poor John Tipping dying of cholera in his Lurgan Workhouse bed. I think of all the Protestant dead of Tartaraghan. The children lying in the Antrim Presbyterian churchyard would have tethered the Morrisons to the town, whether they liked it or not. Whether the north of Ireland was, for them, a place of nostalgia or good riddance.

Five of the Morrison children survived into adulthood, and the youngest of these, Jane, born at Ashville in 1855, went on to marry, in England, an Andrew Davitt. In due course Jane Morrison became the grandmother of Donald Maclean of mid twentieth-century, Burgess-and-Maclean defector fame. I don't think many people are aware that Donald Maclean's great-grandfather was an Ulster Presbyterian minister who fell foul of his congregation – and I mention the fact simply because it adds a miniscule detail to the web of Northern Irish ironies and interconnections I'm constructing (those that have an oblique bearing on my own life, that is, or on matters that concern me here).

Everyone's life contains copious stories and histories. Throughout this book I've tried to uncover a few from my own life, and tried, as well, to find ways of enlisting these in the service of a broader perspective, and in support of an integrationist overview. I've hoped, from time to time, to light on a true Ulster spirit, a spirit of benevolence and inclusiveness. I'd like to dispel the notions that some people have a better right than others to be in Northern Ireland, that some are native and some are not, or that an eternal opposition exists between two clear-cut sections of our society, with a licence conferred on each to be at the other's throat ad nauseam. Because of our mixed inheritances, the battle of the ideologies boils down to a battle with the self, of which the only possible outcome is self-mutilation, or self-destruction. And so it proved. Anyone who spent any time in the North, in the 1970s or '80s (say), would have witnessed desolation and devastation on a scale to daunt any ameliorative heart. Though many of its inhabitants never wavered in the belief that the north of Ireland is the most beautiful place on earth, they'd have had, with Derek Mahon, to add a rider to that assessment:

> Portrush, Portstewart, Portballintrae,
> *Un beau pays mal habité.*

Those among us distrustful of hopes for the future might continue to stress the *mal habité* side of things. They might point to sinister paramilitary images still disfiguring gable walls (bring back folksy King Billy on his white horse, please), to continuing sectarian murders and other outrages, to horrid habitations and other terrible edifices replacing incalculable losses by bomb, fire, rot and redevelopment. We all have to take responsibility for everything that's happened. We are bound together by a common ancestry, and by our place in the world. Bound too by the whole pungent history of wrongs and suffering and bigotry and poetry and picturesqueness and notoriety and all our shared knowledge of secret local places. If each of us has to be classed under a divisive denominational label – which remains true to some extent, though it carries less weight than it did in the past – our entitlements, and our ghosts, are none the less interchangeable.

Ghosts. I have a whole restive company of these shadowy presences at my back, eager to communicate approval or disapproval, some reproachful about wrong motives attributed, or crucial details mislaid; others livid about traits they've been lumbered with, on scant evidence. ('The dead can't talk,' Douglas Dunn wrote,[19] 'or appear on your doorstep / Or be discovered turning to you from / Beautiful landscapes, wearing smiles of courtship, / Perusals of what you've written about them.') Some may harbour a modicum of assent; but more, I suspect, would vehemently wish to set the record straight, to detach their after-image from lunatic surmise. To these I can only reply that I've done my best to fit each of them into a pattern not outrageously at variance with actualities of the day (their day), and to flesh out just a little – as we've seen – the bare Jacobean, or eighteenth-century, or mid-Victorian bones. Most of these people had to grapple, in one way or another, with forces beyond their control, political, economic, puritanical, above all sectarian forces. ... My own personal ghosts, and others connected to me by a skimpier thread: these were born into wildly differing circumstances, and inherited concomitant stances. All, or most of them, lived according to their lights, and in ways dictated by the times, and I've no argument with them, except to point out a certain blindness in the face of variegation. There were more elements to their identities than some of them recognised.

Skimming through the preceding chapters, I find they embody a kind of edgeways or idiosyncratic approach to aspects of Northern Irish history. Northern Irish – so the title of at least one chapter, 'Scullabogue', is (again) making an ironic point about inclusiveness, and also about invalidating persistent preconceptions.

In May 2010 I was invited to deliver the annual *Irish Pages* lecture as part of the Cathedral Quarter Festival in Belfast. Because *A Twisted Root* was very much on my mind at the time, I decided to talk a bit about the book, mentioning the reasons why I felt impelled to write it, and including a few indications of what it might consist of. A short time later, a friend was attending a social gathering and chanced to overhear a conversation between two men whom she didn't know. One was telling the other that he'd recently attended an interesting talk 'by a republican woman from the Falls Road who discovered that all her ancestors were Protestants'.

Well! I was never a 'republican woman'; during the height of the Troubles I was not to be found anywhere near the Falls Road; and the largest 'Protestant' element in my background I didn't 'discover', having known about it all along. However, the person who summarised my lecture so cavalierly was at least right about the gist of it. The pasts of all of us in this small corner of the world are repositories of apparently shattering, but actually (if you think about it) unifying truths. As another friend put it, considering the events of the seventeenth century and their implications, if the native Irish had been white and the Planters black, our complexions would all by now be a uniform shade.

NOTES

INTRODUCTION

1 T.J. Campbell, *Fifty Years of Ulster 1890–1940*.
2 Note the name.
3 In his novel of 1907, *The Unpardonable Sin*.
4 *Portrait of a Rebel Father.*
5 All right, I admit I'm prone to favour this mode as a narrative strategy.
6 *The Speckled People.*
7 R.F. Foster, *Modern Ireland 1600–1972*.
8 I'm indebted to Douglas Carson for this information.

CHAPTER 1

1 *Shakespeare's Wife*, Bloomsbury 2007.
2 The ancient name for a part of south-east Ulster.
3 I'll enlarge on this subject in Chapter Eight.
4 At the top of the Cave Hill in Belfast.
5 Pen name of the poet and editor Anna Johnston McManus (1866–1902).
6 Only published for the first time in the Victorian era.

CHAPTER 2

1 Robert M. Young, *Belfast and the Province of Ulster in the 20th Century*, Brighton, 1909.
2 'The Oul' Orange Flute'.
3 It is possible that the liberal Brownlows of Lurgan favoured Bryan O'Neill because neither he nor his father Hugh had been implicated in violence against the Planter community.

CHAPTER 3

1 Since writing this, I've come across evidence suggesting that 'The first Lett in Ireland was a Captain in Cromwell's army'. Ah me. And it seems he came from Warwickshire, which loosely ties him in with the Tippings.

2   With one or two exceptions.

3   A fluent-Irish-speaking friend
    tells me it's more likely to be an
    adaptation of *Scealbog*, which means,
    among other things, 'a detached
    layer of rock'.

4   His grandfather was Charles Lett
    (they are all called Charles or
    Stephen or Thomas or William …).

5   Reports following the suppression
    of the Rebellion claimed that
    insurgents on the way to slaughter
    Protestant prisoners at Wexford
    Bridge carried a black flag
    emblazoned with a white cross, and
    the letters MWS – Murder Without
    Sin – written across it.

6   A biographical note on Barbara Lett
    which appears in John D. Beatty's
    *Protestant Women's Narratives of the
    Irish Rebellion of 1798* claims that
    Joshua Lett was her father-in-
    law. But this information is flatly
    contradicted by Katherine Lucy
    Lett in her *History of the Lett Family*,
    written for private circulation in
    1925. Barbara's father-in-law was
    Charles Lett (another one!), says
    Katherine Lucy. Since she was the
    family historian, I'm inclined to go
    along with her version.

7   The third of a trio of brothers
    alongside William (father of
    Benjamin) and Charles (subject
    of the Reverend Henry Lett's
    biographical account). Whew!

8   I have to add a note about William.
    Despite his Orange credentials,
    says the Reverend Henry, William
    in later life 'became a PERVERT
    to the Church of Rome' (his
    outraged capitals). He suggests
    that expediency, not conviction,
    was behind it. But here at last is
    a 'Catholic' Lett to underscore
    my point about denominational
    interchangeability.

9   Actually, I can discard this
    possibility; see note 17.

10 According to Katherine Lucy
    Lett, the Charles who joined the
    yeomanry in 1798 did have a son
    named Thomas by his second wife,
    whose dates would fit. But alas,
    no information about this Thomas
    exists. (It may have been lost when
    the Four Courts was burnt.) And,
    since I can't find any reference to
    Clonleigh or my grandmother's
    ancestors in any Lett family
    documents, I think it's possible that
    my branch of the family stemmed
    from some illegitimate offshoot,
    now undiscoverable.

11 'By all accounts, lower-class
    Protestants were the original
    aggressors.' Marianne Elliott, 2000.

12 Blacker Diaries.

13 So called because of his campaign
    against cruelty to animals.
    He was the principal founder
    of the RSPCA.

14 Tim Robinson, *Connemara: Listening
    to the Wind*.

15 Seamus Heaney, 'Station Island',
    Canto 11.

16 May God have mercy on them all.

17 Another irony: the Irish rebel later
    joined the British Navy (and died at
    seventeen).

CHAPTER 4

1   *Contemplations on the Power, Wisdom,
    and Goodness of God*, Belfast, 1843.

2   Given William Blacker's much

publicised attitude to the Catholic church, it's hard to understand why these were present; but they were.

3 Not only do we have James and John incessantly recurring as family names, but they're attached to the streets and terraces they live in too.

CHAPTER 5

1 Not to be confused with Henry's father Matthew.
2 He was educated at Foyle College, Derry, before going on to Shrewsbury School and Magdalen College, Cambridge. His mother was Elizabeth Sinclair of Fort William, Belfast.
3 *Changes and Chances of a Soldier's Life*, London, 1925.
4 Rimbaud, *Le Bateau Ivre*.
5 I'm aware that Olivia May was dead at this point, but some female relative would doubtless have taken over the management of domestic affairs, at least until Charlotte Olivia, the eldest daughter and Marie Heller's exact contemporary, was in a position to do it.

CHAPTER 6

1 *A History of the Town of Belfast* (1880).
2 Basically, revival.
3 See Marnie Hay, *Bulmer Hobson and the Nationalist Movement in Twentieth-Century Ireland*.
4 George Buchanan, *Green Seacoast*.
5 The Reverend T.L.F. Stack, quoted in James Winder Good, *Ulster and Ireland*.
6 Both descended from a long line of Brookes and Chichesters.
7 He may not have been in the country at the time.
8 I have to be careful here, since my own name suggests an affiliation I'm far from embracing. I'm pointing this out myself before someone else does, and presenting it, moreover, as a corroborating, not an undermining, factor in my basic thesis.
9 Rea is joking, of course, while Whitman wasn't; but underlying the jocular tone is a refusal to concede superiority or unquestionable rectitude to one political persuasion over another.
10 See Len Graham, *Joe Holmes: Here I Am Amongst You*.
11 In the 1940s or '50s, she conducted a correspondence with Bishop Mageean on the subject of his ban on married women teachers, to which she was opposed.
12 I think Catherine inherited these aunts after her husband's death, since my mother in old age occasionally mentioned three old women who lived upstairs in her grandmother's house, and whose identity puzzled her.
13 Stevie Smith, 'It was a cynical babe. Reader, before you condemn, pause / It was a cynical babe, / Not without cause.'
14 W.B. Yeats, 'Easter 1916'.
15 Third son of Henry and Mary Anne.
16 *Forward the Rifles*, 2009.

17 From a cousin. No one who'd experienced it ever spoke to me of Lily's death. I barely knew that an aunt Lily was missing from the roster of my relations.

18 I think by Christmas they had moved from Edward Street to North Street, perhaps to get away from the setting of the tragedy.

19 It bothered some of the latter, like Francis Ledwidge, 'To be called a British soldier while my country / Has no place among the nations...'. (Quoted by Seamus Heaney.)

CHAPTER 7

1 The term 'Irish Volunteers' soon gave way to 'IRA' - Irish Republican Army.

2 Once I understand that the Barracks is a former Georgian house, I feel my conservationist hackles begin to rise in protest. But before the incident is over, police and military have burned and wrecked half the village. In the destruction stakes, the forces of law and order win hands down.

3 Then joint Hon. Secretary of Sinn Féin. He committed suicide in 1925.

4 The Tipping referred to is Jimmy.

5 Probably the Mater, where Dr Moore, father of the future novelist Brian Moore, had recently been appointed senior surgeon.

6 Well, for practical purposes. You could say it begins with the Plantation of Ulster, if you wanted.

7 One of Jim McDermott's sources

for his book *Northern Divisions,* from which I'm quoting.

8 See Lawlor, *The Burnings.*

9 One of these young men later became a commandant in the Free State army, while the other was executed by the Free State government in December 1922.

10 Only one of the subsequent accounts of the shooting mentions RIC men on the heels of the getaway car, with the mishap calling to mind the doings of the Keystone Cops.

11 I'm indebted to Glenn Patterson's book for this information.

12 He is tried and condemned to death, though the sentence is later commuted to twelve years' imprisonment.

13 *On Another Man's Wound.*

14 I'm quoting from *Northern Divisions* by Jim McDermott. This valuable book provides a day-to-day account of IRA active service units and their operations during this period.

15 Only the second son John, a married man with domestic responsibilities, stayed away from active involvement.

16 Note the name, and think of long-ago Katherine Rose uprooted from Warwickshire and planted in the 'boiling' Ulster countryside.

17 He'd been elected to a County Armagh constituency in addition to Cork in the Provisional Government, Dáil Éireann.

18 Thirty-year-old Collins has less than a year to live. The shock occasioned by news of his assassination, in August 1922, would

have been complicated, for the Tippings, by their position vis-à-vis the Treaty. They were among the northern republicans who opposed it, while others were willing to regard it as a means to an end.

19 Indicating active and armed service. In total 15,224 medals with bar were issued, and 47,644 without.

20 Appointed Divisional Signaller, 4th Northern Division, in 1921.

21 In the words of an official at the Ministry of Home Affairs.

22 A slogan of the reconstituted, late-twentieth-century IRA. At least Gerry has it in English, not the bad Irish in which it was framed later.

23 There is, of course, quite a large irony here as far as the Tipping family is concerned.

24 On a recent visit to the Tower of London, my cousin Jerome Tipping was intrigued to find the name 'John Tipping' inscribed on the wall of a prison cell.

25 From an anonymous verse written in the nineteenth century.

CHAPTER 8

1 There wasn't much talk of my father's alma mater the Charley Memorial, or his later Lisburn Tech, but that circumstance hadn't particularly struck me either.

2 *Asking for Trouble*, 2007.

3 Oxford University Press, 1924.

4 Two daughters of Henry and Mary Anne's son John Tipping were pupils at the school in the 1930s.

5 No relation. Neither, I am sorry to

say, is the more obscure poet Julius McCullough Leckey Craig, author of the lines, 'On Carrick shore I stood, I stood,/And gaped across at Holywood;/And as I gaped I saw afar/My love upon the Kinnegar.'

6 At least, only Catholics availed themselves of it.

7 Elliott, op cit.

8 One, I would say, rather jolly in a Margaret Rutherford kind of way, the other a bit fluttery and timid (I'm going by their photographs).

9 I'm quoting from an article on Beechmount in his *Rushlight* magazine.

10 I am doubtful about its authenticity, since no one, as far as I know, has actually come up with documentary evidence in relation to the excluding clause.

11 A literal translation of Beechmount.

12 Their niece had married her uncle.

13 Robert Johnston, letter in the *Ulster Echo*, October 1891.

14 I'd like to think that 'Drennan' and 'Thornberry' were different versions of the same name, both derived from the Irish *Ua Dhroighnean*: one translated, the other transliterated. (The Thornberrys, you remember, were Lurgan republican associates of the Tippings.) And Duffin – like Duff – comes from the Irish word for black.

15 John Swanwick Drennan was Ruth Duffin's grandfather.

16 *Northern Voices*, 1975.

17 The district, not the house.

18 Air Raid Precautions.

19 See Stephen Douds, *The Belfast Blitz*.
20 *Counties of Contention*.
21 The other two had married and gone elsewhere.
22 In *Belfast Confetti* (1989).

CHAPTER 9

1 Paul Muldoon, 'The Biddy Boys'.
2 It arrived later in Northern Ireland than it did in Great Britain.
3 Tom Paulin.
4 Hanged in Greyabbey in 1797.
5 It wasn't the only route to success. People who failed the eleven-plus or equivalent examination should take heart from the story of eleven-plus failure Martin McGuinness who, in the course of his upward progress, held the post of Minister of Education, in an inspiriting instance of the 'reversal-of-fortune' parable.
6 Eamonn McCann, *War and an Irish Town*.
7 See *A Place Apart* (1978).
8 Not her real name, but it's as suitable for present purposes as it was then.
9 This was a common observation and it contributed greatly to Catholic disaffection.
10 *Time in Armagh* (1993).
11 The original architect was Thomas Cooley.
12 I should stress that I'm not opposed to prison as a punishment for those who *have* committed crimes.
13 *No Mate for the Magpie*, Virago, 1985.
14 A residual family loyalty, or embarrassment, may have kept him out of it.
15 But the history of Irish republicanism and nationalism is filled with Protestants, as I've stressed throughout.
16 *Lost Lives*.
17 Interesting to find the same surnames shared by marchers and attackers: Moore, McGuinness, for example.
18 *Asking For Trouble*.
19 In the poem, 'Disenchantments'.

SELECT BIBLIOGRAPHY

Bardon, Jonathan, *A History of Ulster* (Blackstaff Press, 1992)

Beatty, John D. (ed.), *Protestant Women's Narratives of the Irish Rebellion of 1798* (Four Courts Press, 2001)

William Blacker Manuscripts, Armagh County Museum

Brown, Terence, *Northern Voices: Poets from Ulster* (Gill & Macmillan, 1975)

Buchanan, George, *Green Seacoast* (Gaberbocchus Press, 1959)

Byrne, John, *An Impartial Account of the Late Disturbances in the County of Armagh* (Dublin, 1792)

Campbell, Captain David, *Forward the Rifles: The War Diary of an Irish Soldier, 1914–1918* (Nonsuch Publishing, 2009)

Campbell, T.J., *Fifty Years of Ulster 1890–1940* (The Irish News Ltd, 1941)

Carr, Peter, *The Night of the Big Wind* (White Row Press, 1991)

Cloney, Thomas, *A Personal Narrative of 1798* (Dublin, 1832)

Colfer, Billy, *Wexford: A Town and its Landscape* (Cork University Press, 2008)

Devlin, Anne, *The Way-Paver and Other Stories* (Faber, 1986)

Devlin, Paddy, *Straight Left* (Blackstaff Press, 1993)

Devlin, Polly, *All of Us There* (Weidenfeld & Nicolson, 1983)

Dickson, Charles, *The Wexford Rising in 1798* (The Kerryman Ltd, 1955; Constable, 1997)

———, *Revolt in the North* (Clonmore & Reynolds, 1960; Constable, 1997)

Donaldson, John, *A Historical and Statistical Account of the Barony of Upper Fews in the County of Armagh, 1838* (Dundalk, 1923)

Douds, Stephen, *The Belfast Blitz* (Blackstaff Press, 2011)

Dunne, Tom, *Rebellions: Memoir, Memory and 1798* (Lilliput Press, 2004)

Egan, Bowes and Vincent McCormack, *Burntollet* (LRS Publishers, 1969)

Elliott, Marianne, *The Catholics of Ulster* (Allen Lane, 2000)

Farrell, Michael, *The Orange State* (Pluto Press, 1976)

Geary, Laurence M. (ed.), *Rebellion and Remembrance in Modern Ireland* (Four Courts Press, 2001)

Good, James Winder, *Ulster and Ireland* (Maunsel & Co., 1919)

Graham, Len, *Joe Holmes: Here I Am Amongst You* (Four Courts Press, 2010)

Hay, Marnie, *Bulmer Hobson and the Nationalist Movement in Twentieth-Century Ireland* (Manchester University Press, 2009)

Hickson, Mary, *Ireland in the Seventeenth Century* (Longmans, Green, 1884)

Hughes, Andrew, *Lives Less Ordinary: Dublin's Fitzwilliam Square 1798–1922* (The Liffey Press, 2011)

Johnston, Sheila Turner, *Alice: A Life of Alice Milligan* (Colourpoint Press, 1994)

Kane, James S., *For God and the King: The Story of the Blackers of Carrickblacker* (Ulster Society, 1995)

Kiely, Benedict, *Counties of Contention* (Mercier Press, 1945)

Lawlor, Pearse, *The Burnings, 1920* (Mercier Press, 2009)

Lett, Reverend Henry, *Memoir of Charles Lett of Balloughton, Kilcavan, Co. Wexford* (Ms. *c.*1871)

Lett, Katherine Lucy, *A History of the Lett Family* (for private circulation, 1925)

Macardle, Dorothy, *The Irish Republic* (Gollancz, 1937)

McCafferty, Nell, *The Armagh Women* (Co-op Books, 1981)

McCann, Eamonn, *War and an Irish Town* (Penguin, 1974)

McClelland, Gillian, *Pioneering Women* (Ulster Historical Foundation, 2005)

McDermott, Jim, *Northern Divisions: The Old IRA and the Belfast Pogroms, 1920–22* (Beyond the Pale, 2001)

McGuffin, John, *Internment* (Anvil Books, 1973)

May, Major-General Sir Edward S., *Changes and Chances of a Soldier's Life* (Philip Allen & Co., 1925)

Molloy, Frances, *No Mate for the Magpie* (Virago, 1985)

Moore, Brian, *The Emperor of Ice-Cream* (Andre Deutsch, 1966)

Murphy, Dervla, *A Place Apart* (John Murray, 1978)

Myers, Kevin, *Watching the Door* (The Lilliput Press, 2006)

O'Faolain, Sean, *Vive Moi!* (Sinclair Stevenson (revised edition), 1993)

————, *The Great O'Neill* (Longmans, 1942; Mercier Press (revised edition), 1981)

O'Hagan, Andrew, *The Missing* (Picador, 1995)

O'Malley, Ernie, *On Another Man's Wound* (Rich & Cowan, 1936)

Patterson, Glenn, *Once Upon a Hill* (Bloomsbury, 2008)

Rice, Adrian 'The Lonely Rebellion of William Drennan'. In G. Dawe and J.W. Foster (eds), *The Poet's Place* (Institute of Irish Studies, Queen's University, 1991)

Rowe, David and Eithne Scallan, *Houses of Wexford* (Ballinakella Press, 2004)

Stewart, A.T.Q., *The Narrow Ground* (Faber, 1977)

———, *The Summer Soldiers* (Blackstaff Press, 1995)

———, *The Shape of Irish History* (Blackstaff Press, 2001)

Witherow, Thomas, *Derry and Enniskillen in the Year 1689* (Wm. Mullan & Son, 1873)

ACKNOWLEDGEMENTS

I am grateful to the Arts Council of Northern Ireland, and especially to Damian Smyth and Craig Corsar, whose award of a grant in 2010 helped enormously in the preparation of this book. I should also like to thank the Society of Authors for much appreciated financial assistance.

A *Twisted Root* (whose working title was *Scullabogue*), grew out of its predecessor, *Asking for Trouble*, and out of the researches and family papers of two cousins, Harry Tipping (the dedicatee of *A Twisted Root*) and George Hinds, both of whom supplied encouragement as well as practical information. I owe them an inestimable debt.

I am also grateful, as ever, to Douglas Carson who read the early chapters and made valuable suggestions; and, for various kinds of help, to Jerome Tipping, Brian Tipping, Erskine Holmes, Margaret Gatt, Yvonne Lloyd, Sally Craig, Dave Fisher, David Parks, Fiona Coyle, Mary Cosgrove, Polly Devlin, Maire Mac Sheain, Maire Nic Mhaolain, Angelique Day, Derek Mahon, Joe Graham, Tom Dunne, Joan Maguire, George McDowell, Anne Devlin, Jim Campbell, Michael Longley, Val Warner, Naomi May and Patricia Mallon.

I should like to thank Chris Agee who published a version of the Introduction in *Irish Pages*. Thanks are due, as well, to John Killen of the Linen Hall Library, Belfast; to Patricia Walker of Belfast Central Library; and to Diarmuid Kennedy of the McClay Library at Queen's University, Belfast.

I am fortunate in benefiting from the expertise of the inspired and indefatigable Blackstaff team, in particular Helen Wright and Patsy

Horton (and if I haven't always acted on their advice – on my own head be it). No publishers could be more supportive or enthusiastic.

Finally, the project would never have come to fruition without the intellectual sustenance and invigorating encouragement of my husband Jeffrey Morgan. I am grateful for this, and for much else besides.